D0860404

JEROME LIBRARY
CURRICULUM RESOURCE CENTER
BOWLING GREEN STATE UNIVERSITY
BOWLING GREEN, OHIO 43403

First Edition

Colonial America and the Revolutionary War

The Story of the People of the Colonies, From Early Settlers to Revolutionary Leaders

BOWLING GREEN STATE UNIVERSITY
DISCARDED
LIBRARY

Laurie Lanzen Harris,
Editor

Favorable Impressions

P.O. Box 69018 • Pleasant Ridge, MI 48069

JEROME LIBRARY
CURRICULUM RESOURCE CENTER
BOWLING GREEN STATE UNIVERSITY
BOWLING GREEN, OHIO 43403

BOWLING GREEN STATE
UNIVERSITY LIBRARIES

Laurie Lanzen Harris, *Editor*
Laurie Collier Hillstrom, Ann E. Merry,
Claire A. Rewold, PhD, *Contributing Editors*
Dan R. Harris, *Senior Vice President, Sales and Marketing*

Library of Congress Cataloging-in-Publication Data

Colonial America and the Revolutionary War : the story of the people of the colonies, from early settlers to revolutionary leaders / Laurie Lanzen Harris, editor.
p. cm. — (Biography for beginners)
Includes index.
ISBN 978-1-931360-34-0 (alk. paper)
1. United States—History—Colonial period, ca. 1600–1775—Juvenile literature. 2. United States—History—Revolution, 1775–1783—Juvenile literature. 3. United States—History—Colonial period, ca. 1600–1775—Biography—Juvenile literature. 4. United States—History—Revolution, 1775–1783—Biography—Juvenile literature. I. Harris, Laurie Lanzen.
E188.C6972 2009
973.2—dc22
2008049193

ISBN-13 978-1-931360-34-0

Copyright © 2009 Laurie Lanzen Harris

The information in this publication was compiled from the sources cited and from other sources considered reliable. While every possible effort has been made to ensure reliability, the publisher will not assume liability for damages caused by inaccuracies in the data, and makes no warranty, express or implied, on the accuracy of the information contained herein.

This book is printed on acid-free paper meeting the ANSI Z39.48 Standard. The infinity symbol that appears above indicates that the paper in this book meets that standard.

∞

Printed in the United States

Juv
973.2
C719r

Contents

Part III: Biographical Profiles

Preface

Welcome to *Colonial America and the Revolutionary War*. Since beginning the *Biography for Beginners* series in 1995, we have published several monographs in areas of high interest for young readers, including U.S. Presidents, world explorers, authors, inventors, and African-American leaders. Three years ago we surveyed librarians for additional areas of interest for young readers, and they suggested a volume on Colonial America and the Revolutionary War era.

The Plan of the Work

Like other monographs in the Biography for Beginners series, *Colonial America and the Revolutionary War* is written for early readers, ages 7 to 10. The volume is especially created for young students in a format they can read, understand, and use for assignments. The volume begins with entries on the major early immigrant groups. The next section includes essays on the Revolutionary War, including causes, political history, and the most important battles. This section concludes with sections on the conclusion of the war and the establishment of the new U.S. government. The next part includes 28 biographical profiles, arranged alphabetically. In this section, each entry begins with a heading listing the individual's name, birth and death dates, and a brief description of his or her importance to American history. Boldfaced headings lead readers to information on birth, youth, growing up, education, marriage and family, and the nature of the individual's accomplishment. The entries also include portraits of the individual, as well as paintings, photos, and other illustrations to enhance the reader's understanding of the person's achievement. The volume concludes with a section describing the most important symbols of the revolutionary era, with information on their origins and importance.

Entries end with a list of World Wide Web sites. These sites have been reviewed for accuracy and suitability for use by young students. A bibliography of works used in the compilation of the entries is at the end of this Preface.

Audience

This book is intended for young readers in grades two through five who are studying American history for the first time. Most children will use this book to study one individual or group at a time, usually as part of a class assignment. Within the entries, the names of individuals who appear in the biographical section are boldfaced, to act as a cross-reference. A Glossary of terms common to colonial American history appears at the end of the book. These Glossary terms appear in the text in bold-faced capitals. This section concludes with a group of "Brief Biographies," featuring short profiles of people prominent in the early colonial era.

Index

An Index covering names and key words concludes the volume. The Index has been created with the young reader in mind, and therefore contains a limited number of terms that have been simplified for ease of research.

Our Advisors

Colonial America and the Revolutionary War was reviewed by an Advisory Board that includes school librarians and public librarians. The thoughtful comments and suggestions of the Board members have been invaluable in developing this publication. Any errors, however, are mine alone. I would like to list the members of the Advisory Board and to thank them again for their efforts.

Nancy Margolin Chapel Hill, NC	McDougle Elementary School
Deb Rothaug Plainview, NY	Pasadena Elementary School
Laurie Scott Farmington Hills, MI	Farmington Hills Community Library
Joyce Siler Kansas City, MO	Westridge Elementary School

Your Comments Are Welcome

Our goal is to provide accurate, accessible historical and biographical information for early readers. Please write or call me with your comments.

Acknowledgments

I would like to thank the Library of Congress Prints and Photographs and American Memory division for textual and visual material. Thank you to Sans Serif for outstanding design and layout.

Bibliography

This is a listing of works used in the compilation of the volume. Most of the works cited here are written at the high school reading level and are generally beyond the reading level of early elementary students. However, many librarians consider these reliable, objective points of departure for further research. Special thanks to my friend and colleague Helene Henderson, for her outstanding work in the area of holidays and symbols.

Columbia Encyclopedia, 2005 ed.

Compton's Encyclopedia, 2005 ed.

Fischer, David Hackett. *Albion's Seed: Four British Folkways in America*, 1989.

Hawke, David Freeman. *Everyday Life in Early America,* 1988.

Henderson, Helene. *Holiday Symbols and Customs*, 2008.

Henderson, Helene. *Patriotic Holidays of the United States*, 2006.

Ichord, Loretta Frances. *Hasty Pudding, Johnnycakes, and Other Good Stuff: Cooking in Colonial America,* 1998.

McCullough, David. *John Adams*, 2001.

McCullough, David. *1776*, 2005.

Laurie Harris, Editor and Publisher
Favorable Impressions

Introduction

The Settling of the New World

By 1750, the area we call Colonial America had been settled by waves of European immigrants who began arriving in the 1600s. The area stretched along the Atlantic coast from present-day Maine to Georgia. The 13 original colonies—Massachusetts (including what is now Maine), New Hampshire, New York, Rhode Island, Connecticut, New Jersey, Pennsylvania, Delaware, Maryland, Virginia, North Carolina, South Carolina, and Georgia—were by then united by British rule. But they were from several distinct ethnic and cultural groups, and they brought to the New World those ways of life, as they settled in their new American homeland.

In 1750, more than 80% of American colonists were from British backgrounds. Some were from families that had come in the first waves of migration that took place in the 1600s. Others were more recent arrivals.

Jamestown, the first permanent English settlement in the New World, was established in 1607. The area that would become Massachusetts was the site of the next small group of immigrants. They were the Pilgrims, and settled Plymouth. The next, much larger wave of immigrants, the Puritans, left East Anglia for the New World beginning in 1629. Their way of life became the greatest influence on the colonial culture of New England. From 1645 to 1670, thousands of Royalists left England and settled what is now Virginia. They would influence the life of colonial Virginia for decades. Beginning around 1675, immigrants from the English Midlands, many of them followers of the Quaker faith, settled Delaware, Pennsylvania, and parts of New Jersey. The Quakers' way of life became the dominant culture in their area of settlement. The last major wave of immigrants, many of them of Scots ancestry, came from north Britain and Northern Ireland and migrated to Appalachia in the 1700s. Their way of life influenced the Appalachian area and the frontier settlements. There were also important internal migrations. In the late 1600s, colonists migrated from Virginia to settle what became North and South Carolina. One of the latest colonies settled was Georgia, founded by James Oglethorpe in 1732, as a land of second chance for impoverished Englishmen and women.

In addition to these English immigrants, there were large groups of Germans who migrated to the colonies in the 1700s. Many of them settled in Pennsylvania, and became known as the "Pennsylvania Dutch." (They weren't Dutch, they were "Deutsche," the German word for "German." That little mistake has become part of our American vocabulary.) Another major immigrant group were the real Dutch, who settled New York City and the Hudson River Valley in the 1600s. By 1750, however, they had come under English rule.

Each of these immigrant groups established their own cultures in the New World. They followed different religions, had different ideas about raising families, education, land owning, and work. This book begins with an exploration of these major cultural groups.

We explore where the colonists came from, and where they settled. We discuss their religious beliefs, and the structure of their settlements and governments. We explore what it was like to be part of a family, go to school, and belong to a community. We talk about meals, manners, houses, and foods. We discuss games and sports that colonial children played, and how they celebrated holidays. We explain how these major groups differed from one another, and how that affected their lives.

It is important to note that we have not, by any means, been able to tell the story of *all* immigrant groups who came to the New World in the pre-Revolutionary War era. Nor can we claim that all individuals in each major group shared all the folkways or ways of life outlined here. What we have attempted to provide is an introduction to the major colonial folkways, relying on widely accepted historical understanding of the major immigrant groups.

The volume also includes sections on the impact of colonization on two other populations: Native Americans and African-American slaves. When the first settlers came to the shores of the New World in the 1500s, Native American tribes had been living in North America for thousands of years. How were their lives effected by the mass migration? And what was life like for African-American slaves? Most had come as the property of wealthy colonists, some were stolen from their homelands and separated from their families. What were their lives like, as the colonies readied for war in the name of freedom denied to them?

The American Revolution

In 1770, most of the area that is now the eastern United States were colonies of England. The American colonists paid taxes to the British government and were ruled by a king, George III. The next portion of this book describes the historical, social, and political atmosphere of the era, focusing on what led the colonists to break with their English rulers, declare themselves independent, and fight a war to secure their freedom. We include summaries of the major battles of the Revolution, the war's conclusion, and the peace that followed. This section also includes information on the writing and ratifying of the U.S. Constitution.

The next section features biographical profiles of major figures of the Revolutionary War era, and follows the familiar format of previous Biography for Beginners titles. These men and women played pivotal roles during the era, and many went on to become leaders of the new nation.

The final section explains the major symbols of Colonial America and the Revolution. It describes the historical backgrounds of our most treasured early American symbols, including the flag, the eagle, the Liberty Bell, the Liberty Tree and Pole, the Liberty Cap, and Yankee Doodle.

The Appendix contains the text of several documents important to the history of Colonial America and the founding of the United States. It includes the text of the Mayflower Compact, William Penn's Charter of Privileges, the Declaration of Independence, the Constitution of the United States, and the Bill of Rights. A note on the texts: the text included in each case is the original, with original spellings and capitalizations. While they may be unfamiliar to a modern reader, they are significant artifacts of an earlier era, and are offered in that context.

Part I:

Colonial America

The Early Colonial Era

The Earliest European Explorers and the First Settlements

When we think of the Colonial Era, we often think first of the Pilgrims of New England. But the era actually began much earlier, with the first European explorers. And that first explorer was Leif Erikson.

Leif Erikson

Erikson was a Viking explorer and the first European to reach North America. Some time around 1,000 A.D., Erikson and his men traveled to what was probably Baffin Island, Labrador, and Newfoundland. Archeologists have found what they believe are Viking ruins on Newfoundland that date from about 1,000 A.D.

Christopher Columbus and the Spanish Explorers

The next Europeans to travel to what became known as the "New World" were explorers from Spain. Christopher Columbus is the most famous of these explorers. Although we say that Columbus "discovered America," he never got to the continental United States. Instead, his journeys took him to several spots in the Caribbean, and in Central and South America.

Still, Columbus is tremendously important to understanding Colonial America. Although he didn't realize it, he proved to the world that there was a huge land mass—North America—between Europe and Asia. More importantly, unlike other explorers who only wanted to trade or travel, Columbus built settlements in the New World. The settlements were created with the intention of having a continuing relationship with the people of the New World. Thus, the first permanent European colony in North America was founded in 1565 by the Spanish, in St. Augustine, Florida.

Columbus's explorations made it possible for Europeans to begin a new life in the colonies of the New World. His discoveries started the migration of Europeans and their ways of life to what would become the United States.

Columbus is important in other, more controversial ways, too. He fought with and enslaved some of the native populations he encountered. Later Spanish explorers, like Hernando Cortes, conquered native populations and destroyed them. The Europeans also brought diseases to which the natives had no resistance. These diseases killed entire tribes.

The European explorers also claimed the Native American tribes' land and any material wealth, such as gold, as their own. In so doing, they began a hostile relationship with the native populations of the New World that would echo down the centuries.

FURTHER RESEARCH:

Biography for Beginners: World Explorers, pp. 133-150 (Columbus); pp.225-232 (Erikson).

The Beginning of English Settlements in the New World

By the 1600s, the influence of the Spanish was waning. It was the beginning of the era of English influence in the New World. Over the next century, some 80,000 English settlers, would journey to America. Guided by their faith, their quest for a new life or new business ventures, they claimed the colonial sites that would become their home, and eventually the first states of a new nation.

Jamestown: The Early Settlement of Virginia

In 1605, English merchants petitioned the king of England, James I, for the right to build a colony in Virginia. It was a "charter," and granted a group of English merchants, the Virginia Company, the right to settle a specific area. From the beginning, it was a business enterprise. The charter spoke of bringing Christianity and "human Civility" to the "Infidels and Savages." But it clearly stated another purpose: "to dig, mine, and search for all Manner of Mines of Gold, Silver, and Copper."

Who Were the Jamestown Settlers?

In May 1607, a group of 105 settlers landed on Jamestown Island, 60 miles from the mouth of the Chesapeake Bay. This first group of Jamestown settlers included 101 men and four boys, ranging in age from 9 to 57 years old. There were no

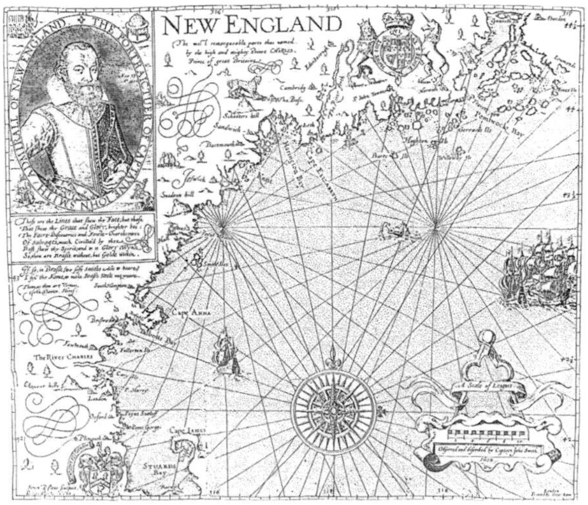

Captain James Smith's map of New England, from 1624.

women or girls in that first group. They came largely from the area around London. About half of them were "gentry." That means they were landowning men. Others were craftsmen, carpenters, masons, and blacksmiths. Some were general laborers. There was also a preacher and a doctor.

Like all the settlers who came to the New World, they came for many different reasons. Some wanted to search for gold. Some wanted to own land, which they couldn't do in England because only the wealthy owned property. Some were seeking better economic opportunities than were available to them in England.

This was the group that founded Jamestown. It was the first permanent English colony in the New World. They settled and built a fort. But they chose to live in an area where there were several problems. The swamp-like climate harbored malaria and other diseases. The local Algonquin tribe, the Powhatan, was hostile to the settlers, and attacked them. At the end of the first year, only 32 of the original colonists had survived.

There were other problems, too. The colony was established under a charter that gave control of Jamestown to a few owners of the company. The people who worked the land were hired laborers, not owners. The merchants of the Virginia Company also didn't provide guidance to the colonists. They didn't set up a local authority to oversee the growth of the settlement and provide necessities like food and housing. Instead of promoting farming and building, they encouraged the laborers to try to find gold and silver.

The lack of leadership, planning, and vision for the colony almost led to its failure. **CAPTAIN JOHN SMITH** helped save the colony. One of the more colorful figures in early American history,

Pocahontas saving Captain John Smith's life.

Smith was a soldier of fortune before he came to Jamestown. He helped the colonists plant crops and defend themselves against the hostile Algonquin people. But he is best known to history as the prisoner of Wahunsunacock, Chief of the Powhatan, and his rescue by the chief's daughter, **POCAHONTAS**.

Pocahontas is an important figure in American history. ("Pocahontas" was a nickname. Her real name was Matoaka.) In her efforts to free Smith, and her personal life, she brought peace between the English settlers and her people. She married an Englishman, John Rolfe, and converted to Christianity. Tragically, she died very young, at the age of 22. But her descendants live in Virginia to this day.

The exact details of Smith's captivity are unknown. He was known to be a boastful man, who often exaggerated his achievements. But according to his account, he was captured by the

Powhatan and held captive for several weeks. Smith always insisted that it was Pocahantas who rescued him from death. He was eventually returned to the Jamestown colony, where he became its leader.

Pocahontas, pictured in English dress.

The colony was badly in need of leadership. They lacked food and fresh water. Some had squabbled among themselves. Others had deserted the colony. Smith set out to explore the region and find food. He also created rules for the colonists, including an order that everyone had to contribute to raising food. "He who does not work, will not eat," he declared.

Due in part to Smith's contributions, Jamestown survived. He continued to lead the colony until 1609, when he was injured in an accident. Smith went to England for treatment, and never returned to Jamestown.

This was a very difficult time for the colony. It was known as the "starving time." The hardship and suffering were terrible. Of a population of 214 in early 1609, there were only 60 alive by early 1610. The colonists abandoned the settlement. A new governor arrived with supplies, and the colony revived somewhat.

Major Crop—Tobacco

In 1609, tobacco began to be planted and harvested by the colonists. It soon became their greatest cash crop. With the money

Early settlers building the fort at Jamestown.

they earned from exporting tobacco, colonists bought manufactured items from England. The colony grew. The settlement needed new farmers. The leaders decided to allow ownership of farms to bring in more settlers. So planters became owners of the tobacco plantations.

The First Representative Government

In 1619, the settlers of Jamestown and other areas of what would become Virginia created a House of Burgesses. It was the first legislative assembly in America, made up of 22 burgesses who represented 11 plantations. Their job was to advise the colonial governor on local issues. It was the first system of representative government in the land. Most importantly, it offered the model that spread throughout Colonial America.

Slavery

Sadly, 1619 marks another "first" for Jamestown. In that year, the first African slaves were brought to the colony. These Africans were "indentured servants." That means they may have been able to work for several years, then gain their freedom, but their actual fate is not known. Whether they eventually became free, or ended their lives in slavery is uncertain. But within decades, African slavery became a way of life in Virginia, and in other colonies as well.

Virginia Becomes a Crown Colony

In 1622, the Algonquin tribe attacked the plantations and killed over 300 people. King James decided that the Virginia Company should lose its charter. The area became a crown colony, under English control. Most of the settlers moved to an area east of the original settlement.

Life in Jamestown

Recently, researchers have dug in the area of the original settlement, looking for artifacts from the early settlers. These range from old tools to bones of animals, and help modern people understand how the Jamestown settlers lived. From their research, they believe the settlers ate mostly fish, turtles, and other animals native to Virginia. They discovered the tools that settlers used to mine for gold and make buildings. They even found dice and a trumpet mouthpiece, indicating how the settlers may have spent their leisure time.

WORLD WIDE WEB SITES:

http://memory.loc.gov/ammem/
http://ngm.nationalgeographic.com/ngm/jamestown
http://www.apva.org/history/index.html
http://www.historicjamestowne.org/learn/

The Pilgrims of Plymouth Plantation

In 1620, another migration of English settlers reached the New World. They came to be called the "Pilgrims." It is a word used to describe anyone who travels to a place for reasons of faith. And though those early English settlers never called themselves "Pilgrims," that's what we call them now. These early colonists came from England seeking freedom to worship as they pleased, and to start a new life. Some 101 men, women, and children left the English port of Plymouth in September 1620, aboard the *Mayflower*. They landed on Cape Cod, in what would become Massachusetts, on November 6, 1620.

The Pilgrims land in the New World.

Religious Beliefs

The Pilgrims left England because they thought the state religion—the Church of England—was corrupt. They believed that each individual group should be in control of worship, and did not recognize any higher church authority. They also believed that faith was personal. They thought that religious beliefs should be determined by each individual, not by church leaders, or the King. Such beliefs were against the law in England in 1620. So, to safeguard themselves and their beliefs, they had to leave England.

It is important to note that the "Pilgrims" were more correctly "Separatists." Unlike the Puritans, who wanted to "purify" the existing church (see section below), they wanted to "separate" from the Church of England, the official religion of their homeland.

Governmental Organization

Before leaving England, the Pilgrims had formed a joint-stock company. They wanted to establish a colony on land near the mouth of the Hudson River, in what is now New York. This was actually within the area still granted to the London Company. But the *Mayflower* was blown off course, and landed on Cape Cod by accident.

The Pilgrims decided they were outside the area controlled by the London Company. They declared they were free of governmental control. So they decided to create their own governing laws. That set of laws is known as the **MAYFLOWER COMPACT**.

The Mayflower Compact is one of the most important government documents in U.S. history. In it, the colonists agreed to follow

Pilgrims sign the Mayflower Compact.

majority rule, to enact their own laws, and to cooperate for the general good of colony. Here is part of what the document says:

"We whose names are underwritten do by these Presents, solemnly and mutually in the presence of God and one another covenant and combine ourselves under into a civil Body Politick . . . and by Virtue hereof do enact such just and equal Laws . . . as shall be thought most meet and convenient for the general Good of the Colony."

These simple words created both a government for the Pilgrims, and set the standard followed by the other colonies as they established themselves in the New World.

Who Were They?

The 101 men, women, and children who came to Cape Cod in 1620 came for many different reasons. Many came to worship freely; most came to provide a better life for themselves and their children. It is important to note that, unlike the settlers at Jamestown, there were several *families* who settled in Plymouth.

They were from the English middle class, and were neither rich nor poor. They came from a wide variety of backgrounds. Some came from London, some from smaller towns in the countryside. Some were craftsman, some were fisherman, some were farmers. Not all were Separatists; some practiced other faiths. Some of the Separatists had fled England and had lived for a time in Holland.

The Mayflower *at sea.*

When they had the opportunity to start a new life in the New World, they chose it eagerly.

The settlers had signed agreements with the owners of the joint-stock company to work for them for seven years. After that, they would own the land they worked and lived on. This was very important to them. In England, only the very rich were landowners.

The settlers named their new home after their English home, Plymouth (also spelled "Plimouth.") They called their settlement "Plymouth Plantation." The climate was cold, and life was more difficult than they had expected. Over the first winter, nearly half the settlers died of disease.

The early settlers thought they would make their living fishing. At that time, the oceans and rivers teemed with fish. But after living in Plymouth for several years, they became successful farmers and fur traders as well. They learned both of these skills through the local tribe, the Wampanoag.

The Wampanoag

The Wampanoag were the Native people who lived in the area settled by the Pilgrims. Their name means "People of the First Light." They had lived in the area of the Plymouth Plantation for hundreds of years. In the early 1600s, some 40,000 Wampanoag lived in an area covering most of coastal Massachusetts and Rhode Island.

Many colonists had never learned to farm. The Wampanoag helped them prepare the soil and introduced them to the crops that would help them survive in the New World.

Squanto

Of special help to the colonists was **SQUANTO** (1585?-1622). He was a Wampanoag who had been captured and sold into slavery by Spanish explorers when he was a young man. He escaped, and fled to England. There, he learned the language, and returned to his native land aboard an English ship in 1619, one year before the Pilgrims arrived.

He returned to his tribe's area, and when the Pilgrims arrived, he became a helpful friend. Thanks to his help, the colonists learned to farm, to fish, and to survive in their new land. Later, he acted as an interpreter between the settlers and the Wampanoag.

Their Food

First, the colonists cleared the land of trees. Then, the Wampanoag showed them how to fertilize the soil using herring, a local fish. Then, they helped them plant corn, which the Pilgrims called "Indian corn." It had multi-colored kernels, the kind you see in harvest displays today. Back then, it was ground into cornmeal and flour, which were used to bake breads and make cereals. It soon became the most important food crop they grew.

The Wampanoag also helped them plant vegetables, like pumpkins and peas, that grew well and were nutritious. After several years, the settlers were able to grow enough food to sell. They also traded crops with the Wampanoag for furs. They sold these furs to people in England. With the money, they were able to buy things they couldn't make for themselves, and staples like sugar.

The colonists liked to eat meat. They raised cows, pigs, and sheep they'd brought from England. They also ate fish, wild birds, and other game they hunted.

It's hard to imagine in our time, but the Pilgrims didn't think water or cow's milk were healthy to drink. They preferred beer, even for children. They ate three meals a day, like we do, but what they ate was quite different. For breakfast, they ate bread and cheese. Their mid-day meal, called "dinner," was the biggest meal of the day. They often ate meat at dinner, as well as bread or cooked cereal and vegetables. The meal was designed to fill them up for all the hard work of building homes and tending farms. The last meal of the day, called supper, was smaller, perhaps some bread and cheese again, before a long night's sleep.

Their Homes

The Pilgrims began to build houses in Plymouth as soon as they arrived. They needed wood, and cut down trees in the nearby

Plymouth Plantation, as recreated in the modern era, showing the style of Pilgrims' houses.

forests. They used these to fashion the frame of the house, and to make boards for its sides. They had brought nails and woodworking tools from England. The roofs were thatched, made of grasses they collected. They made the interior walls using a mixture of water, clay, and grass. The floors were made of dirt.

The finished homes were quite small; often an entire family lived in just one large room. The homes had large hearths for cooking and heating the house. Any windows were very small. The interiors of the homes were lit by the hearth fire and candles.

Their Clothing

Like the Puritans, the Pilgrims wore clothes that were dark-colored, including brown, dark green, and blue. Boys and girls both wore long gowns, like nightgowns, from the time they were babies until about the age of 6 or 7. At that point, girls and boys began to dress like women and men. Girls began to wear "shifts," which were like a long dress, often with a corset-like vest, a jacket, and an apron on top. To keep their legs warm, they wore "petticoats" under their shifts. Clothing was made of durable fabric, like wool, linen, and canvas.

As girls grew up and changed the way they dressed, they were also signifying their changing roles. They became more like their mothers, and learned to tend to the needs of the household. A cloth apron helped protect a girl's clothes while preparing food, washing clothes, and helping her mother keep house.

Around the age of 6 or 7, boys also began to wear the clothes and take on the roles of men. They started to wear pants, called breeches. They also wore long shirts, and "doublets," which were

This drawing of Pilgrims going to church shows their style of dress.

like jackets. They also often wore an apron. Men's aprons were often made of leather, to protect their clothing as they worked with wood or metal.

Everyone wore stockings and shoes or boots. They wore wool or linen caps or hats made of felt. Coats, cloaks, and mittens were made of wool, which came from their sheep.

Childhood: School and Work

Children were expected to work with their parents, in the home and in the fields. Parents of the time thought is was important to teach their children these life skills, and everyone was expected to contribute to the family's well-being. They were very important to the survival of the colony.

Unlike the Massachusetts Bay Colony, there weren't official public schools in the Plymouth Plantation for many years. So most parents taught their children to read and write at home.

Games and Sports

Versions of many of the games we enjoy today were played by the children of Plymouth Plantation. They played a game like tic-tac-toe, which they called "naughts and crosses." They played

A painting of the first Thanksgiving.

a game like checkers they called "draughts." They also liked running games, and sports like bowling. They didn't have much time for play, though, because their lives were so busy with chores. But they enjoyed games and sports when they could.

The First Thanksgiving

Many people, young and old, think that the Pilgrims held the first Thanksgiving. But recent research tells a different story. Some historians believe that the Spanish explorer Ponce de Leon held Thanksgiving celebrations as early 1513 in Florida, after he had safely landed there.

By the time the Pilgrims arrived, the Wampanoag had held thanksgiving harvest celebrations for generations. They had specific festivals tied to the harvest of a certain crop, like strawberries or corn.

Also, the Pilgrims didn't think of a harvest celebration as "Thanksgiving." For them, that was a term for a religious day of prayer, not a festive celebration.

Yet sometime in the fall of 1621, following their first harvest in the Plymouth colony, the Pilgrims did indeed have a feast, with games and other celebrations. They invited almost 100 of the local Wampanoag, and together they celebrated their first successful harvest in the New World.

There is a quote from a diary of a colonist named Edward Winslow describing that first Thanksgiving. He wrote that: "For three days we entertained and feasted, and [the Wampanoag] went out and killed five Deere which they brought to the Plantation and bestowed on our Governor, and upon the Captain, and others."

William Bradford

The "Governor" mentioned by Winslow is William Bradford (1590-1657). He was the second, and best known, governor of the Plymouth colony. Born in England, Bradford had moved to Holland with the early Pilgrims, in search of religious freedom. He was aboard the *Mayflower* when in landed on Cape Cod in 1620.

In 1621, Bradford negotiated an important treaty with Massasoit, the chief of the Wampanoag. In the treaty, Massasoit granted the tribe's land to the Pilgrims. He also vowed peace between the Native peoples and the colonists. Squanto helped Bradford in drawing up the treaty. He also acted as an interpreter between Bradford and the Wampanoag. Sadly, Squanto died just a year later, while on a scouting party around Cape Cod.

Much of what we know of the early years of the Plymouth colony is from Bradford's writing. His book is titled *The History of the Plymouth Plantation, 1620-1647.* It is full of rich detail of the early Pilgrim settlement.

The next major migration of colonists from England truly transformed the New World. They were the Puritans. They went on to great success in the area that became New England, and in 1691, annexed the Plymouth Colony.

WORLD WIDE WEB SITES:

http://www.plimoth.org
This is the web site of the Plimoth Plantation historical site. It is full of information on the Pilgrims and the Wampanoag.

The Mayflower
http://www.rootsweb.ancestry.com/~mosmd/mayfpas.htm
This remarkable site has much information, including brief biographical facts of all the people who sailed on the Mayflower.

Other:
http://www.loc.gov/exhibits/treasures/trr003.html

Note: There is a complete copy of the Mayflower Compact in the Appendix.

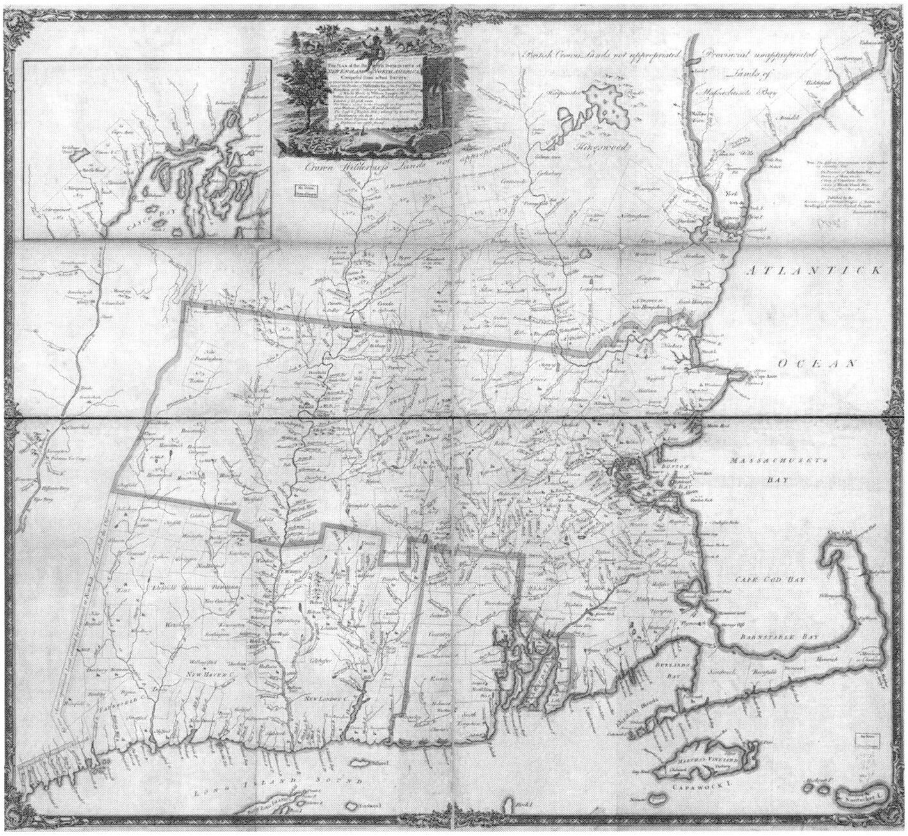

Map of New England, from 1753.

New England

The Puritans

In 1629, a mass migration began from Eastern England to what would become Massachusetts. Over the next 11 years, from 1629 to 1640, more than 21,000 men, women, and children emigrated to settle first Massachusetts, then Rhode Island, Connecticut, Maine, Vermont, and New Hampshire. They were known as the "Puritans."

Religious Beliefs

Most of the Puritans came from an area of England called East Anglia. They came to the New World seeking relief from a desperate political situation. As Puritans, they wanted to "purify" the Church of England, the official religion of their country. They thought that their Christian religion had become corrupt, and needed to be changed. Like the Pilgrims, who were Separatists, they were unable to worship as they wished, and they fled England to escape persecution. (You can read about the Pilgrims in an earlier chapter.)

Seeking religious and political freedom, the Puritans moved to Massachusetts. There, they set up one of the first permanent settlements in the New World, the Massachusetts Bay Colony. Over the next 150 years, their numbers would grow to nearly one million people, as new generations expanded into the areas we now call Connecticut, New Hampshire, Maine, Vermont, New York, and New Jersey.

Who Were They?

In 1630, the first of thousands of Puritans emigrated to Massachusetts. This large group had many things in common. First and foremost, they shared a common faith that was the bedrock of their lives. They believed that they were building a "Bible Commonwealth" in the New World. As the American historian David Hackett Fischer wrote, "Religion was not merely their leading purpose. It was their only purpose."

Also, like the settlers of the Plymouth Plantation, they were mostly families: mothers, fathers, children, and related people.

The Puritans were very selective: not just anybody could join their colony. People wanting to live in the colony had to request permission, have recommendations, and have a skill or trade. Also, those that didn't fit in were banished from the colony. Some of these, like **ROGER WILLIAMS**, would go on to found other colonies. (See information on Williams below.)

The Puritans came from the "middling" classes of England. A few were wealthy landowners, but most were from the middle class. They were yeoman, craftsman, merchants, and artisans. That means that they brought a variety of skills that were needed to build a new society.

The Puritans wanted skilled laborers. Only about one-quarter of the colonists were servants. (In contrast, the Royalists who settled Virginia, described below, had a servant population that included about three-quarters of the total early settlers.)

Most Puritan immigrants were neither rich nor poor, but they had enough money to afford their passage to the New World. That means they did not have years of debt to work off, as other colonists did. They were also able to build homes and start to make a living.

The Climate

The Puritans found a climate in the New World that was much different from East Anglia. It was very cold in coastal Massachusetts. There were certain positive benefits to the cold. It killed diseases, like malaria, that flourished in some of the southern colonies. People lived much longer lives, too. The Puritans became the first society in history in which grandparents were common.

But the climate also led to a shorter growing season for crops. The soil was rich in certain areas. But generally, the land was not rich enough to allow large tract farms to develop. Instead, most of the communities that developed were farm towns, with most of the men working on small farms. This encouraged people who could perform more than one job. For example, an individual developed skills as both a farmer and a blacksmith.

Their Homes

The Puritans built homes in the "Salt Box" style. They were wooden structures, shaped in a rectangle, and two stories high. The roof was distinctive: in the back of the house, it sloped at a steep angle to the ground. The roofs looked like an old-fashioned box of salt, and that's how they got their name.

An example of the "Salt Box" style house.

Family Life

Family was the center of life for the members of the Bay Colony. The leaders encouraged people to marry. They believed that strong marriages meant a strong community. Married couples had large families. Parents were very strict. Children were expected to be obedient to their parents, and a have a deep reverence for their elders. They could be very harsh in punishing their children.

The idea of family was so important to the Puritans that single people were required to live as part of a family. They thought it encouraged good behavior, and the best for the community.

Another custom unique to the Puritans was called "sending out." Parents often sent a child to live with another family. They did this for a number of reasons. Sometimes the parents wanted a child to live closer to school, or to live with another family while working as an apprentice to learn a skill. Sometimes they wanted

A painting of a Puritan family at the dinner table, with the child standing.

the child to learn to behave better. They thought children might learn to act properly in someone else's home.

A book called *The New England Primer. A Guide to the Art of Reading*, published in 1787, gives us a glimpse of what was expected of children of the era:

Good Children must
Fear God all Day,
Parents obey,
No false thing say,
Love Christ alway,
In secret pray,
Make no delay,
In doing Good.

The Meetinghouse

Religion was a part of every aspect of daily life for the Puritans. They were Protestants and called themselves "Congregationalists." They went to services in Congregational "meetinghouses" rather than traditional churches. These were very plain structures. They look very different from Christian churches today. There was no altar, and in the center of the house, there was usually a stairway leading to a pulpit. On Sundays, the entire family spent the day at services. Men and women sat on separate sides of the building, listening to sermons and readings. Children, too, had to sit still and pay attention.

Governmental Organization

The Puritans' system of government included town meetings, town selectmen, and a set of laws. The colonists generally lived

The interior of the Alna Meetinghouse, built in 1789 in Lincoln County, Maine.

close to one another, in a system of farm towns that developed throughout New England. They held town meetings at the meetinghouse. The town "selectmen" were officers elected by the townsmen. At the town meetings, individuals discussed all aspects of life. They made laws about property, taxes, immigrants, and other issues affecting the community.

The meetings allowed townspeople a voice in the government. It was not a representative democracy, as was to develop later. But it did allow for a broad range of opinions. It also established the idea of government working to reach "consensus," or general agreement. Individuals worked together to create a set of laws for their communities. These early principles of government and freedom would in time help form the ideas behind the Revolutionary War and the founding of the United States.

Here is an example, from the 1641 Massachusetts Body of Liberties, that states some of these ideas:

> "Every man whether inhabitant or foreigner, free or not free shall have liberty to come to any public Court, Council or Town meeting, and either by speech or writing to move any lawful . . . question, or to present any necessary motion, complaint, petition, bill, or information."

John Winthrop

John Winthrop (1588-1649) was the first governor of the Massachusetts Bay Colony. He had been elected governor before the Puritans left England, and was re-elected many times. The devout Winthrop famously wrote that he believed that the Puritans were founding "a City on a Hill," to inspire all.

He could be a very stern ruler—he banished dissenters like Roger Williams from the community. But he did bring new ideas to the governing of the colony. He thought that a small group of Puritan leaders needed the popular support of the people to govern effectively. He wanted to extend governmental power to a larger number of colonists. He and the other Puritan leaders made about 100 of the new settlers "freeman." They became part of the governing authority, adding to its success and stability.

Their Food

The Puritans ate simple foods. They didn't like to "indulge" their appetites for tasty foods. They thought that was wrong. By the 1770s, two main dishes made up most of their daily diet: baked beans and brown bread. The "peaseporridge" of nursery rhymes

A modern-day recreation of a Puritan kitchen.

refers to the baked beans they ate every day. Many homes had brick ovens, and these were used to bake breads and pies. Puritan women baked many kinds of pies based on what they grew, including pumpkin and fruit pies. They also ate fresh fruits and vegetables in season. Another favorite was the famous "New England boiled dinner": meat and vegetables boiled together for a long period of time.

Their main beverage was apple cider. It wasn't the kind of cider we have today. It was "fermented," so it had an alcoholic content similar to beer.

It's interesting to note that in many Puritan households, the parents and older adults sat at a table at mealtime, while the children stood behind them. As in every aspect of daily life, children followed a strict set of rules at the table. One book from the 1770s, called *A Pretty Little Pocket Book*, set down some of those rules. Children were supposed to bow to their parents in greeting them. They were never to seat themselves until their parents told them to, and could not speak until spoken to.

Childhood: School and Work

The Puritans valued education. In 1642, members of the Bay Colony made a law requiring all parents to teach their children to read. This law was copied in Connecticut, New Haven, and Plymouth colonies. In 1647, the Puritans created another law that required every town with 50 or more families to have a schoolmaster. Only boys went to school, but many Puritans taught their girls at home. Parents taught their children to read using the Bible.

Over the century, public schools thrived in Massachusetts. By 1770, children in Massachusetts received twice as many years of education as those in Virginia. Also by 1770, more than 80 percent of men and 50 percent of women could make their "mark." That means they could sign wills, deeds, and other documents.

For the Puritans, the instruction of children also included preparing them for lives as adults. Girls were taught to cook, sew, and tend to household duties. Boys were taught to farm, fish, gather wood, and prepare for work of some kind. Some, when they were old enough, apprenticed to a skilled tradesman to learn a trade.

The family farm produced enough food for a family, and enough for them to sell. That helped establish trade between the Bay

Colony and the rest of the world. Boston developed into one of the busiest harbors of the era. Trade allowed the Puritans to sell their agricultural products—wheat, oats, barley, fish, beef, pork, butter, cheese, and lumber. In return, they could get tea, sugar, and goods from the islands of the Caribbean and Europe.

Their Clothing

The Puritans dressed simply. They didn't wear black, which they didn't think was plain enough. Instead, they chose plain clothes in what they called "sadd," or muted colors. They thought that wearing gaudy colors and new fashions was wrong. The Bay Colony had rules for dress, and even for hair length. These rules had to be obeyed by everybody within the community. No long hair, no lace or other adornments, and no short sleeves were allowed. Both men and women wore large black hats made of felt.

By the time they were six or seven, children wore clothing that was very similar to their parents: long shirts and trousers for the boys, long blouses and skirts for the girls. Both wore aprons to protect their clothing while they did chores. They wore clothing made of cotton and wool, and boots made of leather.

An example of Puritan dress.

Games and Sports

Sports were encouraged in the Bay Colony. The Puritans thought it was good for the spirit as well as the body. Children were very busy with house work and farm work, and with their studies, too. When they had time, they were encouraged to play outdoor games, like tag, as well as hopscotch, marbles, hoops, and skating in the winter.

The Puritans encouraged games that required athletic ability, concentration, and teamwork. In fact, two very American games, football and baseball, got their start in Massachusetts.

The Boston Game: The game we know as American football was originally called the Boston Game. It developed from an old English sport that involved teams kicking a ball. By the time of the American Revolution, football was a game with strict rules. It was often associated higher education, and was often played by college teams. There is a monument in Boston Common that celebrates the first football organization in the country.

The Massachusetts Game: The game we call baseball also originated in Massachusetts. Sometimes called "town ball" or "the New England game," it was very much like the sport we have today. Teams of eight to 20 players used a bat to hit a ball thrown by a pitcher. The batter ran four bases, in a square field. It was based on an English game called "bittle-battle." It was hugely popular in New England, and spread throughout the colonies. There are descriptions of soldiers playing baseball at Valley Forge during the Revolutionary War.

The Puritans didn't like gambling games, so card games and horse racing were frowned upon. They also didn't approve of the "blood sports," like cockfighting, that were popular in the Southern colonies.

Celebrating Holidays

The Puritans thought that the Church of England's celebration of Christmas and other religious holidays was wrong. They thought it was a gaudy display for what should be a day devoted to prayer. They saw it as part of the corruption of the faith that had led them to flee England. So they did away with what we would think of the traditional celebrations of religious holidays.

Instead, they developed their own holidays. These included Election Day, Commencement Day, Thanksgiving, and Training Day. These days marked special community activities. Celebrating them brought the community closer together. On Election Day, the community members met to elect their officials. Commencement Day was a holiday linked to the school term. Training Day was established as a day when the local militia marched and did their training exercises.

Thanksgiving was first celebrated in the Bay Colony on February 22, 1630. On that day, a ship came with much-needed food that rescued the colonists from starvation. Over the years, it became a fall festival, and was held on a Thursday. The colonists would fast for one day, then have a Thanksgiving family dinner the next. The Thanksgiving holiday usually involved a sermon. The minister would talk about the founding of the colony, and they would recommit themselves to its ideals and purposes.

The Salem Witch Trials

One of the strangest, and most startling pieces of Puritan history involves the Salem Witch Trials. In 1692, more than 150 women and men from Salem, Massachusetts, were accused of practicing witchcraft. Most were accused by neighbors. Fear and hysteria gripped the community. The accused were jailed, and some were tried by authorities. Twenty people were convicted and executed for witchcraft. More died in prison. It was a dark and tragic time.

The hysteria that fed the witch trials died down within months. By the end of 1692, the governor of Massachusetts had stopped the trials, and those still in prison were released. Now we use the phrase "witch trial" to refer to a circumstance where innocent people are accused without warrant.

Roger Williams and the Founding of Rhode Island

Roger Williams (1603?-1683) was a minister in Salem, Massachusetts. He was a Puritan, but some of his views were too extreme for the Bay Colony leaders. He believed in the freedom of each individual to practice his or her own religion. Because of this, he thought it was wrong for the Puritan church to have any say in the government of the colony.

Williams also believed that the colonists had no right to take the land belonging to the Native American tribes. He thought they should buy it. Because of these two beliefs, Williams was banished from the Massachusetts Bay Colony.

With his followers, he left Massachusetts and moved to the Naragansett Bay Area. There, he founded the city of Providence. In

1643, Williams went to England. He asked for a charter for the settlement. It became known as the Rhode Island and Providence Plantation.

Williams established a democratic form of government. He offered the people of the colony complete freedom of religion. He provided a very strict separation of church and government. This early settlement drew many other dissenters from Puritan New England. Williams's ideals would influence some of the central ideas behind the Revolutionary War.

WORLD WIDE WEB SITES:

http://memory.loc.gov/ammem/
http://www.americaslibrary.gov/cgi-bin/page.cgi/jb/colonial/williams
http://www.digitalhistory.uh.edu/database
http://www.loc.gov/exhibits/religion/

Virginia and Maryland

Royalists from Southern England and Catholics in Search of Religious Freedom

In 1642, another migration began from England to the New World. This group of people was different in many ways from the Pilgrims and Puritans who settled New England. These people were the "Royalists."

The English Civil War

The Royalists got their name from their loyalty to King Charles I, the "Royal" head of England. From 1642 to 1648, England was torn by Civil War. King Charles's supporters fought against a group called the Roundheads, also called the Parliamentarians. These people were largely English Puritans who thought the King and his followers had corrupted their faith and their country. They refused to acknowledge that the King governed by divine right, the will of God. They thought they had the right to rule the country, and were willing to fight for that right.

This bloody war ended with King Charles's execution in 1649. Many of his followers, including those who settled Virginia and parts of Maryland, fled England.

Sir William Berkeley

The leader of Virginia for 35 years was **SIR WILLIAM BERKELEY**. He came to the New World in 1642 from the south of

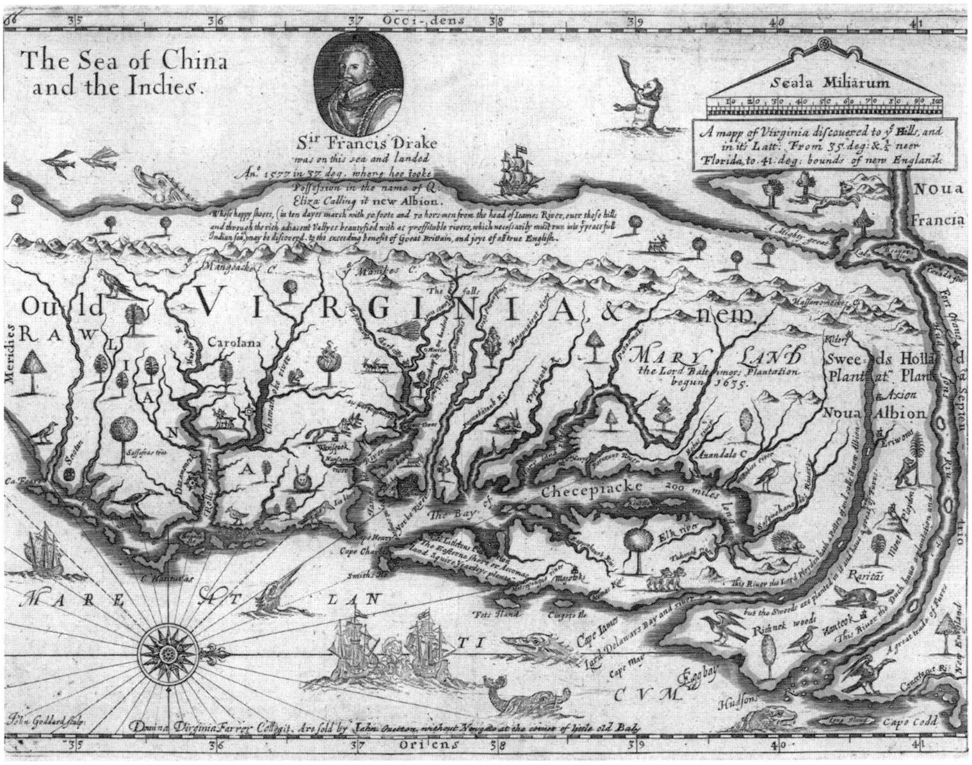

A map of Virginia, from 1667.

England. He brought with him a commission signed by King Charles I, naming him Royal Governor of Virginia.

Berkeley was a Royalist, an Anglican, and a member of the English upper class. As a Royalist, he was deeply loyal to the King. As an Anglican, he had a deep faith in the Church of England. As a member of the English upper class, he created a social and political order based on the one he knew in England. That order established a small ruling upper class and a large servant class.

Over the years, Berkeley had a great impact on the development of Virginia. He helped write its laws, establish its commerce, and shaped the makeup of its society.

Who Were the Royalists?

From 1645 to 1670, some 40,000 to 50,000 people immigrated from England to Virginia. They were very different in their social backgrounds from the Pilgrim and Puritan settlers of New England. The men who became the leaders of Virginia shared Berkeley's background. Like him, they were from the English upper class and Anglican. They were also called the "Cavaliers." After the English Civil War began, they fled their country to avoid persecution. In many cases, Berkeley recruited them to come to the New World.

The upper class Englishmen who settled Virginia made up about 25% of the population. Berkeley, as head of the government, gave this small group most of the land, and political power.

The rest of the immigrants to Virginia were from the lower classes, and most of them were male. Some 75% of them were indentured servants. That means that they had to work for the landowners for years to pay off their passage and living expenses. These were poor, unskilled workers, farming the land owned by the upper classes, as tenant farmers or servants.

The makeup of the populations of Virginia and Massachusetts were very different. In Massachusetts, the society was based on a large middle class, made up mostly of families, with family-owned farms and skilled workers. In Virginia, the largest part of the early population was male, poor, and unskilled.

Religious Beliefs

The Royalist settlers of Virginia were Anglican, members of the Church of England. They were hostile to those of other faiths. They

An example of an Anglican church,
Williamsburg, Virginia.

banished Quakers, Puritans, and others who were not Anglican. It wasn't until the 18th century that religious tolerance came to Virginia.

The Climate

The warm, humid climate of the Chesapeake Bay area was a breeding ground for typhoid, malaria, and other diseases. The unhealthy climate killed many of the new settlers.

The warmer climate did have benefits. It meant a longer growing season. Also, the soil in the areas owned by the wealthiest people was very rich. The area became divided into huge tracts of land called plantations. Over the years, the main crop became tobacco. The plantation owners began to import African slaves to work the land, along with the indentured servants and tenant farmers.

The Royal Governor's Palace in Williamsburg, an example of the houses of the wealthy in colonial Virginia.

Their Homes

The wealthiest landowners in Virginia built homes that were large brick structures, normally two stories high, with large rooms. They included high ceilings and a large central hallway, which helped the flow of air in the hot summer months.

Most of the other colonists lived in smaller homes. These were made of wood, usually one and one-half stories, with two rooms on the first floor, and several rooms on the second. They often had fireplaces and chimneys on each end of the house.

Family Life

The settlers of Virginia valued family highly. For them, "family" often meant cousins, aunts, uncles, and other relations living together. Sometimes, families also built houses close to one another.

Early Virginians often welcomed relatives in need into their homes. At that time, illness claimed the lives of many family members. In the 17th century, more than 75% of children had lost one parent before they reached adulthood. More than one-third of babies died in the first year; almost half never reached adulthood.

That meant that children were often raised in the home of an aunt, uncle, or became part of a step-family.

Virginians were encouraged to marry. Often, the married couple took part in two ceremonies. One was a service in a church, and the other, based on an ancient ritual, was jumping over a broomstick. This rite was the only wedding ceremony that was allowed to African-American slaves.

The children of colonial Virginia were raised to be strong-willed, boys in particular. At the same time, they were raised to control their emotions. The colonists taught their children proper behavior. Children memorized lists of the rules of how to behave.

When he was young, **George Washington** wrote down many of these rules, and lived by them. They included advice on friendship, morality, table manners, and other topics. Here is a sampling:

- What you may Speak in Secret to your Friend deliver not to others.
- Speak not Evil of the absent for it is unjust.
- Put not your meat to your Mouth with your Knife.
- In your hand neither Spit forth the Stones of any fruit Pye upon a Dish nor Cast anything under the table.
- Let your Recreations be Manful not Sinful.

Childhood: School

In Virginia, the amount of education a child received was based on his or her economic and social background. For example, almost all wealthy plantation owners could read and write. Few of the poor and indentured servants could. And it was against the law to teach a slave to read and write.

There weren't many schools in colonial Virginia. The children of the wealthy were tutored at home. In fact, colonial leaders like Governor Berkeley were against public education for all. He thought that it would challenge his control of the people. There were private schools for those who could afford it, but it was many years before Virginia students of all backgrounds were educated in the same numbers as the children of the northern colonies.

Their Food

As in other aspects of life, there was a great difference in the food eaten by the rich and the poor in Virginia. The wealthiest liked eating beef, as well as fresh fruits and vegetables. They often hired chefs trained in Europe to prepare their food. The poorer people of Virginia had a more limited diet, and they often had only one pot to cook in. Many of their meals, like soups, ground corn mush and greens flavored with pork, were prepared in that one pot. People at all levels also liked to add spices to their food.

Their Clothing

In colonial Virginia, wealthy landowners dressed in expensive and fashionable clothes. Wealthy men wore well-made breeches and expensive silk stockings. They wore silver buckles on their heeled shoes, and often carried swords.

Ordinary farm workers wore very simple clothing, made of inexpensive, coarse cloth. Slaves were not allowed to dress in African clothing. They, too, dressed in simple clothing of coarse cloth.

Small children in Virginia wore long shirts or dresses until the age of six or seven. The long shirts often had strings on them, that parents used to guide a child learning to walk. As they got older, children wore clothes like their parents, with girls wearing long fitted dresses, some with hoop skirts. Boys wore shirts, breeches, vests, and long socks.

Games and Sports

Virginians were very fond of sports, but they were of a different type than those played in New England. They particularly liked games they could gamble on, like horse racing. Only the upper classes were permitted to bet, so horse racing remained a game of the wealthy for years.

They were also fond of hunting for sport. The different classes hunted for different game. The wealthy hunted deer, the middle classes went after fox and rabbits, the poor killed birds. It was referred to as "blood sport," and was encouraged in young people, too.

In addition to hunting, children of the middle classes often played games familiar in modern times, like puzzles, cards, hoops, and ninepins (like bowling).

Celebrating Holidays

The Virginia colonists celebrated holidays throughout the year. The tobacco harvest was celebrated, as were religious holidays like Christmas. Christmas celebrations were much like today's, and very unlike those in New England. The Virginians enjoyed exchanging gifts, having parties, and dancing. They also celebrated Christian holidays like Lent, Easter, and Twelfth Night.

Governmental Organization

The same families that owned most of the land also ruled Virginia as members of the Royal Council. There were 12 individuals on the Council, and they had far-reaching powers. They served as one of the legislative groups and also as the supreme court. They also controlled many offices of government and

The court house in Williamsburg, Virginia.

decided how land would be distributed. So most of the power, land, and influence in the colony was held by a small percent of the population.

Virginia also had a House of Burgesses that had been in existence since the early days of Jamestown. Throughout the 18th century, the powers of the elected Burgesses continued to grow. The House of Burgesses was the place where several colonial leaders, including **Thomas Jefferson, Patrick Henry,** and **Richard Henry Lee,** became involved in the political movement leading to the Revolutionary War.

Maryland

In 1634, settlers arrived in what would become Maryland. Maryland began as an English colony when Charles I granted the land under a charter to George Calvert, Lord Baltimore. Calvert was a Catholic, and he hoped his colony would become a haven for persecuted Catholics in the New World.

George Calvert died before the colony was established. His son, Cecilius, led the early colony. He originally wanted the colony strictly controlled by a small group of men. When he realized that he couldn't get colonists to settle without giving them more freedoms, he changed his mind. Calvert allowed the settlers to own their own land and have a say in local government.

In 1649, Calvert signed a Toleration Act that included freedom of religion to all Christians. But this religious liberty didn't last. In 1689, after the English Glorious Revolution, the Anglican Church became the official religion of Maryland. After that, Catholics were again persecuted, even in their own colony. They weren't allowed to worship, vote, or hold office. This persecution continued until the Revolutionary War.

WORLD WIDE WEB SITES:

http://americaslibrary.gov/cgi-bin/page.cgi/jb/colonial/maryland
http://www.history.org/Almanack/life/trades/
http://www.loc.gov/exhibits/religion/

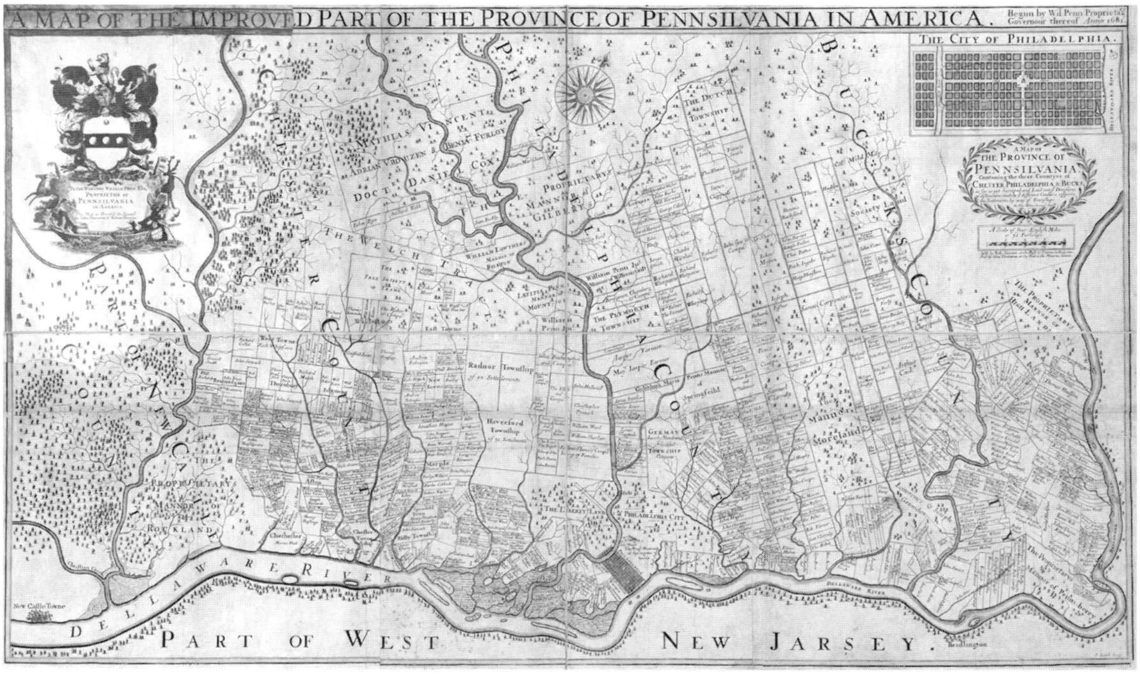

A map of Pennsylvania, from 1681.

Pennsylvania, Delaware, and Eastern New Jersey

Quakers from the Midlands

In 1675, another large group of immigrants left England for the New World. They were mainly from the Midlands region of England, and most were members of the Society of Friends, called the Quakers. From 1675 to 1725, over 23,000 of them settled what would become Pennsylvania, Delaware, and Eastern New Jersey.

Religious Beliefs

The Quakers were members of a faith called the Society of Friends. Their religious beliefs were very different from the Anglicans, Pilgrims, and Puritans. Their faith was centered on a "God of

Love and Light." They believed that each person was capable of being saved by "the inner light." For them, this light was represented in Jesus.

The Quakers didn't believe in the authority of clergy. They also didn't believe that God should be worshiped in churches. Instead, they created an organization based on the equality of individuals. They held meetings in meeting houses rather than religious services in churches.

The Quakers believed that war was wrong. They refused to support a military, unlike many other colonists. Also, they were one of the first American colonial groups to condemn slavery. They believed in the natural equality of all people under God.

Like the Puritans, the Quakers had suffered from persecution because of their faith, in both England and America. The ruling Anglicans in England imprisoned Quakers because they didn't believe in paying taxes. In Virginia, they banished them. The Puritans of Massachusetts banished Quakers, and, in some cases, burned them as witches.

The Quakers themselves developed a different approach to those who didn't share their beliefs. In their own colony in the New World, they promoted religious freedom. People in Quaker settlements were allowed to worship according to their own Christian beliefs. However, Quakers didn't allow people who did not believe in God to settle in their colonies.

Other Immigrants

In this spirit, the Quakers welcomed several different immigrant groups to share their settlements. William Penn, founder of the colony, actually recruited many of these people from their native lands. There were German, French, Dutch, Swedish, and Danish settlers in the Delaware Valley. Some of them were Quakers, and some were from other religious backgrounds. The Germans especially found the area welcoming. In fact, the term "Pennsylvania Dutch" refers to the German word for "German": "Deutsche."

Who Were the Quakers?

Most of the Quaker settlers had come from the northern Midlands area of England. There were also some that immigrated from Ireland and Wales. About half of them came as family groups.

Their economic and social backgrounds were very different from the Pilgrims, Puritans, and Anglicans. Most of them were poor to middle class. Very few came from the upper classes. Most made their living as craftsmen, farmers, and manual laborers.

Although many were poor, they found the means to come to the New World. Some had been given the money for their passage by Quakers in England. That means they came to this country without a large debt to pay off.

They brought their manner of speech from the Midlands, too. The colonial Quakers used the forms of speech "thee" and "thou" for "you," as did their English relatives. This form of speech is still used among the Amish people of Pennsylvania. They are descendants of the early German settlers.

The Delaware Valley

The Delaware River Valley was an area full of promise for the Quaker colonists. The Delaware and the river systems around it

William Penn making a treaty with Native Americans in Pennsylvania.

were good settings for mills and commercial trading by boat. There were many natural resources in the area, too, with coal, iron, and copper. The fertile soil was good for farming.

The climate of the area was temperate. This was good for farming, and for the health of the colonists. They did have malaria and yellow fever epidemics, but not to the extent the Virginians did.

The Delaware Indians

The Native American tribes in the Delaware Valley were friendly to the new settlers. They were very different from the warring tribes who had threatened the Jamestown settlers in

Virginia. The Lenni Lenape (called the Delaware Indians by the Quakers) did not fight the new colonists. Also, the Quakers *bought* land from the Delaware; they did not claim it as their own. Founder William Penn learned the language of the tribes so he could communicate with them.

William Penn

William Penn (1644-1718) was one of the most important colonists of the era. He was an English Quaker who received the land that became Pennsylvania from the English king, Charles II. It was in payment of a debt owed Penn's late father. It was Charles II who named the new area "Pennsylvania," for the man who was its most important early leader. Penn developed its laws, society, and commerce, and also oversaw its growth. He established a colony built on the idea of harmony and love among the people.

William Penn.

Their Homes

Most Quakers made their homes of fieldstone, with slate roofs and windows and doors made of wood. They came in two styles. One was a two-story house with rooms on each floor and fireplaces on one side. The other was called a "Four-over-Four" house. This was a two-story house with four large rooms on each floor. They were simply furnished and full of light. The simple lines of this furniture are still popular today. It is the style of

An example of a Quaker house, from Quakertown, Bucks County, Pennsylvania.

Shaker furniture, named after a 19th century religious group related to the Quakers.

Family Life

As in other colonial cultures, family was the center of life for the Quakers. They thought that the family was the center of love. For them, that love included both the traditional family and the "family" of all members of their faith.

The Quakers encouraged marriage within their community. But they discouraged Quakers from marrying non-Quakers. People who did that were often banished from the community.

Raising children was of great importance to Quaker family life. Their upbringing was a serious responsibility for parents and the whole community. Children were taught to obey their parents. But the Quakers didn't agree with the Puritan's harsh punishment of children. Instead, they used reason to reinforce good behavior. Nor did they agree with the Puritan idea of "sending out." They encouraged their children to stay at home among family. They were very strict in certain areas, however. For example, they didn't allow dancing, which they thought was wicked.

The Quaker idea of equality was part of their understanding of family. Children were considered to be equal to adults in many ways. In the home, children sat at the dinner table with their parents. In the meeting house, children as well as adults preached to the members.

The Quakers's idea of equality extended to women, too. In the 18th century, most cultures and religions considered women inferior to men. But the Quakers celebrated equal roles for women and men, especially in practicing their faith.

Quaker Meetings

The Quakers held meetings several times a week in a meeting house. Like their homes, the Quakers' meeting houses were simple buildings. In them, they held worship services, as well as the community's business meetings. Women and men held separate meetings. They worshiped together, in separate areas.

The Quaker services were very different from other Christian services. They quietly gathered together in the meeting house. Then they each "turned their mind to the light." There was no altar or pulpit. They didn't have a minister to lead them in worship,

A painting showing a Quaker meeting, with a woman preaching.

because they didn't believe it was necessary. They didn't have a set of rituals to follow, either.

Often individuals, young and old, male and female, would rise and begin to preach. Their belief in the equality of Friends led them to believe that anyone could be inspired to preach.

Childhood: School

While the Quakers were great believers in the power of reason, they had many different approaches to education. Children were encouraged to learn to read by reading the Bible. But they weren't encouraged to spend years in school, as the children of the Puritans were.

The interior of the Plymouth Quaker Meeting House in Montgomery County, Pennsylvania, built in 1708.

Still, literacy was encouraged, and about one-half of adult colonists could sign their names. There were laws establishing schools, and requiring that children learn to read and write by the age of 12. Many schools were part of local Quaker meeting houses, and were run by them.

The Quakers favored "natural knowledge," and learning by doing. They also encouraged children to learn a trade. Boys and girls were encouraged to learn, in the classroom and in the world around them.

Their Food

As in so much of their life, the Quakers stressed that food should be simple. Like the Puritans, they didn't believe in indulging their appetites, so feasting was discouraged.

The Quakers liked simple food, prepared simply. They usually boiled their food, and made different kinds of puddings and dumplings. Through boiling, they created a food we still eat today: Philadelphia cream cheese. They made it by boiling cream, then drying it in cloth. They also made foods like apple butter in a similar way.

In keeping with their religious beliefs, the Quakers avoided foods that were created with slave labor. At that time, sugar came from sugar plantations, worked by slaves. Many Quakers refused to buy it. Also, salt was taxed, and the taxes used to pay for the military. The Quakers were pacifists—they did not believe in war—so many did without salt, too.

Their Clothing

The Quakers dressed plainly. They believed that clothing should be as simple as possible, in cut and color. Even hats and hairstyles were discouraged. Most clothes were made of gray homespun fabric. Men wore leather breeches or simple trousers, shirts, and aprons to protect them while working.

Women's clothing was also extremely simple. Their clothing didn't have buttons, pockets, or decorations of any kind. Women wore simple homespun dresses, with aprons and a simple shawl. Their clothing was grey or another dark color. Children dressed like their parents, in very simple clothing.

Games and Sports

The Quakers didn't like sports. They thought they corrupted the natural order of life. They had laws that forbade them. They especially condemned the "blood sports" and gambling favored in Virginia. They believed that killing for sport was evil, and that an animal's life should be taken only to provide food.

The Quakers also condemned ball games enjoyed by the Puritans of New England. But they did believe that exercise was good for people, especially children. They encouraged activities like swimming and ice-skating, which they found "useful." They also liked to garden, which they considered useful, too.

Celebrating Holidays

Like the Puritans, the Quakers didn't believe in celebrating religious holidays. They believed that all days should be devoted to God. They also believed that gaudy displays on Christian holy days was wrong. The Quakers also refused to celebrate old folk holidays, like May Day. Instead, they treated all days equally, dedicating them to hard work, simple living, and faith.

Organization

The Quaker ideals of equality are seen in the way their colony was organized, including the division of land, and the structure of society and government. William Penn was in charge of selling the land to raise money. Then, he oversaw the dividing up of the land into independent family farms. This he did in a manner that land, and the wealth that land brought, would be evenly distributed. This ensured that there would not be a small number of very wealthy landowners.

Most Quakers lived on a family farm, with other Quaker farms nearby. This encouraged neighborhoods. Quakers often helped out their neighbors, including non-Quaker families, in building homes and barns.

The Quakers elected officials, like sheriffs, judges, and peace makers, to enforce laws and keep order in the settlements. The Quakers encouraged political activity among the settlers of all backgrounds. They held elections, and elected an Assembly in Pennsylvania.

The Quakers also believed in a minimal government, because that allowed greater individual freedom. And, significantly, they believed that a person was free to follow one's own conscience. Even those who disagreed with Quaker ideals were allowed that important freedom within their communities. The first law passed in Pennsylvania established freedom of conscience, and of worship to all.

William Penn outlined three major freedoms: (1) the right to one's life, liberty, and estate, (2) the right to representative government, and (3) the right to trial by jury. Also, taxes could not be imposed without the approval of the people.

Slavery: It is important to note the difference among the colonists on the issue of slavery. While many Quakers owned slaves at the founding of the colony, by the late 17th century, colonial Quakers were fighting for its abolition. In 1758, the Philadelphia Quaker Meeting issued the first anti-slavery document in history.

One of the great symbols of freedom in the U.S. is the Liberty Bell. It was created by the Pennsylvania Assembly in 1751 to celebrate the 50th anniversary of William Penn's "Charter of Privileges." That list of laws and rules outlined the goals of the Quaker colony.

The inscription is taken from the Bible. It states, simply and profoundly, the beliefs of the Quakers: "Proclaim liberty throughout all the land unto all the inhabitants thereof." The great bell was rung on July 8, 1776, to celebrate the birth of a new nation. The Quaker ideal of liberty for all would inspire the colonists as they waged war against those who would deny them their liberties.

WORLD WIDE WEB SITES:

http://www.americaslibrary.gov/cg-bin/page.cgi/jb/colonial/penn
http://www.chaddsfordhistory.org/history/quaker.htm
http://www.loc.gov/exhibits.religion/
http://www.quakerinfo.org/history

Note: There is a complete copy of William Penn's Charter of Privileges in the Appendix.

Settling Appalachia: Virginia, Pennsylvania, North and South Carolina, and Georgia

North Britons from the Borderlands of Britain and Ireland

In 1717, the last, and largest, migration from England to Colonial America began. Over the next 60 years, until the 1770s, more than 250,000 people from Northern England and Ireland arrived in the New World. They settled in the rural areas of Pennsylvania, Maryland, Virginia, Georgia, the Carolinas, and in the areas that would become Tennessee and Kentucky.

Who Were They?

The people who migrated to what became the Appalachian areas of the New World were generally from the border areas of England and Scotland, and Northern Ireland. They were mainly of Scottish ancestry. Most were very poor tenant farmers.

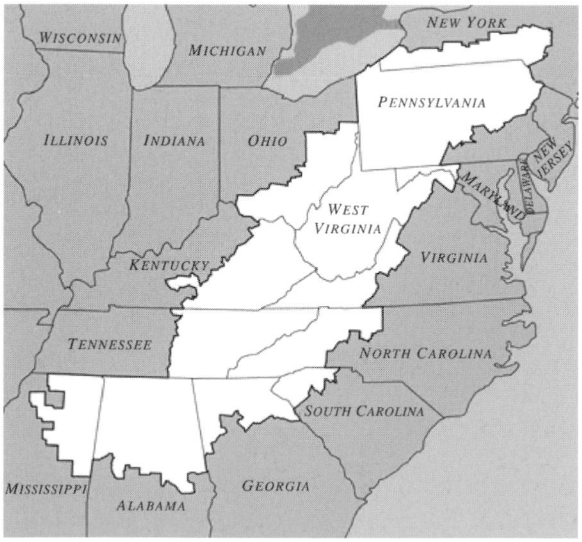

The Appalachian Region.

The border region where they had lived had been fought over for centuries. For hundreds of years, English and

Scottish armies had battled for control of the land. These were bloody and brutal conflicts that had a great impact on the people of the borderlands. They came to rely on a close-knit system of family relations, or clans, to help protect them against violence.

When England and Scotland were united in the early 1700s, many border people were forced from the land they lived on. A large number of them moved to Northern Ireland. For this reason, this group of people are often called the "Scotch-Irish." In Ireland they became part of another border conflict, fighting with the people of Ireland for the right to settle. Adding to their problems, crop failures led to starvation.

Many people decided to migrate again, this time to the New World. They were largely families, and they were seeking a place where they could make a better life for themselves.

A small minority of the immigrants were wealthy landowners from the borderlands. Another small group were artisans and craftsmen. The great majority were very poor tenant farmers and mill workers.

Among the settlers of the Appalachian countryside were immigrants from other countries. Some were German settlers, some were Swedish, and some were French.

Religious Beliefs

Unlike the Puritans, Pilgrims, and Quakers, the people of the borderlands didn't come to the New World primarily for religious freedom. Many of them were Presbyterian, and some were followers of the Church of England (Anglican). When they reached the New World, many joined the reform movements within their religions. They were suspicious of the more established faiths. Many joined the evangelical movements within their faiths.

Their Settlements

The Scotch-Irish immigrants settled in the rural areas to the west of the major cities of colonial America. They settled in areas of what would become Pennsylvania, Maryland, Virginia, North and South Carolina, Kentucky, Tennessee, and Georgia. Many built homes in the valleys of the Appalachian Mountains.

The land was heavily forested and received a great deal of rainfall. The fertile land and moderate climate helped small family farms to flourish. Family gardens provided a wide variety of vegetables for the settlers, too. They mainly made their living by raising crops and livestock, especially pigs and cattle.

Their Homes

The people of the area were among the first in the New World to live in log cabins. The cabins were very simple structures, made

An example of a log cabin home, in West Virginia.

of logs that were notched at the ends so that the logs fit together. The spaces were filled with clay to seal the walls. The cabins were usually one large room, with a fireplace for heating and cooking. They had dirt floors and small windows.

Families sometimes built several cabins together, so relatives could live close together. They also built simple barns for their animals. They kept their cattle in "cowpens." These structures were early versions of the corrals that became popular in the West.

Family Life

The people who settled the Appalachian area brought their strong ties of kin to the New World. It was based on the idea of "clan." People related to one another often settled together. They were also committed to protecting one another. Settlements were small, and sometimes separated by many miles, so there wasn't a

An example of an Appalachian settlement.

system of neighborhoods. The backwoods areas could be unsafe and violent, and people relied on kin to protect them.

The culture encouraged marriage, and couples tended to have large families. Extended families were very close to one another. This helped to protect families, but it also helped start family feuds between clans. Some, like the Hatfields and McCoys, went on for generations.

Conflicts with Native American Tribes

The area settled by the Scotch-Irish had been the home of many Native American tribes for centuries. Unlike the Delaware Indians and the Quakers, these tribes fiercely fought the settlers for control of their land. Among the tribes were the Cherokee, Creek, and Shawnee, who battled the settlers for generations.

Childhood

Boys and girls were raised differently in the Appalachian culture. Their roles were similar to those of their parents. Boys, like men, were encouraged to be strong-willed, courageous, and to fight for themselves. They often played at war, and learned to use weapons at a very young age. Girls were raised to be obedient, as wives were to their husbands, and to run the household.

School

The settlers of the Appalachian countryside had different ideas about education. The wealthier families had their children educated at home or sent them to boarding schools. In most poor families, children didn't attend school on a regular basis.

In general, the settlements didn't promote the building of schools or specific years of education. On average, children only went to school for a few weeks each year. Some children were educated in schools taught by traveling educators who held classes for several weeks, then moved on. Because of this, there was a lower rate of literacy. They did, however, send to England for Presbyterian ministers. Some built schools to educate and train members of the ministry.

Their Food

Corn was an important food for people of the Appalachian countryside. It was one of the many vegetables, like potatoes and squash, they grew in family gardens. They ate sweet corn, and ground it into cornmeal to make "mush" ("grits"), cornbread, and pancakes. They also ate products made of milk. Their main meat was pork.

Many people of the countryside ate only two meals each day: breakfast and a mid-day meal. Stews and soups were made in big kettles, heated over the fire. Many people ate their meals on "trenchers" instead of plates. Trenchers were blocks of wood that had a bowl-shaped section hollowed out, where the food was placed. Some people also had a distinctly different choice of beverage. They often drank whiskey with their meals.

Their Clothing

The people of Appalachia had a distinct clothing style. The women wore more fitted and colorful clothing than the Pilgrims, Puritans, or Quakers. Their blouses, vests, and skirts were made of home-spun linen and wool. The men wore long hunting shirts and trousers. Their clothing was made of home-spun linen and also of

An example of clothing worn by people of the Appalachian frontier.

deerskin. Children wore long shirts, and only rarely wore shoes. One famous American from this area, explorer Meriwether Lewis, recalled that he hunted barefoot, even in winter.

Games and Sports

The colonists of the southern countryside liked sports that showed strength and courage. Wrestling was a favorite, as were sports like running and jumping. They also had competitions throwing spears, much like the sport of javelin. In fact, many of the sports in track and field contests today would have been known to those early settlers. Like the colonists of Virginia, they enjoyed hunting and blood sports.

Celebrating Holidays

The people of the Appalachian countryside enjoyed celebrating holidays in their own unique way. During the Christmas holiday season, they had a major celebration on January 6th. That date, known as Twelfth Night, or Epiphany in Christianity, is still celebrated as the day that the Wise Men visited Jesus in Bethlehem. The settlers believed it to be the true holiday, and they called it "Old Christmas." They celebrated with feasting, bonfires, and firecrackers. They also celebrated Easter with feasting and games.

Organization: Property and Politics

Many people moved to the Appalachian area in search of land of their own. It was something they could never have had in England, where only the wealthy were landowners. But when they moved to the New World, they learned that most of the area had already been bought by a small number of wealthy landowners. Many were forced to become tenant farmers again. Some became "squatters," and lived on land they didn't own. So unlike Puritan New England, or Quaker Pennsylvania, there were few landowners among the common people in Appalachia.

Instead, land, wealth, and power were held by a small group. They controlled politics, too. The majority of political offices were held by this same small group of men.

Unlike Puritan Massachusetts or Quaker Pennsylvania, most Appalachian settlements were small, and very far apart. This didn't promote the development of regular meetings where settlers could discuss local problems, as in other areas. Instead, the colonial governments of what became the 13 colonies were centered in the older, more established areas of each colony. Many were in coastal towns, like Boston, New York, and Philadelphia.

Yet, the people of the Appalachian countryside believed in a liberty that many considered a right from birth. One member of the society who gave voice to this belief was **Patrick Henry**. He believed that too much government constrained the true liberty of men. His famous speeches outline this clearly. His concept of liberty would influence the course of the Revolution, as it became a rallying cry for like-minded colonists.

WORLD WIDE WEB SITES:

http://www.digitalhistory.uh.edu
http://xroads.virginia.edu/~UG97/albion/aclan.html

Pennsylvania Dutch: German Immigrants

There were several places in the colonies where German immigrants made their homes. As outlined above in the section on the Quakers, many Germans settled in Pennsylvania and the Delaware Valley.

The German migration began in the 1680s. From then until the mid-1700s, thousands of German people from the Rhineland area and Switzerland traveled to Pennsylvania. They established farming communities, with many built around their churches.

Some of the German immigrants were seeking religious freedom, which they found in Pennsylvania. **WILLIAM PENN**, the founder of the colony, actively recruited Germans to come to Pennsylvania. He offered religious freedom, and a chance at a new life. Some of the Germans were Pietists, a Protestant sect. In the 1680s, the section of Philadelphia called "Germantown" was settled by a Pietist group headed by Franz Daniel Pastorius (1651-1720).

The Germans immigrated during a time when they faced political and religious persecution in their homeland. Many came as families. It was a very expensive journey. Those who couldn't afford the fee for their passage came as indentured servants. That meant that they had to work off the cost of their passage over a term of several years. Then, they would be free to own land and farm, or run a business of their own.

This barn in Pennsylvania is an example of the Pennsylvania Dutch decorative style, with hex symbols.

Germantown became an important point of entry for many thousands of German immigrants to the New World. In addition to the Pietists, other German religious groups that immigrated to Pennsylvania included the Lutherans, Mennonites, and Amish.

Because there were so many Germans in the area, they became known as the "Pennsylvania Dutch." But of course they weren't "Dutch" and that name is based on an error. The German word for "German" is "Deutsche." Over the years, people started using the word "Dutch" instead, and the name stuck.

The Germans brought many of their traditions with them. Some of these have became part of American culture. One is the Christmas tree, which became a widely accepted tradition throughout America. Another is quilt-making, which also spread throughout the country.

A poster from the 1930s shows the Pennsylvania Dutch costumes and handicrafts.

The Pennsylvania Dutch were also admired for their decorative household goods, including pottery and furniture. They also used symbols from their native Germany that dated back to medieval times. These include the "Hex" symbols still seen on barns, featuring tulips, four-leaf clovers, and wheel-shaped motifs. These hexes were supposed to keep away bad weather, especially lightning, as well as witch's spells, which some believed could sicken cows and livestock. Today, these symbols still appear on barns all over the country, an emblem of an old colonial culture.

While Pennsylvania remained the site of the largest German immigrant population, some also chose to live in upstate New York, Virginia's Shenandoah Valley, as well as in parts of Georgia and North and South Carolina.

WORLD WIDE WEB SITE:

http://www.ulib.uipou.edu/kade/merrill/lesson2.html

New York: Dutch Immigrants

In the 1600s, another immigrant group, the Dutch, began to settle New York. They represented one of the largest non-English migrations to the New World. The area they settled covered much of what is now the Hudson River Valley.

The Dutch based their claim to the area on the explorations of Henry Hudson in 1609. The Dutch settlers made their living as farmers and as merchants, especially in the fur trade. As early as 1610, the Dutch trade with Native Americans was thriving. Many boats took furs from the New World back to Holland. The first Dutch settlers arrived in Manhattan in 1623. Their colony was headed by Peter Minuit.

In 1624, Dutch settlers founded Fort Orange, near what is now Albany. Peter Minuit bought what became Manhattan in 1626 for the small sum of $24. That same year, New Amsterdam was founded at the entrance of the Hudson River. The area settled by the Dutch became known as "New Netherlands."

The Dutch came to the New World seeking a better life for themselves and their families. Many of them were members of the Dutch Reformed Church. They built their churches in several styles. Many of the churches built on Long Island were six-sided, or eight-sided, called "hexagonal" and "octagonal." The settlers built their homes—in a style still called Dutch Colonial—in small neighborhoods surrounding their churches.

A painting showing early Dutch merchants from New Amsterdam trading with Native Americans.

The Dutch lost control over their colony in 1664, at the end of a war between England and Holland. New Amsterdam became "New York."

By the time of the American Revolution, people of Dutch background made up nearly 75% of the Hudson River Valley population. But their numbers didn't grow as quickly as the English colonies. Gradually, the English began to dominate the Dutch influence in New York. The Anglican church had the largest congregations. English became the dominant language. By the end of the Revolution, they only numbered 98,000 in a country of 3,900,000 people.

Yet the Dutch cultural influence in New York has become part of our American lives in several ways. Our modern Santa Claus is related to the Dutch tradition of "Sinter Klaas." Our cookie is a direct descendent of the Dutch “koekje.” And today’s cole slaw comes to us from the Dutch dish they called “koolsla.”

WORLD WIDE WEB SITES:

http://www.nps.gov/nr/travel/kingston/colonization.htm

A map of North and South Carolina and Georgia, 1755.

North and South Carolina: The Proprietors

In 1663, King Charles II of England granted a charter to eight members of the English aristocracy. They had remained loyal to Charles during the English Civil War. He did this in part to thank them for helping him regain power.

King Charles granted the men, called "Proprietors," a huge tract extending south of Virginia to Florida. They named the colony "Carolina," which is a form of the name "Charles." These eight men and their families would control most of the growth in the colony for most of the next 60 years. They made land grants to settlers, and also chose the leaders of the colony.

The Proprietors did not recruit settlers from England or Europe. Instead, the area was populated from settlers moving from existing colonies. Many of the settlers who moved to the northern part of Carolina came from the Tidewater area of Virginia. They settled in a section called Albermarle, and most of them made their living as farmers.

The settlers of the southern part of Carolina were Englishmen who moved there from Barbados in the West Indies. They settled in what became Charleston, which became a wealthy center of trade, in furs and food.

From 1692 to 1712, the colonies of North Carolina and South Carolina were part of one government. In 1712, they became two separate colonies.

North Carolina

Family Life

Most of the settlers in North Carolina had moved to the colony from Virginia. Some were wealthy families whose family lives were similar to the Royalists, who had settled Tidewater Virginia. Most were poor farming families, looking for a better life for themselves. Their lives were similar to those of the poorer families of Virginia, from both the Tidewater area and the Appalachian countryside.

Marriage was encouraged, and couples tended to have large families. The colonists of every background valued family highly. And, as in Virginia, "family" often meant several generations of a family living together. Because of illness, family members often died young. Many children grew up without parents, and only 60% of children lived beyond the age of six. This means that there were many step-families living together, and relatives raised children from several related families.

As in other colonial cultures, the husband and father was considered the head of the household. He had legal control over all members of a family, because women, once they married, had no legal rights. Wives were expected to be obedient to their husbands. Children were expected to be obedient to their parents.

Childhood

As in other colonial cultures, children in North Carolina were raised to be helpful members of the family at a very young age. Boys were taught the work ways of their fathers. If a boy's father was a farmer, he learned to farm. If the father was a carpenter, the boy learned that trade. Girls learned all the household chores of women in the culture. They learned to sew and make clothing. They learned to cook, take care of livestock, and tend the garden.

Life was very busy and active for children in North Carolina. There was little time for formal schooling. Instead, a boy might be sent away as an apprentice to learn a trade. Because so many of the colonists in North Carolina were farmers, they relied on their children to help out on the family farm.

As in so many aspects of life, the years of education, and the kind of education a young person received, had a lot to do with a family's wealth. The sons of the wealthy were sometimes sent to England for school. The sons of the poorer folk received little education. Some religious groups, like the Quakers and Presbyterians, provided schools. But these schools could be expensive, and often their main goal was to train young boys to become ministers.

Family Farm

As elsewhere in the colonies, the settlers of North Carolina learned to plant corn from the local Native Americans. It was a plentiful and tremendously useful plant. A hundred bushels of corn could feed a family of six for a year.

There were many uses for corn, too. It could be ground into meal for bread, pancakes, or grits. The husks were used to make brooms and chair seats. Livestock were fed leaves and stalks. Cobs could be used as fuel for fires, too.

Lumber

The pine tree forests of North Carolina were another important source of income for the colonists. The trees were made into ships, and their byproducts, tar and pitch, were used in building, too. They supplied much of the wood, tar, and pitch that built the British Navy in colonial times.

Rice and Slavery

Rice was South Carolina's most important crop, and soon it became a major crop for North Carolina, too. But the success of rice in the New World was based on slavery. English settlers didn't know how to grow rice. They relied on West African slaves, who had grown the crop for centuries, to raise and harvest the grain.

This meant that North Carolina became a major destination for the slave trade. As with tobacco in Virginia, the difficult and back-breaking labor was done by slaves, while white landowners reaped the profits.

Governmental Organization: North Carolina

The Proprietors who had created the Carolina colony sold their interests to the English king in 1729. North Carolina became a Crown Colony. It remained under the supervision of England until 1775.

But at the same time, a representative government was taking shape in North Carolina. There were two parts of the government: the governor and governor's council, and an assembly. The governor and all officials were appointed by the British government. The assembly was made up of people elected by settlers from various counties and towns. But not all counties were allowed, by the British, to have representation. The assembly passed laws and established taxes.

South Carolina

South Carolina's development as a colony was similar in some ways to North Carolina. But in several important ways, it was different.

Charleston, its main city, was one of the busiest ports in the colonies. Many of the first people to settle in Charleston were traders from the Caribbean island of Barbados. Over the years, they became some of the wealthiest men in the colonies.

Rice and Slavery

One of the greatest influences on the economy of South Carolina was its reliance on the rice trade. Rice was brought to the New World from Europe. Soon, rice production was the major source of income for the colony. But it came at an inhuman cost. Rice was a

The port of Charleston, South Carolina, in the colonial era.

crop that required a huge amount of human labor. It also meant huge profits for the rice plantation owners. And it was supported almost exclusively by slave labor.

South Carolina became one of the central ports in the colonies for the importation of slaves. English settlers didn't know how to grow rice. They relied on West African slaves, who had grown the crop for centuries, to raise and harvest the grain. These men and women came as slaves, not as owners of the land they farmed.

By 1720, 65% of the people living in South Carolina were slaves. In some areas, African slaves made up 80% of the population. The plantations grew indigo, used as a dye, as well as rice. This crop, too, was produced by slave labor, with the white plantation owners growing rich as the Africans suffered. This led to several events in South Carolina history. The first slave rebellion took place in South Carolina. This led to an unstable, volatile political and social atmosphere in the years leading up to the Revolutionary War.

WORLD WIDE WEB SITES:

http://statelibrary.dcr.state.nc.us
http://www.learnnc.org/

Georgia: James Oglethorpe's Ideals

The colony of Georgia was founded in 1732. James Oglethorpe, a member of the British Parliament, and several of his colleagues came up the idea. They wanted to create a colony where people in debtor's prison could have a new start. (In England at that time, people who couldn't pay what they owed were put into prison. Some worked for years to try to pay off their debts.)

The British government granted Oglethorpe a charter for the colony in 1732. It was a grant to land south of the Carolinas and north of Florida. The British government thought it would provide a buffer between the English and the hostile Spanish colonies in Florida.

Statue of Georgia's founder, James Oglethorpe.

In 1733, a group of 116 men and women traveled from Britain to Georgia. They were not the debtors Oglethorpe had originally intended to bring to the New World. Instead, they were from many different backgrounds. They landed in what would become Savannah, Georgia.

They were not the first settlers in the area. Over the years, other people had moved to the area, including Puritans, Quakers, and

German immigrants. The people were allowed to worship as they wished, so early Georgia did offer a certain amount of religious freedom to the colonists.

Oglethorpe and his trustees had been granted a charter to run the colony for 21 years. He created several laws for orderly rule. He settled the people on 50-acre farms. He outlawed slavery and liquor. The early settlers rebelled against the rules. Some wanted to own their own land. Others wanted to have slaves to work the land.

In 1739, the Georgians became involved in border battles with the Spanish colonists of Florida. These went on for several years. By 1750, it was clear the colony was not doing well economically. So, in 1752, Georgia came under control of the English king. Slavery was instated. Some Georgian colonists were furious with the decision, while others favored it. It was just one issue on which the colonists disagreed. In the north and south, on the coast and in the back country, Georgian colonists held different opinions of their English rulers, and their colony's future.

WORLD WIDE WEB SITES:

http://www.ourgeorgiahistory.com

Native American Tribes and Colonial America

When the first European explorers reached the New World in the 1400s, they encountered Native American tribes. These native peoples had lived in North America for thousands of years when the Europeans first arrived. They were divided into many different tribes and had many different cultures and ways of life.

Historians think that almost 40 million Native Americans lived in the New World at the time the first explorers arrived. For many of the native peoples, the arrival of the Europeans changed their lives forever. The Europeans could be brutal and destructive. They fought with and enslaved the native populations. Some explorers, like Hernando Cortes, conquered native populations and destroyed them.

The Europeans also brought diseases to which the natives had no resistance. Diseases like smallpox and measles were unknown in the New World. These diseases killed entire tribes.

Europeans also claimed lands for themselves and their countries. They treated the natural wealth of the lands as their own. In Christopher Columbus's time and later, they forced the Indians to work for them as slaves, and enriched themselves.

Between the destruction by disease and war, thc Native American population dropped sharply. Historians believe that by the 1600s, their numbers had fallen from 40 million to somewhere between two and 18 million.

Pocahontas saving Captain John Smith's life.

When the mass migration of English settlers began in the 1600s, each group encountered different tribes, with different results. Some native people were friendly with the new settlers. Others were hostile and fought with them. The different colonial people also treated the Native Americans differently.

In Jamestown in 1607, the local Algonquin tribe was hostile to the first settlers, and attacked them. Relations between the settlers and the Algonquin remained difficult. In 1622, the Algonquin tribe attacked the plantations and killed over 300 people. The Jamestown colony lost its charter and came under the control of the English king.

A very different relationship developed between the Pilgrims of Plymouth Plantation and the Wampanoag. They were the Native people who lived in the area settled by the Pilgrims. They had

Colonial settlers take arms against Native Americans in King Philip's War, 1675.

lived in what became the Plymouth Plantation for hundreds of years. They shared their knowledge of hunting, fishing, and farming with the Pilgrims, which helped them survive.

Yet this friendly relationship didn't last forever. In 1675, a Wampanoag chief named King Philip tried to unite the local tribes to stop the movement of settlers into their lands. Philip died in the conflict, called King Philip's War.

In Puritan New England, there were clashes with local Native American tribes, too. These were often over land. The major conflict was the Pequot War (1636). The Pequot were a fierce tribe in the Connecticut River valley. There, they had frequent skirmishes with the local settlers. These led to the war, in which the English colonists fought under the direction of Governor John Endicott of the Bay Colony. The colonists attacked a Pequot settlement near what is now New Haven, Connecticut. They burned the settlement to the ground, killing 500 men, women, and children. The remaining tribesmen fled. Some were later captured and killed; some were sold into slavery.

William Penn making a treaty with Native Americans in Pennsylvania.

The Native American tribes in the Delaware Valley were friendly with the first Quaker settlers. They were very different from the warring tribes who had threatened the Jamestown settlers in Virginia, or the Pequots in Connecticut. The Lenni Lenape (called the Delaware Indians by the Quakers) did not fight the new colonists. Also, the Quakers *bought* land from the Delaware; they did not claim it as their own. Founder William Penn learned the language of the tribes so he could communicate with them. Yet by the time of the Revolution, the Delaware tribes were often in armed conflict with the settlers. As settlement expanded into the Ohio valley and across the mountains, Native peoples and colonists came into conflict again and again.

The people of the frontier area—those who had settled in the Appalachian area—had a history of conflict with Native Americans. Many tribes had moved inland as the settlers took land as their own. On the one hand, the tribal peoples benefitted from trade with the colonists. They were able to exchange furs for tools, weapons, and other things they did not have. But they were also losing their traditional way of life, and means of making a living. The settlers moved into their lands, and competed with them for resources like animals for food and furs. This led to frequent conflicts up to the era of the Revolutionary War and beyond.

The Iroquois League was a group of five tribes from upper New York to Pennsylvania. The original tribes were the Mohawk, Onondaga, Oneida, Cayuga, and Seneca. In the early 18th century, the Tuscarora joined the league.

The Iroquois League was run by a council made up of representatives of each tribe. One of their main goals was to find a way to stop settlers from taking all the land on which they lived, hunted, and trapped. The League also sided with the British in the **FRENCH AND INDIAN WAR**. Their support helped the British defeat the French in that war.

When the colonies declared war on Britain, the Iroquois could not agree which side to support. Instead, the alliance ended. Some tribes fought with the British. Others fought on the side of the Americans. The alliance ended at the end of the Revolutionary War.

WORLD WIDE WEB SITES:

http://usinfo.state.gov/products/pubs/historyotln/

African-American Slavery in Colonial America

Slavery existed in every colony at the time of the American Revolution. Although the greatest number of slaves lived in the southern colonies, they were also held in bondage in every settled area.

The first law regarding slavery was passed in Puritan Massachusetts in 1641. Although New England was the center of the anti-slavery abolitionist movement in the 19th century, that wasn't the case in colonial times. New England took part in the slave trade from the mid-1600s to the 1780s. By the time of the Revolution, 20% of the people in Boston were slave owners. In Kingston, Rhode Island, 30% of the population were slaves. In New York, they were 7% of the population.

In the northern colonies, slaves were used in farming and for domestic labor. They raised livestock, farmed land, and did the majority of housework for landowners and city dwellers. They also worked in industry, mining salt, and working in iron foundries.

In New York, they worked in skilled trades, like shipbuilding and construction. They did this for their owners, not for themselves. They did not profit by their labor, their owners did.

Unlike plantation slaves in the south, northern slaves didn't live in slave quarters. Instead, they often lived in the attics or back alleys of their owners' homes. They also suffered poorer health than white people, with higher rates of disease and early death.

This painting depicts Africans aboard a slave ship, bound for the colonies.

The slaves living in the north also were able to develop certain celebrations of their own. One was called " 'Lection Day." It began around 1750 and continued for another 100 years. The slave population elected their own "governors" and "kings" on "Lection Day." These people became leaders of the black community.

In the southern colonies, slaves made up more than half the total population. They were brought from Africa in brutal conditions. In Virginia and Maryland, especially in the Chesapeake area, blacks were 60% of the population. A small percentage of these African-Americans were freemen or descendants of freeman. These were people who had bought their freedom, or, in some cases, been emancipated by their masters. But most of the blacks were slaves.

The slave population in the Chesapeake worked mainly on the tobacco plantations. This was back-breaking work, and the slaves were forced to work at least six days a week, from sun up to sun down. They lived in poorly made shacks and often didn't have enough to eat.

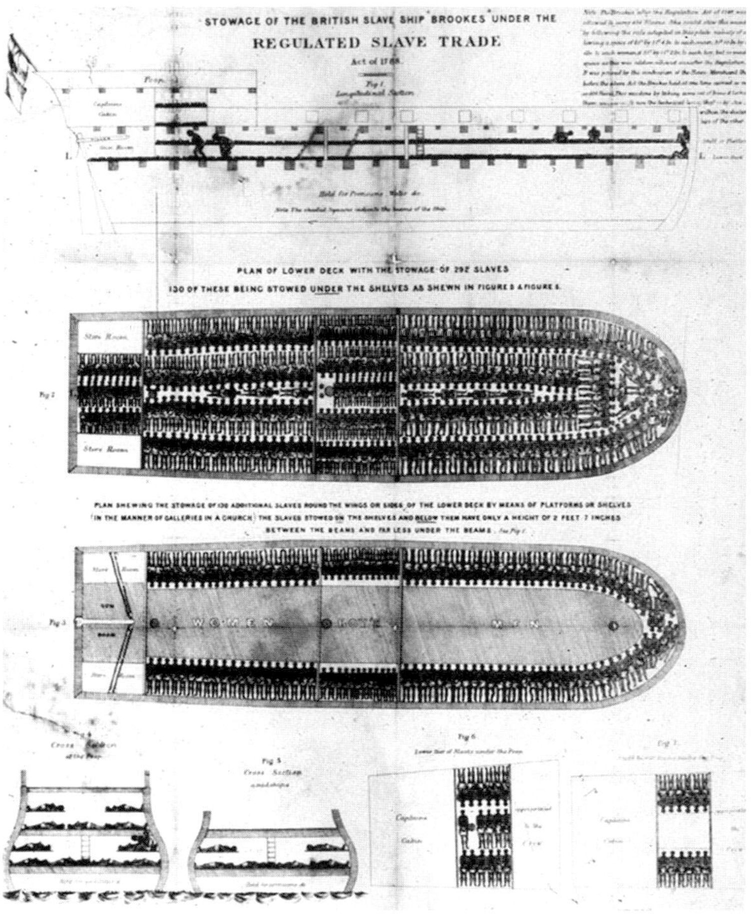

This diagram shows the wretched conditions aboard a slave ship, with Africans forced into severely cramped areas, on their journey to the colonies.

In South Carolina, slaves made up as much as 80% of the area where the rice plantations flourished. Colonial landowners had enslaved rice farmers from West Africa. They forced them to work, preparing the land, then planting and harvesting the grain. This made the slave owners of Charleston some of the wealthiest men in the colonies. Their slaves were among the most brutally treated. The first major slave rebellion in the colonies took place in South Carolina.

Every aspect of a slave's life was controlled by the slave owner. They had no rights, not even to marry or own property. Slaves did

This is an example of houses for slaves on a rice plantation in South Carolina.

often marry in secret, but they, and any of their children, could be sold at any time. There were also laws that gave slave owners the right to punish their slaves, even to kill them, for almost any reason.

It was slavery that made the wealth of the southern plantation owners. Over the years, the southern colonies developed laws to restrict the lives of the slaves. Slaves could not travel where they wished, gather for a funeral, earn money, or learn to read.

By the time of the Revolutionary War, slavery influenced every aspect of work life in the South. Slaves not only provided the labor that ran plantations, they also worked on farms of all types, in skilled trades like shipbuilding, and in industry. It is a shameful legacy of American history that many of the men who called for freedom from British oppression were blind to the injustice of slavery in their midst.

During the Revolution, some slaves decided to fight with the British, and some with the Patriots. In November 1775, Lord Dunmore, the British Governor of Virginia, promised slaves owned by Patriots their freedom if they would fight for the British. (Runaway slaves belonging to Loyalists were returned to their slave masters.)

Some slaves agreed to fight with the Loyalists, but after the British lost the war, most were treated terribly. The victorious

Americans demanded that slaves be returned to their masters. The British had promised them freedom; what many actually received was a return to bondage. Many were sent to the Caribbean, thinking they would be made free. They were enslaved instead. Several thousand were given passage to Canada, England, and Jamaica.

Some slaves fought bravely for the American side in the Revolution. In fact, the first person killed at **THE BOSTON MASSACRE**, **Crispus Attucks**, was an escaped slave. Some were promised their freedom if they fought; others fought simply because they felt it was right. In some cases, the slaves were granted freedom at the end of the war. But some owners went back on their promises. Slaves who had risked their lives for the nation's freedom once again found themselves in bondage.

It would not be until the 19th century, with the abolitionist movement and the Civil War, that the issue of slavery would be decided in the new United States. It is an uncomfortable but true fact of our history that the freedom from tyranny fought and won by the new nation would not be extended to all its people for many more years.

WORLD WIDE WEB SITES:

http://www.digitalhistory.uh.edu/
http://www.history.org/Almanack/people/african/
http://www.pbs.org/wgbh.aia/

was a continuation of the ongoing hostilities in Europe between Britain and France, where it was called the Seven Years War.

In 1754, France controlled a huge amount of land, from Quebec to New Orleans. It included most of the land west of the Appalachian Mountains to the Mississippi River. France had forged partnerships with the Native American tribes in the Great Lakes region and Canada. The French built a series of forts to limit the British movement into the area. At that time, Britain controlled the colonies stretching from Maine to Georgia, reaching inland from the Atlantic coast to the Appalachian Mountains.

The major conflicts of the French and Indian War took place in the Ohio valley. In 1754, British and French forces met at Fort Duquesne (it is where Pittsburgh, Pennsylvania is now). One of the British officers was a young Virginian named **George Washington**. The British lost the battle, but it brought about an important event.

The threat of the French led the British to call a meeting to discuss their goals. The meeting, called the Albany Congress, would be crucial to the colonies. **Benjamin Franklin**, a delegate to the Congress, created a plan. It called for a president (named by the King) and delegates chosen by the colonial assemblies.

Franklin's plan included several ideas that became central to the ideas behind the Revolutionary War. He proposed a union of colonies that would control their own defense, trade, and settlement. They would have the right to raise taxes and develop the western lands. The individual colonies weren't interested in Franklin's plan at the time. But it laid the groundwork for what would come later.

The British finally defeated the French, and in 1763, the Peace of Paris was signed, ending the War. Canada and all of North America east of the Mississippi River became British territory. Most of the British colonists were happy with the results and grateful to the British government and army.

Acts of Parliament

At that point, many of the colonists were still loyal to the British monarch, George III, who became king in 1760. However, the colonial wars had been expensive, and King George needed money to support the British troops that remained in America after the wars ended.

The British Parliament began to pass several acts that created taxes and duties to be paid on goods and services on the colonies. These would eventually drive the colonists to war.

In 1764 Parliament passed the **SUGAR ACT** (or the American Revenue Act). It was the first law created to raise money for Britain from the colonies. The Sugar Act revised a previous tax on sugar, molasses, and other goods imported from the French West Indies. It changed the way in which the money was collected from the colonists, and ensured that the colonists paid high tariffs (taxes) on non-British goods.

Also in 1764, Parliament passed the Currency Act. It stated that the colonies were forbidden to create their own currency (money).

These two acts created protests throughout the colonies. In town meetings, they cried out against "taxation without representation" (being taxed without any say in the political process). For the first time, colonists from several areas called for a unified response to the Acts. Many decided to boycott (refuse) British goods, as a means of protest.

In 1765, Parliament passed the **QUARTERING ACT**. It required the colonies to provide British soldiers with barracks and supplies. (To "quarter" means to provide lodging or shelter.)The colonists strongly resisted the act. In 1766, the New York Assembly refused to assist the soldiers, and a fight broke out in which a colonist was killed. As a result, Parliament threatened to suspend the New York Assembly. Parliament increased the powers of the Quartering Act in 1774. That extension of the Act stated that colonists could be forced to allow soldiers to stay in their individual homes.

Also in 1765, Parliament passed the **STAMP ACT**. This Act made it mandatory that most documents, such as contracts, newspapers, and pamphlets, even playing cards, had to be written on special paper bearing a stamp from the British government.

A political cartoon reflecting the colonists' hatred of the Stamp Act.

The colonists were forced to purchase the stamped paper for most of their documents, because documents on plain paper had no legal standing. The American colonists were enraged. They were especially suspicious of the tax because many thought that the money paid remained in the pockets of the "Stamp Men." Those were the stamp agents who sold the paper to them.

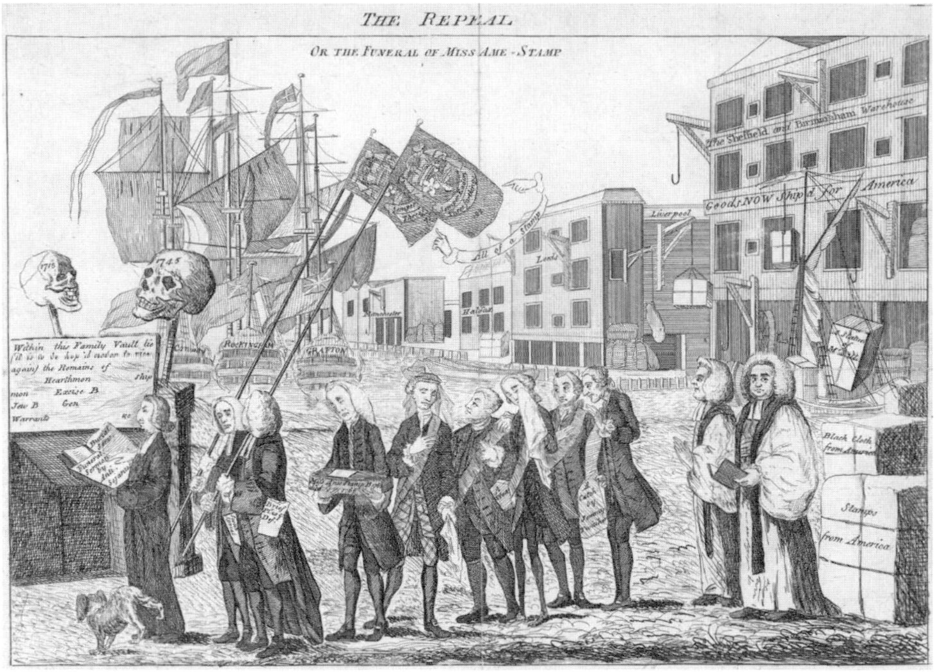

A political cartoon about the repeal of the Stamp Act, with caricatures of the English political leaders responsible for the Act.

Throughout the colonies, groups of men, calling themselves **THE SONS OF LIBERTY**, met to discuss the Act. They developed ways of intimidating the stamp agents. The stamp agents resigned in every colony.

The angry colonists went further in their protests. They formed the Stamp Act Congress. This group created a document, "The Declaration of Rights and Grievances." The Declaration outlined their claims: that the colonists were equal citizens to those in Britain, and that Parliament had no right to tax them without granting them representation.

The colonists protested so much that in 1766, the Stamp Act was repealed. But the Parliament still wanted to maintain their control over the colonies. They passed an act that claimed that Parliament had the right to pass any laws they chose.

The **TOWNSHEND DUTIES** were enacted in 1767. The colonists now had to pay duties on glass, lead, paints, paper, and tea, as they had under the Sugar Act. Again, the colonists refused to pay the duty and protested passage of the law. And again, they protested by boycotting English imports. By 1770, the Townshend Duties were repealed.

In 1768, **Samuel Adams** wrote the Massachusetts Circular Letter. It was approved by the Massachusetts Assembly. It challenged Parliament's right to taxation without representation, and rallied the other colonies to unite. The British response was swift: they dissolved the Assembly, and troops were brought in.

Next, Virginia declared its intentions. In 1769, the Virginia House of Burgesses issued the Virginia Resolutions. They condemned Parliament for dissolving the Massachusetts Assembly. They claimed that the power to tax was in the hands of the Burgesses and the governor. In response, the House of Burgesses was also dissolved by the British.

The next major event took place in Massachusetts. On the evening of March 5, 1770, a rumor began to fly around Boston. A British soldier had supposedly struck a young barber's apprentice. Armed only with snowballs and sticks, a group of citizens confronted the soldiers. With **Crispus Attucks** at the head of the crowd, they marched to the Boston Customs House.

The soldiers fired into the crowd. When the smoke cleared, Attucks and three others lay dead. Eventually five men—Attucks, Samuel Gray, James Caldwell, Samuel Maverick, and Patrick Carr—died of their wounds.

Paul Revere's engraving of the Boston Massacre.

The people of Boston were furious. They claimed that Attucks and the other men were martyrs in the cause of independence. Attucks and Caldwell were given funerals attended by thousands of Boston's citizens.

Patriots like **Samuel Adams** called their murder **"THE BOSTON MASSACRE."** It became a rallying cry throughout the colonies. Within two years, Adams had helped create "Committees of Correspondence" to spread the news of actions taken against the British among all the colonies.

Probably the most famous law passed by Parliament was the **TEA ACT.** Passage of this law, and the events that occurred after it, were the stepping stones to the Revolutionary War. The Act was passed in 1773. The East India Company was a large importer/exporter of tea. The tea was stored in English warehouses and shipped to America. In order to sell more tea to the colonists, the British government reduced the tax on tea imported by East India. The company could sell the tea at a much reduced price to the Americans.

Even though the Tea Act did not impose additional duties or taxes on the colonists, they were suspicious of Parliament's motives. The colonists felt that the British would not stop increasing taxes and that it was time

Americans throwing the Cargoes of the Tea Ships into the River, at Boston

A painting showing the Boston Tea Party.

to resist as best they could. On December 16, 1773, in what was to become known as **"THE BOSTON TEA PARTY,"** a group of men disguised as Indians, most of them from the Sons of Liberty, dumped 342 chests of tea into the harbor.

The British were furious. They closed the port of Boston to all trade in March 1774, and passed the **COERCIVE ACTS** in May. (They were called "The Intolerable Acts" by the colonists.) These were intended to restrict the colonists and their government in Massachusetts. Boston Governor Thomas Hutchinson had authority to appoint judges, and he severely restricted town meetings.

The remaining colonies were not intimidated by the British government's actions. Rather, they became more determined to declare their independence from Britain once and for all.

In September of 1774, the First **CONTINENTAL CONGRESS** met to protest the Coercive Acts. Of the 13 colonies, all but Georgia sent representatives to the Congress. At that time, the colonies included Massachusetts (including what is now Maine), New Hampshire, New York, Rhode Island, Connecticut, New Jersey, Pennsylvania, Delaware, Maryland, Virginia, North Carolina, South Carolina, and Georgia. They decided as a group to promote a boycott of British goods, and to refuse to allow them to be imported, throughout the colonies.

In 1775, Parliament passed another act to force the colonists to comply with their laws. The New England Restraining Act prohibited the colonies from trading with one another. They were only allowed to trade with Britain. The colonists continued their boycott.

The new Governor of Massachusetts, Thomas Gage, tried to disband the Continental Congress. He was unsuccessful. He could see that the people were preparing to fight for freedom. In Boston, the Committee of Safety began raising militias. They called themselves, the "Minute Men," because they could be ready to fight in a "minute." They readied themselves for war.

Gage knew the colonists were collecting and storing weapons in the town of Concord. In an effort to discourage the colonists, Gage planned a secret attack on Concord, sending British troops to destroy their weapons.

The Battles of Lexington and Concord

On the night of April 18, 1775, **Paul Revere**, William Dawes, and others rode from Boston. They had discovered the British plan. With one light hanging in the belfry of Christ Church, Revere warned the Patriots that the British were coming by land to Concord. He set off to warn **Samuel Adams** and **John Hancock** that the British were also on their way to capture them.

Revere reached Lexington and informed Adams and Hancock. Along the way, he stopped by each house, warning them of the

A painting portraying the Battle of Lexington, April 19, 1775.

The "Minute Man" statue, in Philadelphia, commemorating "The Shot Heard Round the World."

British soldiers' approach. He then set off to warn Patriots at Concord.

On the morning of April 19, 1775, British troops reached the village of Lexington. There, they met 77 Minutemen. The head of the British, Major John Pitcarin, yelled, "Disperse you damned rebels! You dogs, run!"

American Captain John Parker carefully instructed the Minutemen. "Let the troops pass by," he told them. "Do not shoot, without they being first." Then, someone fired a shot. The British began firing on the Americans, and then charged them. When it was over, there were eight Americans dead. This was the famous "Shot heard round the world." The War for Independence had begun.

Next, the British set off for Concord. By the time they reached it, the Americans had stored the weapons elsewhere. The British destroyed what they could find. As they marched back to Boston, they began to be fired on. Militiamen from the area ambushed the

BLOODY BUTCHERY,

BY THE

BRITISH TROOPS;

OR THE

RUNAWAY FIGHT OF THE REGULARS.

Being the PARTICULARS of the VICTORIOUS BATTLE fought at and near CONCORD, situated Twenty Miles from Boston, in the Province of the Massachusetts-Bay, between Two Thousand Regular Troops, belonging to His Britannic Majesty, and a few Hundred Provincial Troops, belonging to the Province of Massachusetts-Bay, which lasted from sunrise until sunset, on the 19th of April, 1775, when it was decided greatly in favor of the latter. These particulars are published in this cheap form, at the request of the friends of the deceased WORTHIES, who died gloriously fighting in the CAUSE OF LIBERTY and their COUNTRY, and it is their sincere desire that every Householder in the country, who are sincere well-wishers to America, may be possessed of the same, either to frame and glass, or otherwise to preserve in their houses, not only as a Token of Gratitude to the memory of the Deceased Forty Persons, but as a perpetual memorial of that important event, on which, perhaps, may depend the future Freedom and Greatness of the Commonwealth of America. To which is annexed a Funeral Elegy on those who were slain in the Battle.

The front page of a Massachusetts newspaper describing the Battles of Lexington and Concord.

British soldiers throughout their retreat to Boston. When it was over, the British had 250 dead or wounded. The Americans had lost 93 men.

The Battles of Lexington and Concord actually took place before war had officially been declared. That next step was taken by the Second Continental Congress, on May 10, 1775.

The New Nation at War

The Second Continental Congress

On May 10, 1775, delegates to the Second Continental Congress met in Philadelphia. **John Hancock** was elected president. The members had to respond to the news from Lexington and Concord. British and American soldiers had met in two battles, and there were deaths on both sides. The same day the Congress had its first meeting, **Ethan Allen** and **Benedict Arnold** took the British Fort Ticonderoga.

The Continental Congress voted to go to war with the British. **John Adams** recommended **George Washington** as commander-in-chief of the army on June 15. Washington accepted. Congress approved the forming of the Continental Army, to be under his direction. Just two days later, another battle took place.

Bunker Hill

On June 12, 1775, General Gage, the British commander in Boston, stated that anyone aiding the American cause would be charged with treason. The Americans set up fortifications against the British on Bunker Hill, outside Boston. British commanders on ships in Boston Harbor saw what was going on. They fired on the Patriots.

In the battle that followed, 2,400 British soldiers fought against 1,000 Americans. The Americans lost many men. They also lost the battle and their fortifications.

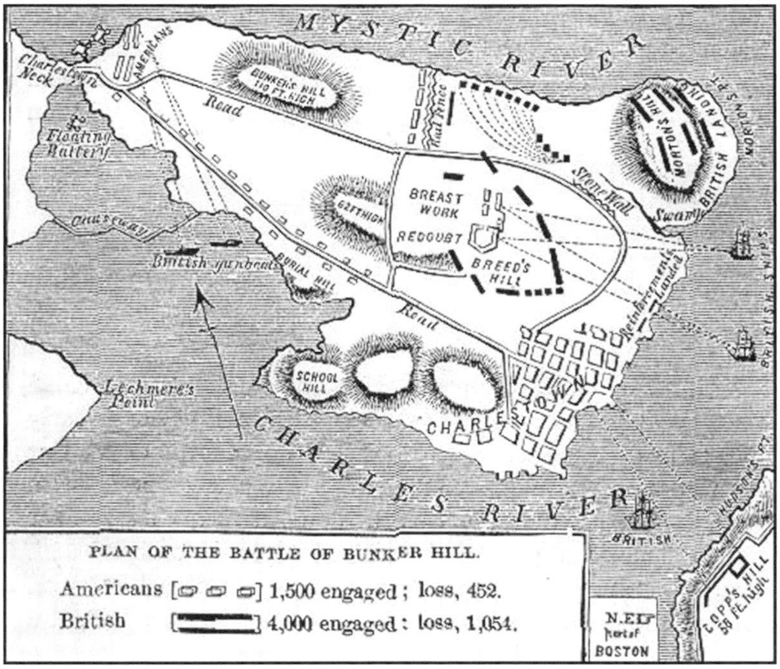

The Loyalist Cause

At this point, even though the Americans had declared war, there were many colonists who wanted to remain loyal to the king. Unlike the Patriots, they didn't want independence. They wanted to continue to be part of England. The issue divided families, including some famous ones. **Benjamin Franklin's** son William refused to follow his father in approving the Revolution. Instead, he remained a "Loyalist."

The "Loyalists" got their name for their loyalty to the English king, George III. A group of Loyalists in the Congress decided to write a letter to the king. It was called the "Olive Branch Petition." The Loyalists pled with George III to stop the fighting and resolve the problems. But when the king received it, he rejected it. On August 23, 1775, King George issued a proclamation. It stated that the colonies were in "a state of rebellion."

There were Loyalists in all the colonies. They were from every walk of life and background. Many Loyalists lived in the South. The British thought that Southern plantation owners would remain loyal because they feared independence would mean the end of slavery. Lord Dunmore, the Royal Governor of Virginia, even offered freedom to all slaves who would fight for the British. But Dunmore's plan didn't work, and many Virginians became Patriots.

In North Carolina, Royal Governor Josiah Martin rallied the people to the British cause. But those he convinced to back the Loyalist cause soon found themselves battling Continental Army soldiers, and losing.

The Quaker community of the Delaware Valley was especially divided over the war. One of the central values of their faith was pacifism—they were against war. Yet some Quakers enlisted and served in the Continental Army. Others chose to be "conscientious objectors." That is someone who, because of their beliefs, refuses to go to war. Some were persecuted and lost their land. Some left Pennsylvania and moved to the West.

Thomas Paine's *Common Sense*

Thomas Paine was an English writer living in America who was deeply committed to the Patriot cause. In January 1776, he published *Common Sense*. He used his powerful prose to outline the argument for war with Britain. It was a sensation. Soon, there were more than a half a million copies in print in the colonies. Newspapers and magazines published sections, too.

Paine urged a revolutionary way of thinking about government. He believed that governments by kings and a rich aristocracy were corrupt and wrong. That form of government didn't value common people, or grant them power. Paine believed that only independence and a new government was right for Americans.

Paine's book helped inspire many Americans to join the cause for independence. As the colonists moved toward that way of thinking, their political leaders were preparing an important statement. It was a unified expression of grievances and aspirations: The Declaration of Independence.

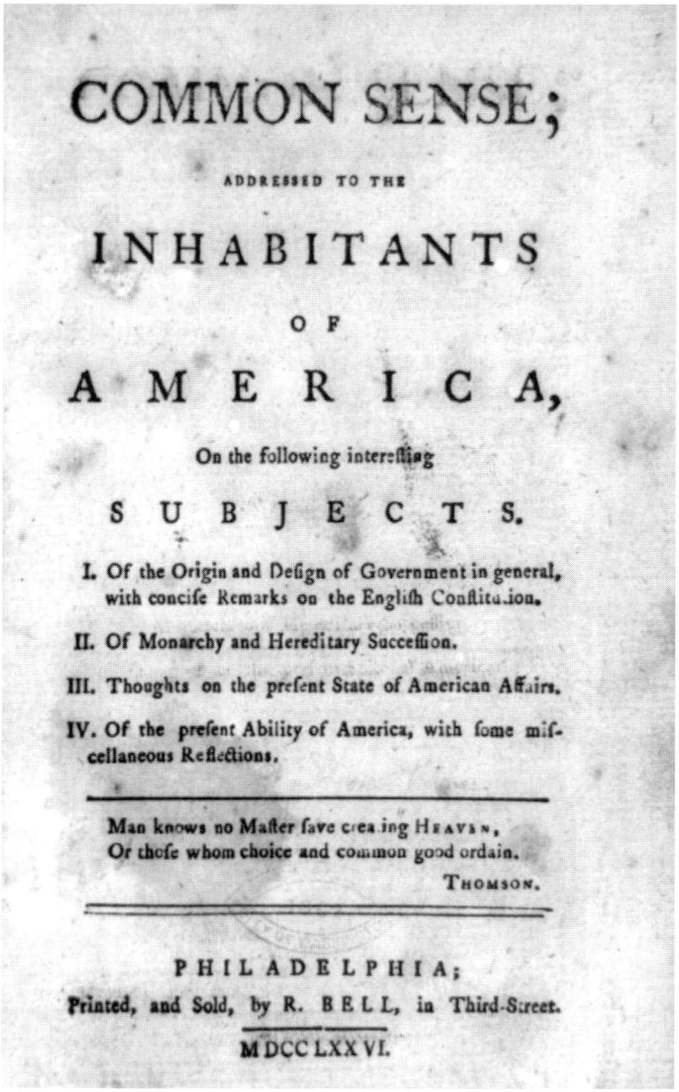
COMMON SENSE;

ADDRESSED TO THE

INHABITANTS

OF

AMERICA,

On the following intereſting

SUBJECTS.

I. Of the Origin and Deſign of Government in general, with conciſe Remarks on the Engliſh Conſtitution.

II. Of Monarchy and Hereditary Succeſſion.

III. Thoughts on the preſent State of American Affairs.

IV. Of the preſent Ability of America, with ſome miſcellaneous Reflections.

Man knows no Maſter ſave creating HEAVEN,
Or thoſe whom choice and common good ordain.

THOMSON.

PHILADELPHIA;
Printed, and Sold, by R. BELL, in Third-Street.
MDCCLXXVI.

The Declaration of Independence

On June 7, 1776, **Richard Henry Lee** introduced a resolution to the Second Continental Congress.

> RESOLVED: That these United Colonies are, and of right ought to be, free and independent states, that they are absolved from all allegiance to the British Crown, and that all political connection between them and the State of Great Britain is, and ought to be, totally dissolved.

IN CONGRESS, JULY 4, 1776.

The unanimous Declaration of the thirteen united States of America,

When in the Course of human events it becomes necessary for one people to dissolve the political bands which have connected them with another, and to assume among the powers of the earth, the separate and equal station to which the Laws of Nature and of Nature's God entitle them, a decent respect to the opinions of mankind requires that they should declare the causes which impel them to the separation. —— We hold these truths to be self-evident, that all men are created equal, that they are endowed by their Creator with certain unalienable Rights, that among these are Life, Liberty and the pursuit of Happiness. — That to secure these rights, Governments are instituted among Men, deriving their just powers from the consent of the governed, — That whenever any Form of Government becomes destructive of these ends, it is the Right of the People to alter or to abolish it, and to institute new Government, laying its foundation on such principles and organizing its powers in such form, as to them shall seem most likely to effect their Safety and Happiness. Prudence, indeed, will dictate that Governments long established should not be changed for light and transient causes; and accordingly all experience hath shewn, that mankind are more disposed to suffer, while evils are sufferable, than to right themselves by abolishing the forms to which they are accustomed. But when a long train of abuses and usurpations, pursuing invariably the same Object evinces a design to reduce them under absolute Despotism, it is their right, it is their duty, to throw off such Government, and to provide new Guards for their future security. — Such has been the patient sufferance of these Colonies; and such is now the necessity which constrains them to alter their former Systems of Government. The history of the present King of Great Britain is a history of repeated injuries and usurpations, all having in direct object the establishment of an absolute Tyranny over these States. To prove this, let Facts be submitted to a candid world. —— He has refused his Assent to Laws, the most wholesome and necessary for the public good. —— He has forbidden his Governors to pass Laws of immediate and pressing importance, unless suspended in their operation till his Assent should be obtained; and when so suspended, he has utterly neglected to attend to them. —— He has refused to pass other Laws for the accommodation of large districts of people, unless those people would relinquish the right of Representation in the Legislature, a right inestimable to them and formidable to tyrants only. —— He has called together legislative bodies at places unusual, uncomfortable, and distant from the depository of their public Records, for the sole purpose of fatiguing them into compliance with his measures. —— He has dissolved Representative Houses repeatedly, for opposing with manly firmness his invasions on the rights of the people. —— He has refused for a long time, after such dissolutions, to cause others to be elected; whereby the Legislative powers, incapable of Annihilation, have returned to the People at large for their exercise; the State remaining in the mean time exposed to all the dangers of invasion from without, and convulsions within. —— He has endeavoured to prevent the population of these States; for that purpose obstructing the Laws for Naturalization of Foreigners; refusing to pass others to encourage their migrations hither, and raising the conditions of new Appropriations of Lands. —— He has obstructed the Administration of Justice, by refusing his Assent to Laws for establishing Judiciary powers. —— He has made Judges dependent on his Will alone, for the tenure of their offices, and the amount and payment of their salaries. —— He has erected a multitude of New Offices, and sent hither swarms of Officers to harrass our people, and eat out their substance. —— He has kept among us, in times of peace, Standing Armies without the Consent of our legislatures. —— He has affected to render the Military independent of and superior to the Civil power. —— He has combined with others to subject us to a jurisdiction foreign to our constitution, and unacknowledged by our laws; giving his Assent to their Acts of pretended Legislation: — For Quartering large bodies of armed troops among us: — For protecting them, by a mock Trial, from punishment for any Murders which they should commit on the Inhabitants of these States: — For cutting off our Trade with all parts of the world: — For imposing Taxes on us without our Consent: — For depriving us in many cases, of the benefits of Trial by Jury: — For transporting us beyond Seas to be tried for pretended offences — For abolishing the free System of English Laws in a neighbouring Province, establishing therein an Arbitrary government, and enlarging its Boundaries so as to render it at once an example and fit instrument for introducing the same absolute rule into these Colonies: — For taking away our Charters, abolishing our most valuable Laws, and altering fundamentally the Forms of our Governments: — For suspending our own Legislatures, and declaring themselves invested with power to legislate for us in all cases whatsoever. — He has abdicated Government here, by declaring us out of his Protection and waging War against us. —— He has plundered our seas, ravaged our Coasts, burnt our towns, and destroyed the lives of our people. —— He is at this time transporting large Armies of foreign Mercenaries to compleat the works of death, desolation and tyranny, already begun with circumstances of Cruelty & perfidy scarcely paralleled in the most barbarous ages, and totally unworthy the Head of a civilized nation. —— He has constrained our fellow Citizens taken Captive on the high Seas to bear Arms against their Country, to become the executioners of their friends and Brethren, or to fall themselves by their Hands. —— He has excited domestic insurrections amongst us, and has endeavoured to bring on the inhabitants of our frontiers, the merciless Indian Savages, whose known rule of warfare, is an undistinguished destruction of all ages, sexes and conditions. In every stage of these Oppressions We have Petitioned for Redress in the most humble terms: Our repeated Petitions have been answered only by repeated injury. A Prince, whose character is thus marked by every act which may define a Tyrant, is unfit to be the ruler of a free people. Nor have We been wanting in attentions to our Brittish brethren. We have warned them from time to time of attempts by their legislature to extend an unwarrantable jurisdiction over us. We have reminded them of the circumstances of our emigration and settlement here. We have appealed to their native justice and magnanimity, and we have conjured them by the ties of our common kindred to disavow these usurpations, which, would inevitably interrupt our connections and correspondence. They too have been deaf to the voice of justice and of consanguinity. We must, therefore, acquiesce in the necessity, which denounces our Separation, and hold them, as we hold the rest of mankind, Enemies in War, in Peace Friends.

We, therefore, the Representatives of the united States of America, in General Congress, Assembled, appealing to the Supreme Judge of the world for the rectitude of our intentions, do, in the Name, and by Authority of the good People of these Colonies, solemnly publish and declare, That these United Colonies are, and of Right ought to be Free and Independent States; that they are Absolved from all Allegiance to the British Crown, and that all political connection between them and the State of Great Britain, is and ought to be totally dissolved; and that as Free and Independent States, they have full Power to levy War, conclude Peace, contract Alliances, establish Commerce, and to do all other Acts and Things which Independent States may of right do. —— And for the support of this Declaration, with a firm reliance on the protection of divine Providence, we mutually pledge to each other our Lives, our Fortunes and our sacred Honor.

John Hancock

Button Gwinnett
Lyman Hall
Geo Walton.

Wm Hooper
Joseph Hewes,
John Penn

Edward Rutledge 1.
Thos Heyward Junr.
Thomas Lynch Junr.
Arthur Middleton

Samuel Chase
Wm Paca
Thos Stone
Charles Carroll of Carrollton

George Wythe
Richard Henry Lee
Th Jefferson
Benja Harrison
Thos Nelson jr.
Francis Lightfoot Lee
Carter Braxton

Robt Morris
Benjamin Rush
Benja Franklin
John Morton
Geo Clymer
Jas Smith
Geo. Taylor
James Wilson
Geo. Ross
Caesar Rodney
Geo Read
Tho M:Kean

Wm Floyd
Phil. Livingston
Frans Lewis
Lewis Morris
Richd Stockton
Jno Witherspoon
Fras Hopkinson
John Hart
Abra Clark

Josiah Bartlett
Wm Whipple
Saml Adams
John Adams
Robt Treat Paine
Elbridge Gerry
Step Hopkins
William Ellery
Roger Sherman
Samel Huntington
Wm Williams
Oliver Wolcott
Matthew Thornton

The Signing of the Declaration of Independence.
John Adams is the figure at the far left. Thomas Jefferson is second from the right. Next to Jefferson is Benjamin Franklin.

The resolution didn't pass right way. The Congress created a committee to outline the reasons for independence in a longer, more official document. That committee included **Thomas Jefferson**, **John Adams**, and **Ben Franklin**. Jefferson became the main author of what became the Declaration of Independence.

The Declaration is made up of two parts. In the first section, it sets out the reasons why the colonists had the right to revolt against their king. The second part is a long listing of the grievances of the colonists. In this part, Jefferson outlined what George III had done. He describes how he had interfered with the representative governments of the colonies, taken away their civil rights, quartered troops in their homes, taxed them, and restricted trade, all without their consent.

But it is Jefferson's statement outlining the natural rights of the people that still inspires readers around the world.

> "We hold these Truths to be self-evident, that all Men are created equal, that they are endowed, by their Creator, with certain unalienable Rights, that among these are Life, Liberty, and the Pursuit of Happiness.—That to secure these Rights, Governments are instituted among Men, deriving their just Powers from the Consent of the Governed, that whenever any Form of Government becomes destructive of these Ends, it is the Right of the People to alter or to abolish it, and to institute new Government, laying its Foundation on such Principles, and organizing its Powers in such Form, as to them shall seem most likely to effect their Safety and Happiness."

Jefferson wrote later that he had not felt that it was his purpose to "invent new ideas." Rather, he wanted "to place before mankind the common sense of the subject, in terms so plain and firm as to command their assent. It was intended to be an expression of the American mind."

In words that still ring with power and clarity, he fulfilled those goals.

On July 4, 1776, the Continental Congress accepted the Declaration of Independence. The United States was born. Now a war would be fought to determine whether the new nation would remain free.

Note: There is a complete copy of the Declaration of Independence in the Appendix.

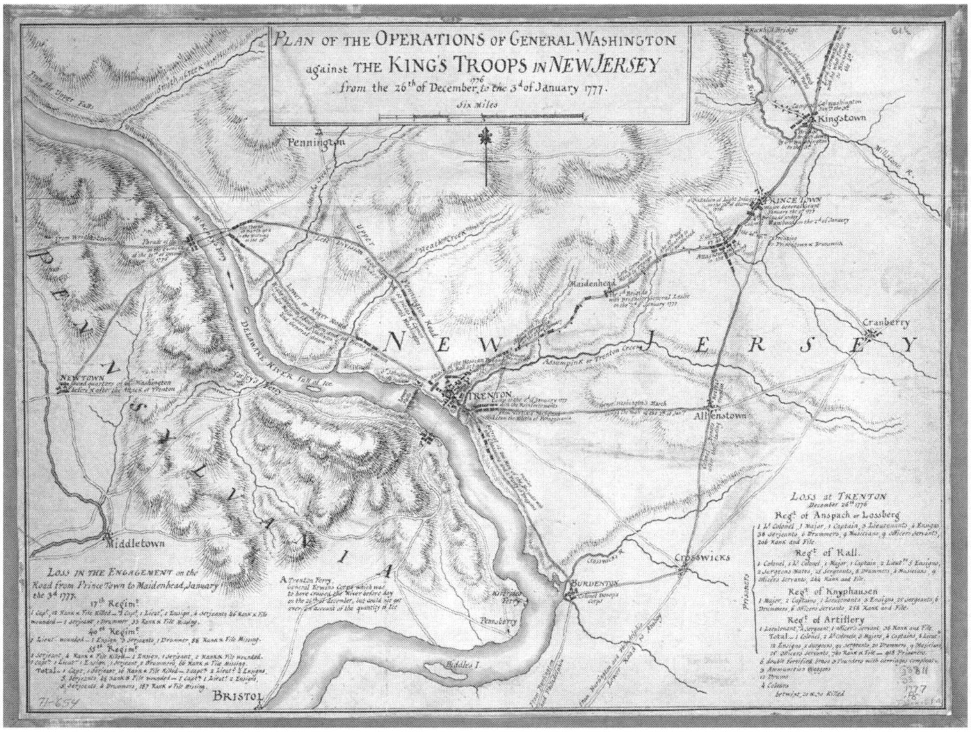

A map of the battles of Trenton and Princeton.

The Battles of Trenton and Princeton (1776-1777)

In August 1776, British General Howe had built up his forces in New York to 32,000 men. They had beaten the American forces on Long Island and Brooklyn Heights. Washington and his weary army of 3,000 retreated to White Plains, New York. Then, two American forts on the Hudson River fell to the advancing British troops. New York was now in British hands.

Washington and his men continued to retreat. **Thomas Paine** was with Washington's troops as they pulled back across New Jersey to Pennsylvania. With all that in mind, Paine wrote one of the best-known pieces of the era, "The American Crisis, Number 1." It begins:

This famous painting shows Washington crossing the Delaware River to New Jersey, December 25, 1776.

"These are the times that try men's souls. The summer soldier and the sunshine patriot will, in this crisis, shrink from the service of their country. But he that stands in now, deserves the love and thanks of man and woman. . . . The harder the conflict, the more glorious the triumph."

Paine's new pamphlet spread throughout the colonies like wildfire. According to another writer of the time, it was "read in every camp." Its first line became a battle cry.

Washington had his troops listen to Paine's new essay on Christmas Eve, 1776. His words rallied the weary troops. Armed with new strength, the army fought on, rowing across the Delaware River from Pennsylvania and surprising the British at Trenton. They attacked, and captured more than 1,000 soldiers.

After a brief retreat back to Pennsylvania, Washington crossed to Trenton again. His troops now numbered more than 6,000. They engaged the British troops under General Cornwallis, who was unable to stop their advance. Washington and his troops reached Princeton and defeated the British forces there. It was an important victory for the Americans. Their next major battle, at Saratoga, would bring them one of the greatest triumphs of the war.

The Battle of Saratoga (1777)

In 1777 General John Burgoyne was in command of the British army in Canada. He created a plan he thought would win the war for England. According to the plan, his army would march south from Lake Champlain in Canada down the Hudson River Valley. At the same time, another force of British soldiers, Loyalist militias, and Indians under the command of Colonel Barry St. Leger, would march down the Mohawk Valley. General William Howe's army would march north from New York City. All three forces would meet at Albany, New York. This would cut off New England from the rest of the colonies.

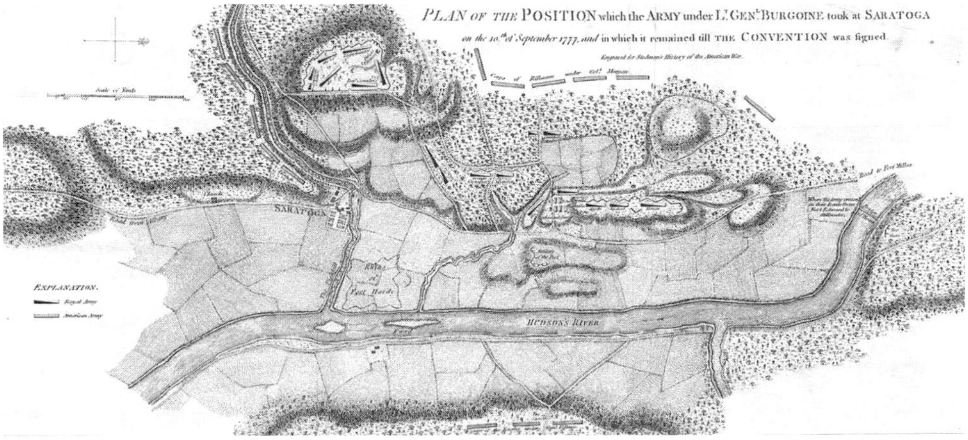

A map of the Battle of Saratoga.

This painting describes the surrender of British General Burgoyne and his troops to American General Horatio Gates after the Battle of Saratoga, October 17, 1777.

Burgoyne began his march south from Lake Champlain in June 1777. His plan began to unravel almost immediately. The rough terrain along the river valley caused the troops to advance at a very slow pace. The American forces slowed them down even further by cutting down trees and putting other obstacles in their way. Meanwhile, General Howe decided not to march north to Albany. Instead he boarded his troops onto ships, and sailed south to capture the city of Philadelphia. Colonel St. Leger's troops were forced to retreat to Canada after they were defeated by the American forces at Fort Stanwix in Oriskany, New York.

When Burgoyne finally reached the Hudson River in August, he was running short of supplies. He sent a raiding party of 1,000 troops to seize food and supplies. But they were defeated and captured by American militias at Bennington, Vermont. Burgoyne continued his advance until he got to Saratoga (now Schuylerville). There he was blocked by the American army under the command of Horatio Gates.

During the summer, militiamen throughout the northern colonies came to join Gates' force. **George Washington** also sent reinforcements from his Continental Army in Pennsylvania. Gates now commanded over 15,000 troops, greatly outnumbering Burgoyne's force.

On September 19, 1777, the two armies clashed at the Battle of Freeman's Farm. After much fierce fighting, the British succeeded in driving the American troops from the battlefield. They suffered heavy casualties. Burgoyne tried a second advance on October 7, 1777. They were met by the American forces at Bemis Heights, and forced to retreat. Burgoyne attempted to cross over the Hudson River, and return to Canada, but found his army surrounded by Gates' forces. On October 17, 1777 Burgoyne surrendered. His surviving 5,791 men laid down their arms.

The Battle of Saratoga is considered one of the most important American victories of the Revolutionary War. It eliminated the threat of British invasion from the north. More importantly, it convinced the French government to support the American cause with financial and military aid. This aid ultimately turned the tide in the American's favor.

The Winter of 1777-78: Valley Forge and Aid from France

In September 1777, the Americans were defeated at the battle of Brandywine. British commander Howe marched into Philadelphia and took the city. The Continental Congress fled.

Washington and his men were forced to endure the hard winter of 1777 and 1778 in Valley Forge, Pennsylvania. The winter at Valley Forge has become a famous piece of Revolutionary War history.

The outlook was bleak for the young nation. Despite the victory at Saratoga, things had not gone that well in the battlefield. Washington's men, 11,000 in all, were tired, hungry, and close to despair. Congress hadn't sent the money for the soldiers' food, clothing, and weapons.

Some 3,000 of the soldiers had no shoes. Many died of starvation. Horses and oxen died of starvation, too. When that happened, the men had to pull the wagons themselves. Over 2,000 of the soldiers deserted that winter.

It was up to Washington to lift the mens' spirits and inspire them to continue the fight for independence. Washington was helped in his task by several European volunteers, especially the **Marquis de Lafayette**. He joined the fight for independence and offered supplies to the army, which he paid for himself. Another volunteer, Baron von Steuben, helped to drill the soldiers and ready them for battle.

The soldiers' devotion to Washington, and to the cause of independence, got them through this bleak time. There was also news from France to cheer them.

Lafayette and George Washington visit the suffering troops during the hard winter at Valley Forge, 1777.

In the spring of 1778, the Americans learned that the French had signed a treaty with the U.S. to give them aid. They sent money, ships, and weapons. The British commander of Philadelphia, Sir Henry Clinton, feared the power of the French navy. He left the city with his troops and advanced to New York.

Benjamin Franklin was partly responsible for encouraging France to support the Americans. He had been sent to France in 1776, and met with leaders to convince them to send aid to the U.S. Also, France was willing to help the Americans against their enemy, the British.

The agreement between the U.S. and France included several key issues. First, France recognized the U.S. as a nation. They agreed that if France entered the war, they would fight with the

U.S. until they had won. Also, if the U.S. won, they agreed that France would hold on to its current colonies in North America.

France's actions made the war a larger conflict. Britain declared war on France in 1778. In 1779, Spain decided to back France in the conflict. At that time, the Dutch had continued to trade with the U.S. So, in 1780, Britain declared war on the Dutch. So Britain was fighting a war on several fronts, and the U.S. had more support and allies than ever.

The British decided to concentrate their forces on the southern colonies. There, they would clash with the armies of **Nathanael Greene**, **George Washington**, and **Lafayette**. The fate of the new nation would be decided, first in South Carolina, then in Virginia.

The Southern Campaigns and Yorktown

The British forces had captured Savannah, Georgia, in December 1778. In 1780, the British increased their attacks in the South. Generals Clinton and Cornwallis attacked Charleston, South Carolina, in May 1780. The first time they tried to seize the city,

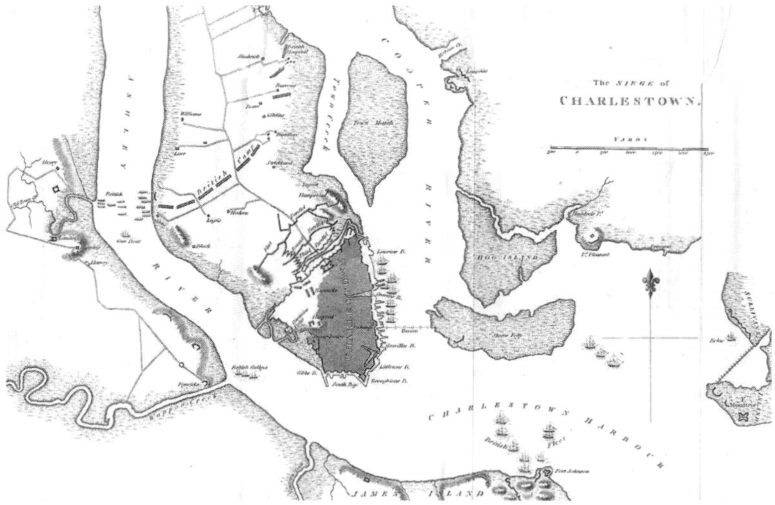

A map of the siege of Charleston, 1780.

This painting shows Patriot leader Francis Marion, known as "The Swamp Fox," and his men on their way to battle the British in South Carolina.

they failed. But on their second attempt, Charleston fell to the British.

Hearing about the fall of Charleston, American General Gates brought a force of 3,000 soldiers and fought Cornwallis's men at Camden. But he lost, and had to retreat to North Carolina.

Meanwhile, Isaac Shelby and John Sevier led a group of frontiersmen in Kings Mountain, South Carolina. They won against a group of 1,000 British soldiers. There were similar raids led by the legendary "Swamp Fox," Francis Marion, and Thomas Sumter.

General **Nathanael Greene** took over the forces in the South in December 1780. At the Battle of the Cowpens in January 1781, 950 American troops under General Daniel Morgan defeated the British soundly.

The next major battle took place at Guilford Courthouse in North Carolina. Some 4,500 American soldiers overwhelmed 2,200 British troops, for another important victory. Greene moved his troops into South Carolina, and bested the British at Hobkirk's Hill and Eutaw Springs.

Cornwallis moved north to Virginia with 6,000 men. There, he hoped to defeat Lafayette and a force of 3,000 Americans. Lafayette retreated to the north. Soon, he was joined by General Anthony Wayne and his force of 1,000 men. Cornwallis decided to head for the coast of Virginia, to Yorktown.

Yorktown

When Cornwallis moved his forces to Yorktown, Lafayette followed, and kept him there. Soon, Lafayette was joined by a massive force, including Washington, and the French army and navy.

A map of the Battle of Yorktown, 1781.

The French navy, under Admiral Francois de Grasse, brought 24 ships into Yorktown harbor. The British fleet fled, leaving Cornwallis without reinforcements. The combined American and French forces on land and on sea, 16,000 in all, trapped Cornwallis. He had nowhere

This painting shows British General Cornwallis surrendering to General Washington after the British were defeated at Yorktown, October 19, 1781, marking the end of the Revolutionary War.

to retreat. He knew he was defeated. On October 19, 1781, Cornwallis surrendered. He and 7,247 soldiers laid down their arms. The Revolutionary War was essentially over, although some fighting went on for the next two years.

Now, the country looked to its diplomats, **John Jay**, **Benjamin Franklin**, and **John Adams**. They would spend the next two years working out the terms of the peace with Britain.

The New Nation at Peace

The Treaty of Paris

Although the final battle of the Revolution ended at Yorktown with the British surrender in 1781, the war was not officially over. That happened with the signing of the "Treaty of Paris."

John Jay, **Benjamin Franklin**, and **John Adams** represented the new United States in the negotiations that ended the war. They met with representatives of the British government for several months, working out an agreement. Finally, in September 1783, the treaty ending the Revolutionary War was finished.

This map shows the new boundaries of the United States after the signing of the Treaty of Paris, 1783.

Called the Treaty of Paris, the document outlined several important issues. Britain officially recognized the former colonies as the United States of America. The treaty also established the boundaries of the U.S. The new United States stretched from the Atlantic Ocean west to the Mississippi River, and from the Canadian border south to Florida.

The Constitutional Convention

After the Treaty of Paris ended the Revolutionary War, there was much to do in the new United States. One of the most important tasks of the new government was the creation of the Constitution.

The Constitution is the plan of the national government. It outlines the structure and the powers of the government. When it was written in 1787, there were many different ideas of what the government should be. But the leaders knew there was an urgent need for a Constitution. They knew they had to create a plan that would unite the states, speak to the needs of the people, and provide protection for the liberty and freedom they had so dearly won in the Revolutionary War.

At that time, the states were governed by the laws outlined in the **ARTICLES OF CONFEDERATION**. They were the ruling laws of the U.S. before the Constitution was adopted. They were written in 1777 by the **CONTINENTAL CONGRESS**, and served as the national constitution from March 1781 until the U.S. Constitution went into effect. There were many problems and weaknesses in the Articles, notably regarding the size and power of the federal government, the rights of the states, taxation, and boundaries of the states. So

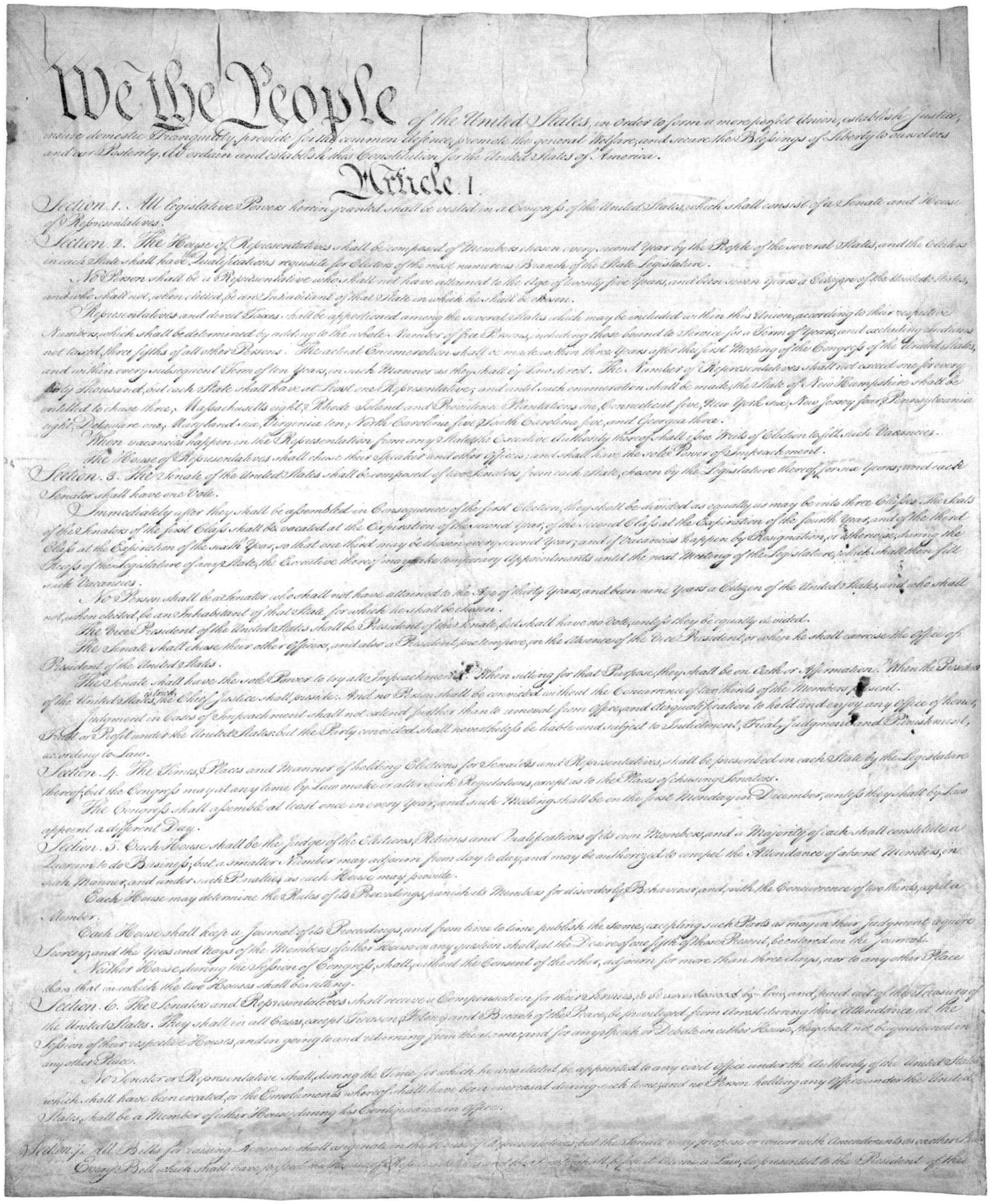

We the People of the United States, in Order to form a more perfect Union, establish Justice, insure domestic Tranquility, provide for the common defence, promote the general Welfare, and secure the Blessings of Liberty to ourselves and our Posterity, do ordain and establish this Constitution for the United States of America.

Article. I.

Section. 1. All legislative Powers herein granted shall be vested in a Congress of the United States, which shall consist of a Senate and House of Representatives.

Section. 2. The House of Representatives shall be composed of Members chosen every second Year by the People of the several States, and the Electors in each State shall have the Qualifications requisite for Electors of the most numerous Branch of the State Legislature.

No Person shall be a Representative who shall not have attained to the Age of twenty five Years, and been seven Years a Citizen of the United States, and who shall not, when elected, be an Inhabitant of that State in which he shall be chosen.

Representatives and direct Taxes shall be apportioned among the several States which may be included within this Union, according to their respective Numbers, which shall be determined by adding to the whole Number of free Persons, including those bound to Service for a Term of Years, and excluding Indians not taxed, three fifths of all other Persons. The actual Enumeration shall be made within three Years after the first Meeting of the Congress of the United States, and within every subsequent Term of ten Years, in such Manner as they shall by Law direct. The Number of Representatives shall not exceed one for every thirty Thousand, but each State shall have at Least one Representative; and until such enumeration shall be made, the State of New Hampshire shall be entitled to chuse three, Massachusetts eight, Rhode Island and Providence Plantations one, Connecticut five, New York six, New Jersey four, Pennsylvania eight, Delaware one, Maryland six, Virginia ten, North Carolina five, South Carolina five, and Georgia three.

When vacancies happen in the Representation from any State, the Executive Authority thereof shall issue Writs of Election to fill such Vacancies.

The House of Representatives shall chuse their Speaker and other Officers; and shall have the sole Power of Impeachment.

Section. 3. The Senate of the United States shall be composed of two Senators from each State, chosen by the Legislature thereof, for six Years; and each Senator shall have one Vote.

Immediately after they shall be assembled in Consequence of the first Election, they shall be divided as equally as may be into three Classes. The Seats of the Senators of the first Class shall be vacated at the Expiration of the second Year, of the second Class at the Expiration of the fourth Year, and of the third Class at the Expiration of the sixth Year, so that one third may be chosen every second Year; and if Vacancies happen by Resignation, or otherwise, during the Recess of the Legislature of any State, the Executive thereof may make temporary Appointments until the next Meeting of the Legislature, which shall then fill such Vacancies.

No Person shall be a Senator who shall not have attained to the Age of thirty Years, and been nine Years a Citizen of the United States, and who shall not, when elected, be an Inhabitant of that State for which he shall be chosen.

The Vice President of the United States shall be President of the Senate, but shall have no Vote, unless they be equally divided.

The Senate shall chuse their other Officers, and also a President pro tempore, in the Absence of the Vice President, or when he shall exercise the Office of President of the United States.

The Senate shall have the sole Power to try all Impeachments. When sitting for that Purpose, they shall be on Oath or Affirmation. When the President of the United States is tried, the Chief Justice shall preside: And no Person shall be convicted without the Concurrence of two thirds of the Members present.

Judgment in Cases of Impeachment shall not extend further than to removal from Office, and disqualification to hold and enjoy any Office of honor, Trust or Profit under the United States: but the Party convicted shall nevertheless be liable and subject to Indictment, Trial, Judgment and Punishment, according to Law.

Section. 4. The Times, Places and Manner of holding Elections for Senators and Representatives, shall be prescribed in each State by the Legislature thereof; but the Congress may at any time by Law make or alter such Regulations, except as to the Places of chusing Senators.

The Congress shall assemble at least once in every Year, and such Meeting shall be on the first Monday in December, unless they shall by Law appoint a different Day.

Section. 5. Each House shall be the Judge of the Elections, Returns and Qualifications of its own Members, and a Majority of each shall constitute a Quorum to do Business; but a smaller Number may adjourn from day to day, and may be authorized to compel the Attendance of absent Members, in such Manner, and under such Penalties as each House may provide.

Each House may determine the Rules of its Proceedings, punish its Members for disorderly Behaviour, and, with the Concurrence of two thirds, expel a Member.

Each House shall keep a Journal of its Proceedings, and from time to time publish the same, excepting such Parts as may in their Judgment require Secrecy; and the Yeas and Nays of the Members of either House on any question shall, at the Desire of one fifth of those Present, be entered on the Journal.

Neither House, during the Session of Congress, shall, without the Consent of the other, adjourn for more than three days, nor to any other Place than that in which the two Houses shall be sitting.

Section. 6. The Senators and Representatives shall receive a Compensation for their Services, to be ascertained by Law, and paid out of the Treasury of the United States. They shall in all Cases, except Treason, Felony and Breach of the Peace, be privileged from Arrest during their Attendance at the Session of their respective Houses, and in going to and returning from the same; and for any Speech or Debate in either House, they shall not be questioned in any other Place.

No Senator or Representative shall, during the Time for which he was elected, be appointed to any civil Office under the Authority of the United States, which shall have been created, or the Emoluments whereof shall have been encreased during such time; and no Person holding any Office under the United States, shall be a Member of either House during his Continuance in Office.

Section. 7. All Bills for raising Revenue shall originate in the House of Representatives; but the Senate may propose or concur with Amendments as on other Bills.

Every Bill which shall have passed the House of Representatives and the Senate, shall, before it become a Law, be presented to the President of the

The first page of the U.S. Constitution, 1787.

the delegates to the Constitutional Convention knew they had a lot of work to do.

The Constitutional Convention took place in Philadelphia. It began on May 25, 1787, with 55 delegates from 12 states. Rhode Island sent no delegates, because it didn't like the idea of a strong central government that could tell the states what to do. So from the very beginning, those delegates who believed in a strong central government were opposed by those that believed in giving the most governmental power to the states.

The delegates to the Convention included some of the most famous, and heroic, figures of the Revolutionary War. **George Washington** was president of the Convention. **Benjamin Franklin** was the delegate from Pennsylvania, **Alexander Hamilton** represented New York, and **James Madison** represented Virginia. Because they were overseas on diplomatic work, neither **John Adams** nor **Thomas Jefferson** attended the Convention.

But Adams and **John Jay** had both helped write the constitutions for their states, so the Convention had a guide to follow in creating the document. Almost all the delegates had served during the Revolutionary War, as soldiers, officers, or in the government. They brought all those experiences to creating the new government.

James Madison is considered "The Father of the Constitution." He worked well with the other members, and was able to suggest compromises when delegates were unable to resolve their differences. He helped shape the different sections of the document, and Gouverneur Morris actually wrote down the words.

The Constitution divides power between three branches. The Executive Branch is made up of the President and the Cabinet. The Legislative branch, or Congress, is made up of the House of Representatives and the Senate. They make the laws for the country. The Judicial Branch is made up of the U.S. Court system, including the Supreme Court.

One of the greatest debates over the Constitution concerned the system of representation in the Legislative branch. Small states with small populations wanted to be guaranteed powers equal to large states with large populations. The compromise that settled that was the creation of the two-part Congress. The House of Representatives has representation based on population. In the Senate, each state has two representatives. So both small states and large states were satisfied.

The Constitutional Convention completed their debate and voted on the document on September 17, 1787. Not all members voted in favor of the Constitution. Some thought it was too flawed. But enough voted for it that it then went on to the states for approval.

The Constitution had to be "ratified"—voted on—by all the states. Madison wanted to convince the country to adopt the new Constitution. Along with Alexander Hamilton and John Jay, he wrote many articles, called the Federalist Papers. In the articles they tried to persuade people to vote for the new Constitution. Finally, in 1788, enough states had voted to ratify the Constitution to guarantee that it would become the governing document for all the people.

But the issue of states' rights versus a strong central government remained for many people. In response, Madison wrote additions, or "amendments" to the Constitution. These are called the "Bill of Rights."

The Bill of Rights guarantees specific freedoms to all Americans. Some of the major rights we enjoy—like freedom of speech and religion—are outlined in the Bill of Rights.

The opening words, or preamble, to the Constitution are:

> "We the People of the United States, in Order to form a more perfect Union, establish Justice, insure domestic Tranquility, provide for the common defence, promote the general Welfare, and secure the Blessings of Liberty to ourselves and our Posterity, do ordain and establish this Constitution for the United States of America."

In these words are the hopes, as well as the experience and wisdom, of the people who brought the United States into being. That it has continued to guide the nation over the past 220 years, through times of tremendous change, is a tribute to their abilities, the flexibility of the document they created, and their commitment to, in the words of Abraham Lincoln, "government of the people, by the people, and for the people."

Note: You can find the full text of the Constitution and the Bill of Rights in the Appendix.

WORLD WIDE WEB SITES:

http://www.digitalhistory.uh.edu/
http://www.historyplace.com/UnitedStates/revolution/
http://www.house.gov/house/Educate.shtml
http://usinfo.state.gov/products/pubs/histryotln/

Part III:

Biographical Profiles

Abigail Adams
1744-1818
American Patriot and Wife of President John Adams

ABIGAIL ADAMS WAS BORN on November 11, 1744, in Weymouth, Massachusetts. Her name at birth was Abigail Smith. When she was born, Massachusetts was one of 13 American colonies that were ruled by the king of England. Abigail's father, the Reverend William Smith, was a minister and community leader. Her mother, Elizabeth Quincy Smith, was a homemaker. Abigail had an older sister, Mary. She also had a younger brother, William, and a younger sister, Elizabeth.

The first home of John and Abigail Adams, in Quincy, Massachusetts, is on the right. John Adams was born in the house on the left.

ABIGAIL ADAMS GREW UP in a rural area. Poor health kept her from being very active as a girl. She spent much of her time reading and writing letters to family and friends.

ABIGAIL ADAMS WENT TO SCHOOL at home. Like most other girls of her time, she did not have a formal education. Girls were expected to become wives and mothers. Abigail mostly learned cooking, sewing, and other skills she would need in these roles. But she was very bright and curious about the world. She read many books in her father's library to expand her knowledge. Later in her life, she became a big supporter of equal education for women.

MARRIES JOHN ADAMS: On October 25, 1764, Abigail Smith married John Adams. John was a well-educated young lawyer. He hoped to get involved in politics. They bought a farm in Braintree (later renamed Quincy), Massachusetts. Abigail gave birth to five children over the next ten years: daughters Abigail ("Nabby") and Susanna, and sons John Quincy, Charles, and Thomas. Sadly, Susanna died before reaching the age of two.

During the early years of their marriage, John often lived and worked in the city of Boston. While he was away, Abigail took care of the children and ran the farm. It was unusual for women to conduct business in those days. But Abigail bought and sold land and livestock, hired farm employees, and supervised the planting and harvesting of crops. She felt proud of her role in supporting the family. "I hope in time to have the reputation of being as good a Farmess as my partner has of being a good Statesman," she wrote.

SUPPORTS WOMEN'S RIGHTS: Whenever they were apart, Abigail and John wrote long letters to each other. Many of these letters discussed the growing tensions between the American colonies and England. Beginning in 1764, English leaders had tried to put the colonies under tighter control. They charged high taxes on products that people in America needed, like sugar, paper, and tea. Many colonists felt that it was not fair for England to charge them taxes without giving them a say in government.

Some colonists, known as Loyalists, wanted to work out their differences and remain part of England. But many others, known as Patriots, wanted to break away from England and form a new country. In 1774, leaders of the 13 colonies got together in Philadelphia, Pennsylvania, to decide what to do. John Adams was chosen to represent Massachusetts at this meeting of the **CONTINENTAL CONGRESS**.

This is the kitchen at the Adams' house in Quincy.

Abigail wrote letters to John during his time in Philadelphia. In one famous letter, she asked her husband to expand legal rights for women. Abigail argued that women should be allowed to own property and get a good education. "In the new code of laws which I suppose it will be necessary for you to make, I desire you would remember the ladies and be more generous and favorable to them than your ancestors," she wrote. "Do not put such unlimited power into the hands of husbands. Remember, all men would be tyrants if they could."

THE REVOLUTIONARY WAR: The tensions between England and the American colonies eventually exploded into war. The fighting started in Lexington, Massachusetts, on April 19, 1775. Although the war did not threaten the Adams farm, Abigail found even distant battles upsetting. "The constant roar of the cannon is so distressing that we cannot eat, drink, or sleep," she noted. Abigail also struggled to deal with shortages of goods and epidemics of disease during this time.

On July 4, 1776, John Adams and other members of the Continental Congress decided to separate from England and form a new nation. They issued the **DECLARATION OF INDEPENDENCE** to inform the king of their plans. General **George Washington** led the Continental Army into battle against British troops.

In 1778 John Adams traveled to France. He helped convince the French government to give the Americans money and supplies to fight England. Abigail missed her husband terribly during his time in France. They continued writing letters, but it took months for mail to go across the ocean.

With assistance from France, the Americans finally managed to win the war. On September 3, 1783, John Adams and other Americans signed a peace agreement with England. **THE TREATY OF PARIS** recognized the United States as an independent nation. The new country stretched from the Atlantic Ocean west to the Mississippi River, and from the Canadian border south to Florida.

In 1784, Abigail and the children joined John in Europe. By this time, Abigail and her husband had not seen each other in five years. The Adams family lived in France for a while, then moved to England. Abigail served as an advisor to her husband and as a hostess of official gatherings during this time.

BECOMES FIRST LADY: The Adams family returned to the United States in 1788. The new country created a **CONSTITUTION** and formed its own government. **George Washington** was elected as the first president of the United States. John Adams served as Washington's vice president from 1789 to 1797.

After Washington decided to retire, John Adams was elected the second president of the United States in 1797. As First Lady, Abigail hosted social and political gatherings and advised her husband on important issues. Many people knew how much President Adams counted on the First Lady's advice and support. They often went to Abigail when they wanted something from the President. Political opponents sometimes called Abigail "Mrs. President" because she held so much influence.

During John Adams's term as President, the nation's capital moved from Philadelphia to Washington, D.C. The area around Washington was mostly wilderness at this time. Adams was the first President to live in the White House. Abigail had to entertain official guests when the building was not even finished yet.

REMEMBERED IN LETTERS: John Adams lost the election of 1801 to Thomas Jefferson. Abigail and her husband retired to their Massachusetts farm. They spent the next 17 years there together. Abigail suffered from poor health for much of this time. She died at home on October 28, 1818.

Abigail's friends and family saved many of the letters that she wrote during her lifetime. In 1848, one of her grandsons published a book of these letters. It was the first book ever published about a First Lady.

ABIGAIL ADAMS'S HOME AND FAMILY: Abigail lived in Quincy, Massachusetts, until her death in 1818. Six years later, her eldest son, John Quincy Adams, was elected President of the United States. Abigail thus became the first American woman ever to be the wife of one president and the mother of another. She was the only woman to hold this distinction until Barbara Bush in 2000.

HER LEGACY: Abigail Adams is admired for commitment to her family, and the cause of the Revolution. Her letters reveal that she was a bright and capable woman. She was ahead of her time in many ways. For example, she considered herself equal to her husband and freely advised him on many topics. She also argued in favor of women's rights and ending slavery. Her letters provide a vivid picture of the politics and personalities of the Revolutionary War era.

WORLD WIDE WEB SITES:

http://www.whitehouse.gov/history/firstladies/aa2.html
http://www.firstladies.org/biographies/firstladies.aspx?biography=2

John Adams

1735-1826
American Patriot and Statesman
"The Atlas of Independence"
Member of the Continental Congress
Co-Author of the Declaration of Independence
First Ambassador of the U.S. to Great Britain,
Second President of the United States

JOHN ADAMS WAS BORN on October 30, 1735, in Braintree, Massachusetts. (The city is now called Quincy.) His father, John Adams, was a farmer. His mother, Susanna Adams, was a homemaker. John was the oldest of three boys. His brothers were Peter and Elihu Adams.

JOHN ADAMS GREW UP in Quincy in a family that loved reading. "I was very early taught to read at home," John Adams remembered. He also helped out around the farm, chopping wood and milking cows.

JOHN ADAMS WENT TO SCHOOL at a local school. His teacher was named Mrs. Belcher. She "lived in the next house on the opposite side of the road," he remembered. Later, Adams went to the local public school. He worked hard in Greek, Latin, and math. He wanted to go to college, so he had to do well in those subjects.

When he was 15, Adams went to Harvard College. He graduated four years later. In his first job after college, he taught elementary school. He wanted to become a lawyer, so after teaching during the day he studied law at night.

BECOMING INVOLVED IN POLITICS: In 1758, Adams started to work as a lawyer. Around this time, he became interested in politics. In the 1750s, most of the area that is now the eastern United States was a colony of England. That means that the people were ruled by England. They paid taxes to the British government and were ruled by a king, George III.

Some of the colonists were happy being part of England. Some were not. They believed that the colonies should have their own government. They resented the fact that they had to pay taxes to a government they didn't create or control.

The **STAMP ACT** was a British tax that angered Adams and many of his fellow colonists. It forced the colonists to pay an extra tax on things like newspapers and legal papers. It even taxed playing cards. Adams wrote articles in newspapers about the

Stamp Act. He became known as an important thinker and writer in the cause of freedom.

"The Atlas of Independence"

The people who wanted a separate government began to talk about breaking away from England. These were the people who began the American Revolutionary War.

MARRIAGE AND FAMILY: John Adams married Abigail Smith on October 25, 1764. They had five children: Abigail, John Quincy, Susanna, Charles, and Thomas. Susanna died when she was two. All the other children lived to be adults. John Quincy Adams became the sixth President of the United States.

John and Abigail spent many years apart during their long marriage. They wrote each other many letters over those years. Their letters show how much they loved and cared for each other. They also show what an intelligent and witty woman Abigail was. As the founding fathers were writing the **DECLARATION OF INDEPENDENCE**, Abigail wrote to John: "Don't forget the ladies!" She wanted the equal rights and freedoms they were seeking for men in the new country to be for women, too. She is remembered as one of the most intelligent, warm, and witty First Ladies.

The Signing of the Declaration of Independence. John Adams is the figure at the far left. Thomas Jefferson is second from the right. Next to Jefferson is Benjamin Franklin.

JOHN ADAMS AND THE DECLARATION OF INDEPENDENCE: John Adams was part of a group that wrote the Declaration of Independence. It is a document that states that all men are born equal and free. It says that people have the right to revolt against those who will not give them freedom.

Before they began, Adams wrote a letter to **Thomas Jefferson**, one of the men chosen to write the Declaration. In it, Adams encouraged Jefferson to be the main author of the Declaration. Adams could be cantankerous, and he knew it. He told Jefferson that his milder manner, and fine prose, would help the country and the document. Jefferson was indeed the main author of the Declaration, but Adams, and **Benjamin Franklin**, also had major roles. The Declaration was approved and signed on July 4, 1776.

The day the Declaration was signed, John Adams wrote to Abigail. "Yesterday, the greatest question was decided which ever was debated in America, and a greater perhaps never was nor will be decided among men. A resolution was passed without one dissenting colony, "that these United Colonies are, and of right ought to be, free and independent States'."

Just before the Declaration was signed, Adams wrote to his wife about how he thought future Americans would celebrate the Declaration of Independence. It is surprising how it describes the ways we still celebrate the Fourth of July:

"I am apt to believe that it will be celebrated by succeeding generations as the great anniversary of a festival. It ought to be solemnized with pomp and parade, with shows, games, sports, guns, bells, bonfires, and illustrations, from one end of this continent to the other, from this time forward forevermore."

THE REVOLUTIONARY WAR: Unlike **George Washington**, Adams was not a soldier or leader in the army during the war. Instead, he used his talents to write and speak on behalf of the new nation in Europe. So during the war, Adams went to France to try to find money and support for the new United States.

LIFE IN EUROPE DURING THE WAR: Adams lived first in France and then in the Netherlands during the war. He and other Americans, like Benjamin Franklin, worked on agreements with European leaders. These leaders agreed to support the new country and to lend it money.

In 1781, the Revolutionary War finally came to an end. The Continental Army of the U.S. had defeated the British. The United

States was a free country. Adams signed the agreement between the U.S. and Britain that ended the war. For his travels on behalf of the new nation he earned the nickname, "The Atlas of Independence."

In 1783, Adams, along with **Benjamin Franklin** and **John Jay**, drafted the document that formally defined the new nation. Called the Treaty of Paris, the document defined the end of the Revolutionary War, the peace between England and the United States, and the new boundaries of the new country. The new United States stretched from the Atlantic Ocean west to the Mississippi River, and from the Canadian border south to Florida.

Adams's role in helping to define and run the new nation continued. In 1785, Adams became the first minister to Britain from the U.S. He and his family lived in England for three years. Then, in 1788, he came home, and began to serve his country in his native land.

RETURNING HOME: When Adams returned home, he ran in the very first Presidential election. In that first election in 1788, George Washington was elected President and John Adams was elected Vice President. He served as Vice President for eight years, from 1789 to 1797.

FIRST VICE PRESIDENT OF THE UNITED STATES: Adams didn't like being Vice President. He didn't really have much to do. At that time, the only responsibility he had was to attend Senate meetings. He said, "I am Vice President. In this I am nothing, but I may be everything." He realized the job of Vice President had few responsibilities. But if Washington died, he would be responsible for "everything."

THE DEVELOPMENT OF POLITICAL PARTIES: Washington was President when the first political parties came into being. These groups shared similar ideas on how government should work. Washington and Adams were "Federalists." That means that they favored a strong central government. They were opposed by the Democratic-Republicans, led by Thomas Jefferson. Jefferson believed that a strong central government was a bad idea. He thought it limited the power of the states.

PRESIDENT OF THE UNITED STATES: In the election of 1796, Adams ran against Jefferson for President as a Federalist. Today, candidates for President and Vice President are from the same party. They share the same ideas, and they run together. In 1796, the candidates for President ran alone, without a Vice Presidential candidate. The candidate getting the most votes won the presidency, while the second-place finisher won the Vice Presidency. In 1796, Adams won the election and became President. Jefferson got the second highest number of votes. He became Vice President.

Since Adams and Jefferson were from different parties, they didn't agree on many of the major issues facing the young nation. Adams could be tough and stubborn. He didn't mind standing alone.

During the 1790s, England and France went to war. The Federalists wanted the U.S. to get involved on the part of the English. The Democratic-Republicans wanted the U.S. to support the French. Even though it was unpopular politically, Adams kept the U.S. out of the war. He was always a man who stood by what he believed.

Birthplaces of John Adams (right) and John Quincy Adams (left).

He did what he thought was best for the nation, and it cost him political support.

FIRST RESIDENTS OF THE WHITE HOUSE: John and Abigail Adams were the first President and First Lady to live in the White House. It wasn't called the "White House" at the time. It was referred to then as the "President's House.

The Adams didn't like the President's House. It wasn't finished when they moved in, in November 1800. There wasn't even a staircase. The rooms were drafty and cold. Abigail used one room to hang laundry.

Yet despite their discomfort, Adams wished that the new house be the home of honest people always. "I pray Heaven to bestow the best of blessings on this house and all that shall hereafter inhabit it. May none but honest and wise men ever rule under this roof," he wrote.

RUNNING FOR REELECTION: Adams's decisions made him an unpopular President with politically powerful groups. When he ran for reelection in 1800, he was defeated by Jefferson.

RETIREMENT TO QUINCY: Adams left Washington as Jefferson took office in 1801. He never ran for office again. Instead, he and Abigail returned to Quincy. There, Adams enjoyed reading and writing. In 1812 he began to write to Thomas Jefferson. "You and I ought not to die before we have explained ourselves to each other," wrote Adams to Jefferson. They renewed their friendship, and over the years wrote many letters to each other. In them, the two founding fathers discussed many aspects of human nature and politics.

John Adams lived a long, full life. Abigail Adams died before her husband, in 1818. John died on July 4, 1826, at his home in Quincy. The day he died was the 50th anniversary of the signing of the Declaration of Independence. It was the same day his political foe and eventual friend Thomas Jefferson died. He did not know of Jefferson's death when he died. Adams last words were: "Jefferson lives."

HIS LEGACY: John Adams was indispensable in the fight for American independence, and the development of the new nation. He devoted his great gifts as a writer, thinker, and politician to its founding and early years.

WORLD WIDE WEB SITES:

http://www.ipl.org/ref/POTUS
http://www.masshist.org/adams/
http://www.nps.gov/adams/index/htm
http://www.whitehouse.gov/WH/kids/html/kidshome.html

Samuel Adams
1722-1803
American Patriot, Journalist, and Statesman
Rallied the Colonists to the Cause of the American Revolution

SAMUEL ADAMS WAS BORN on September 27, 1722, in Boston, Massachusetts. His parents were Samuel and Mary Adams. Samuel was a brewer and Mary was a homemaker. Samuel was one of 12 children. All but three died as infants. Samuel grew up with a brother and a sister. His most famous relative was his cousin, **John Adams**, his fellow Patriot and the second President of the United States.

SAMUEL ADAMS GREW UP in Boston in a close family. His mother was very strict, and a devout Christian. Samuel was raised to be a responsible, dutiful young man.

SAMUEL ADAMS WENT TO SCHOOL at Boston Grammar School. He went to Harvard College when he was 14 years old. When he graduated, he took part in a debate on liberty. He won. Adams completed a master's degree at Harvard in 1743.

FIRST JOBS: Adams went to work as a businessman. But he wasn't very good at business, and he went broke. Soon, he was working at the family brewery. (There is currently a brewery called "Samuel Adams," but it is not run by any of Adams's descendants.) However, Adams's first love was politics, so his work at the brewery took second place.

Adams took a job as a tax collector in Boston in 1756. He served in the job for eight years, but he didn't keep his mind on his work. He failed to collect almost $10,000 in taxes owed to the government. By this time, he was too involved in politics.

NEWSPAPERMAN: In 1748, Adams started a newspaper, *The Independent Advertiser.* It was his first experience in writing about politics. After his father died in 1748, Adams was supposed to take over the brewery. But he kept his focus on the growing unrest in Boston. His brother and brother-in-law ran the brewery, while he ran the paper. Over the next 30 years, Adams wrote many articles and pamphlets, promoting his political beliefs. Adams's message from the beginning was his firm belief that people had the natural right to self-government.

By this time, the British Parliament had begun to tax the colonists. They did this in part to pay for the expense of the **FRENCH AND INDIAN WAR**. That war took place between 1754 and 1763. Britain defeated France and gained vast territories in North America, but it was also very expensive. They imposed a series of taxes, which infuriated many colonists.

Some colonists, known as Loyalists, wanted to work out their differences and remain part of England. But many others, known as Patriots, wanted to break away from England and form a new country. The growing hostilities between Patriots like Sam Adams and British officials helped spark the Revolution.

OPPOSING THE SUGAR ACT: In 1764, the British Parliament revised a previous tax on sugar, molasses, and other goods imported from the French West Indies. The Sugar Act changed the way in which money was collected from the colonists, ensuring that the colonists paid high tariffs.

Adams reacted with outrage. By this time, he was involved in the "Caucus Club," a group of like-minded Boston Patriots. He challenged the Sugar Act because he felt it limited the colonists' right to self-government. The British were imposing these taxes without giving the colonists a say. So strong was the protest that the British reversed the Act.

SONS OF LIBERTY: Adams was also active in a group of Patriots who called themselves the Sons of Liberty. Members, like Adams and **Paul Revere**, were adamantly opposed to British rule in the colonies. Often in secret, they met to plan the best way to fight the British.

Political cartoon indicating how much the colonists, especially Sam Adams, hated the Stamp Tax.

OPPOSING THE STAMP ACT: In 1765, Adams rallied the colonists against the Stamp Act. This Act of Parliament, passed in 1765, made it mandatory that most documents, such as contracts, newspapers, and pamphlets, had to be written on special paper bearing a stamp from the British government.

The colonists were forced to purchase the stamped paper for most of their documents, because documents on plain paper had no legal standing. The American colonists were suspicious of the tax because many thought that the money paid remained in the pockets of the "Stamp Men." Those were the agents who sold the paper to them.

Adams wrote pamphlets denouncing the British. He and other Patriots rallied the people. The colonists protested so much that in 1766, the Stamp Act was repealed.

ELECTED TO THE ASSEMBLY: Adams was elected to the Massachusetts General Assembly in 1765. By that time, he was already a seasoned and effective political leader. He served as the clerk of the Assembly until 1774.

Adams wrote and spoke to the colonists about the British presence in the colonies. He railed against British rule, which he said was unjust. He stated that the colonists and their government were independent of British control. These rights, he claimed, were the natural rights of all men.

BOSTON MASSACRE: On the evening of March 5, 1770, a rumor began to fly around Boston. A British soldier had supposedly struck a young barber's apprentice. Armed only with snowballs and sticks, a group of citizens confronted the soldiers. With **Crispus Attucks** at the head of the crowd, they marched to the Boston Customs House.

The soldiers fired into the crowd. When the smoke cleared, Attucks and three others lay dead. Eventually five men—Attucks, Samuel Gray, James Caldwell, Samuel Maverick, and Patrick Carr—died of their wounds.

The Boston Massacre.

The people of Boston were furious. They claimed that Attucks and the other men were martyrs in the cause of independence. Adams called their murder "The Boston Massacre." It became another rallying cry of the Patriots.

THE COMMITTEE OF CORRESPONDENCE: In 1772, Adams helped to form the Committees of Correspondence. These important groups shared information about resistance to the British among the colonies. The British authorities were furious. Loyalist Thomas Hutchinson wrote of its effect on Massachusetts. "All of a sudden from a state of peace, order, and general contentment, the province was brought into a state of contention."

TEA ACT: Probably the most famous law passed by Parliament was the Tea Act. The Act was passed in 1773. The East India Company was a large importer/exporter of tea. They were in financial trouble and the British government wanted to help them. In the colonies, East India could sell the tea at a much reduced price to the Americans. This undercut the prices sold by colonial merchants. When the ships loaded with East India tea reached Boston Harbor, the colonists refused to unload them.

BOSTON TEA PARTY: Although the Tea Act did not impose additional duties or taxes on the colonists, they were suspicious of Parliament's motives. The colonists felt that the British would not stop increasing taxes. It was time to

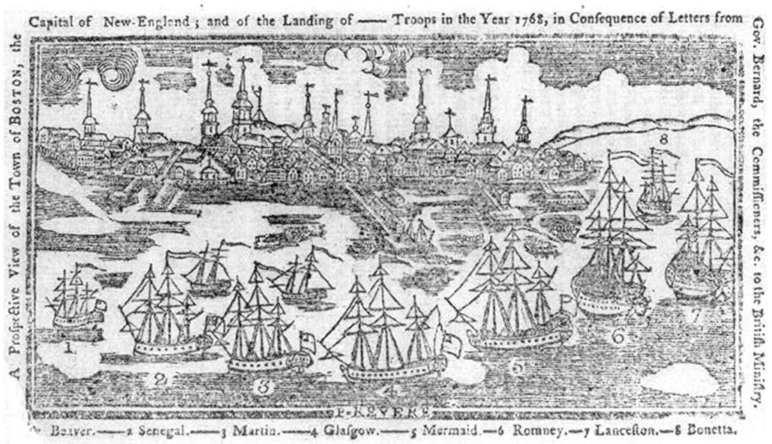

This drawing shows several British ships carrying troops to calm the Colonists of Boston in 1768.

A painting showing the Boston Tea Party

resist as best they could. Led by Adams and Paul Revere, the colonists made a plan. On December 16, 1773, "The Boston Tea Party" took place. A group of patriots, many of them from the Sons of Liberty, dressed as Mohawk Indians and dumped 342 chests of tea into the harbor.

The British were infuriated. They closed the port of Boston to all trade in March 1774. They imposed martial law and martial courts. Adams called for a congress to discuss the colonists' response.

FIRST CONTINENTAL CONGRESS: The First Continental Congress met in Philadelphia in 1774. Adams was elected to represent Massachusetts. He became a leader within the Congress, speaking for a strong response to English rule. The members of the Congress decided to boycott British goods and fight taxes.

PAUL REVERE AND HIS MIDNIGHT RIDE: After Adams returned to Boston, he was once again at the center of the conflict. But he was also in danger. The British authorities wanted Adams and fellow Patriot **John Hancock** arrested for plotting against them. On April 18, 1775, Paul Revere warned Adams and Hancock to the danger during his famous ride. The next day, the battles of Lexington and Concord took place. Soon, Adams was back in Philadelphia, as the call for Revolution spread.

SECOND CONTINENTAL CONGRESS: In May 1775, the colonists called a Second Continental Congress. Adams once again represented Massachusetts. The Congress issued its call to action: the Declaration of Independence.

THE DECLARATION OF INDEPENDENCE: The Declaration outlined the reasons behind the Revolutionary War. It was written mainly by **Thomas Jefferson**, with help from **John Adams** and **Benjamin Franklin**. In simple, powerful language, it describes what the colonists thought about their rights as individuals and as citizens. It states that all men are born equal and free. They have the right to revolt against those who will not give them freedom. On July 4, 1776, the Continental Congress accepted the Declaration of Independence. Adams was among the signers.

THE REVOLUTIONARY WAR: Throughout the Revolutionary War, Adams continued to write and to rally the Patriots. He also continued to serve in the Continental Congress until 1781. After the defeat of the British, the United States came into being.

THE U.S. CONSTITUTION: Adams served as a delegate to the Constitutional Convention, helping to define the new nation. He urged his colleagues to resist the goal of some delegates to build a strong central government. He believed in very limited powers for any government. This was in keeping with his belief in self-government for all. He voted for approval of the Constitution, but insisted on the addition of the **BILL OF RIGHTS**. These guaranteed those individual freedoms—of speech, of the press, of the right to assembly—so dear to his heart.

LATER LIFE: The old Patriot stayed in politics until late in life. He helped draft the state constitution for Massachusetts. He ran for, but did not win, a seat in the U.S. House of Representatives. He was elected lieutenant governor of Massachusetts in 1789. He served in that post until 1794. That year, after the death of his old friend John Hancock, he became governor of the state. He held that job until 1797. Adams died in Boston on October 2, 1803.

MARRIAGE AND FAMILY: Adams was married twice. His first wife was named Mary Checkley. They married in 1749 and had five children. Only two lived to be adults. Mary died in 1757. Adams married again in 1764. His second wife was named Elizabeth Wells. They had no children of their own, but Elizabeth helped to raise Adams's two children from his first marriage.

HIS LEGACY: Adams was one of the most important early Patriots in the fight for independence. His dedication to self-government helped insure that that concept was central to the goals of the Revolution and the Constitution.

WORLD WIDE WEB SITES:

http://www.ushistory.org/Declaration/signers/adams_s.htm
http://www.whitehouse.gov/kids/dreamteam/samueladams.html

Ethan Allen

(1738-1789)

American Patriot and Revolutionary War Hero
Leader of the Green Mountain Boys
Promoter of Statehood for Vermont

ETHAN ALLEN WAS BORN on January 21, 1738, in Litchfield, Connecticut. His father was Joseph Allen and his mother was Mary Baker. Ethan was the oldest of eight children and had seven brothers and sisters. His five brothers were Heman, Heber, Levi, Zimri and Ira. His two sisters were named Lydia and Lucy. Ethan's youngest brother Ira is best known for founding the University of Connecticut in 1791. When Ethan was two years old, his family moved to Cornwall, a frontier village.

ETHAN ALLEN WENT TO SCHOOL at home. Since Cornwall didn't have a school he learned to read from the Bible. Ethan dreamed of one day attending Yale University. When he was 17, he was sent to Salisbury to study with a minister. Unfortunately, his father died shortly after, so he had to return home and take care of his family.

Not going to Yale was a great disappointment for Ethan. He spent much of his time reading, writing and thinking. He also spent as much time as he could with the few educated men he could find.

FRENCH AND INDIAN WAR: By the mid-1700s, most of the colonies in the New World were under British rule. However, there were also areas that were claimed by France, and also areas where Native American populations continued to fight British settlers and refused to acknowledge British control. The British fought several wars in order to claim the territory. The most important of these was the French and Indian War (1754-1763). Allen spent two weeks with the Connecticut army as they tried to stop the French from taking charge of Fort William. This was his only part in the French and Indian War.

MARRIAGE AND FAMILY: Allen married Mary Brownson in 1762 when he was 24 years old. Ethan and Mary had five children together, four girls and one boy.

They lived together first at Cornwall, where they expanded the Allen family farm. In 1763, they moved to a farm in Salisbury. Here Ethan and his brother Heman invested in an ironworks factory. Two years later they sold it.

A ROAMING REBEL: In 1767 Allen's family settled on a farm in Sheffield, Massachusetts, with his younger brother Zimri. Allen began to go away for months at a time to explore the land known then as the "New Hampshire Grants." We know it today as Vermont.

Since the 1600s the land had been claimed by New York, New Hampshire, Massachusetts and Connecticut. Settlers had been given deeds for land from both New York and New Hampshire. In 1767 all settlers who received land from New Hampshire were told they had to reapply for their deeds and pay a tax because the land belonged to New York.

Ethan had spent much time in the area, and knew the land and the settlers well. Because he was a big man with plenty of self-confidence, he was asked to be the leader of the people who now had to fight for their land.

THE GREEN MOUNTAIN BOYS: When the news of the land dispute reached Bennington, Vermont, settlers came together and formed a rag-tag kind of volunteer army. Ethan Allen became the leader of the group that came to be known as the Green Mountain Boys.

In order to protect their interests, Allen and the Green Mountain Boys were determined to drive out the "Yorkers" who were trying to take their land away. In fact, the group took the name Green Mountain Boys from the threat issued by New York—to drive the settlers off the fields and "into the Green Mountains." Although Allen's men used threats, whippings and sometimes crop and cabin burnings, they never shot at or killed anyone during the dispute.

Allen at Ticonderoga.

From 1770 to 1775 the Green Mountain Boys, with Allen as their leader, dedicated their efforts to win independence for the land, and call it Vermont. At one point the governor of New York put a bounty (or price) on Ethan Allen's head. But he was never captured.

FORT TICONDEROGA: In the 1770s, Fort Ticonderoga was the most important British post in eastern North America. Forces here could control Lake Champlain and a waterway all the way north to Montreal, south to New York, or east to Massachusetts or Connecticut. In the spring of 1775, however, the Fort was in disrepair. There were holes in the walls surrounding the Fort and only one sentry was on guard. The two British officers and soldiers had no idea that a skirmish had taken place three weeks earlier at Lexington and Concord.

Meanwhile, Ethan Allen and his Green Mountain Boys had left the Bennington area and moved north to the Champlain Valley. Because Allen and his brothers owned more than 77,000 acres, they were especially interested in making Vermont its own state. When the American Revolution began, Allen planned to take over Fort Ticonderoga and control Lake Champlain.

When Allen received word from a spy that the Fort was not well defended, he and his Boys secretly blocked the roads to the Fort. They crossed the lake in the dead of night and surprised the unsuspecting soldiers. Although the sentry shot at Allen, his gun did not fire and Allen went unharmed.

Joining Allen and the Boys was Captain **Benedict Arnold**, a colonel in the Connecticut Militia. He arrived on the eve of the attack with orders to take the Fort's artillery. He demanded to be the leader of the charge. But the Green Mountain Boys refused to follow anyone but their leader, Ethan Allen. The dispute was settled when Allen invited Arnold to march at his side.

Fort Ticonderoga was captured without a shot being fired. Still, this "battle" was considered to be the first colonial victory of the Revolution. The capture of the Fort not only took away the British chances to control the important waterways, it also supplied the

Colonial Army with cannons and other artillery. The taking of Fort Ticonderoga made Ethan Allen one of the first heroes of the American Revolution.

ALLEN IS TAKEN PRISONER: After the fall of Ticonderoga, Allen was hired as a scout in an unsuccessful expedition to take over Quebec. As the group tried to surprise Montreal, Allen was captured. He was taken in chains by the British to England to be hung. King George III, however, was afraid his hanging would lead Americans to execute captured British soldiers. He ordered Allen to be freed. The hero returned to America.

In 1779, Allen wrote *A Narrative of Colonel Ethan Allen's Captivity, etc.* He described his life as a patriotic American who triumphed over the British attempts to break him.

THE FIGHT FOR INDEPENDENCE FOR VERMONT: Back in Bennington, Allen became the most powerful man in Vermont. He went to Philadelphia three times to plead with Congress to recognize Vermont as a state. Because New York and New Hampshire were still arguing about who really had claim to the land, Allen was unsuccessful.

In 1781, in a message that has become famous with Vermonters, Allen wrote to Congress. He declared he would defend the independence of Vermont. Rather than fail, he and the Green Mountain Boys would move into the mountains and "wage war with human nature at large." His passion was for Vermont to be able to govern itself. Allen vowed he would never live by the rules of New York or Congress.

ALLEN'S LAST YEARS: Allen's first wife died in 1783. In February 1784 Allen married a young widow. They moved to a farm where he raised grain and some cattle.

On February 12, 1789, Allen died suddenly and unexpectedly from a seizure. A large crowd came out in the bitter cold to give him a proper military funeral. Unfortunately, this was two years before Vermont was finally granted statehood. The proud fighter for independence did not live to see his dream.

HIS LEGACY: Revolutionary War hero, burly outdoorsman, brave and cunning soldier, Ethan Allen was called "one of Nature's originals." **George Washington** said "There is an original something in him that commands admiration."

Although he was not a military genius, Allen was a true and fearless Patriot. Although his only contribution to the Revolution was the taking of Fort Ticonderoga, he is a folk hero to this day.

WORLD WIDE WEB SITES:

http://www.ethanallenhomestead.org/
http://www.uvm.edu/~vhnet/hertour/eallen/eahistory.html

Benedict Arnold
1741-1801
American Military Officer Who Betrayed the Revolutionary Cause

BENEDICT ARNOLD WAS BORN on January 14, 1741, in Norwich, Connecticut. His father was Captain Benedict Arnold III, a rich shipowner. His mother was named Hannah. He also had a sister named Hannah. Benedict's great-grandfather had been the governor of Rhode Island.

BENDICT ARNOLD WENT TO SCHOOL at Canterbury. While he was away at school his father began to drink heavily. After some poor business deals the family fortune was gone. Benedict was forced to return home from school.

GROWING UP: Back at home, Benedict began to get into trouble. His mother decided Benedict should become an apprentice to two of his cousins who were very successful "apothecaries"—pharmacists. Benedict worked with his cousins for several years.

When Arnold was 18, his mother died. Two years later, his father died. Arnold went to Europe and bought supplies for his own apothecary shop, which he opened in New Haven, Connecticut. His sister, Hannah, joined him in the business. During this time he also started a trading business. He traveled to the West Indies, trading lumber and horses for molasses, sugar and rum.

MARRIAGE AND FAMILY: Arnold married Margaret Mansfield in 1767 when he was 26 years old. Together they had three sons. Margaret died suddenly when she was only 30 years old of unknown causes.

FIGHTING IN THE REVOLUTIONARY WAR—FORT TICONDEROGA: When the Revolutionary War began, Arnold was eager to fight against the British for freedom. He heard about the battles at Lexington and Concord. He rounded up volunteers, made himself captain, and marched to Cambridge, Massachusetts. Arnold and his men joined other Patriots engaged in the war.

Arnold suggested that Fort Ticonderoga, held by the British, could easily be captured. He explained that by blocking the water routes of Lake Champlain and the Hudson River, the British could be stopped in their advance. The Massachusetts Committee of Safety pronounced him Colonel and Arnold left immediately for upper New York.

Arnold arrived in Castleton, Vermont, and met **Ethan Allen** and his Green Mountain Boys, who were also planning to take Fort Ticonderoga. Arnold and Allen argued about who would be the leader of the expedition. Some say that Allen *allowed* Arnold to march at his side. Others say that Arnold *agreed* to begin the march that way.

Arnold, Allen, and their men arrived at Fort Ticonderoga on May 10, 1775. They found the fort poorly defended, and had no trouble taking control. Not a single shot was fired and the British surrendered.

THE MARCH TO QUEBEC: After Ticonderoga, Arnold and Allen's troops forced the surrender of British soldiers at Crown Point and Fort George. The two leaders continued to argue, however, and after an unsuccessful march by Allen, Arnold took over command.

In June 1775, **George Washington**, the commander of the Continental Army, ordered Benedict Arnold to lead an expedition through Maine to Quebec for a surprise attack. Arnold's soldiers didn't have enough food for the long march. By the end of the month, they were so hungry they ate shoes, candles, and dogs.

They didn't reach Quebec until October. It was a long, hard journey, but Arnold was determined. He wrote that this march would not be "paralleled in history."

On December 30, 1775, Arnold and 600 men marched into Quebec under cover of a blinding snow storm. But the British had found out the Americans were coming, and were ready for battle. Arnold was wounded in the leg and had to be taken to the hospital.

The results of the battle for Quebec were horrible for the Americans. Between 60 and 100 men were killed and wounded; about 400 soldiers were captured. The British defenders of Quebec only lost 20 men.

Thoughts of a second attack were dashed, due to the reduced size of the colonial army. But Arnold was able to block the British from leaving the city. They were trapped in their garrison. In recognition of Arnold's skilled command during the assault on Quebec, he was made a brigadier-general.

In April 1776 Arnold was transferred to Montreal. By May the army was in tatters, and large numbers of British troops were headed toward the city. Arnold was in favor of retreat.

THE ROAD TO SARATOGA: Arnold returned home for a while. He learned that he had been passed over for promotion to the rank of major general. Five men below him had received the honor. This was a disappointment from which Arnold never really recovered. George Washington talked him out of resigning.

Arnold joined the fight at Danbury, Connecticut. After his heroism at that battle, Congress promoted him to major general. In August of 1777, outnumbered two to one, Arnold commanded a victory at Mohawk Valley.

Arnold marched to the Saratoga area. With General Horatio Gates, he engaged the British under General Burgoyne. He received a horrible wound to his leg and almost had to have it amputated. The British were forced to retreat, and Arnold emerged a hero. It was the first major American victory in the war. Even the British admitted that he was responsible for the rout.

ARNOLD IN PHILADELPHIA: When the British were forced out of Philadelphia, Washington sent Arnold to command the city as military governor of Pennsylvania.

Arnold began to spend money recklessly, and soon found himself in debt. He was also facing accusations of having used his military status for private gain. Washington was forced to reprimand him.

Arnold felt that he deserved better treatment. He had been an important force in many important battles in the Revolution. He was angry that people had turned against him.

BENEDICT ARNOLD THE TRAITOR: Arnold began telling the British what he knew about the American army. This was an act of treason. Some of the secrets he told included troop movements and the state of supplies. To get more information, Arnold asked Washington to send him to the fort at West Point, New York. In August 1780, Arnold was transferred there.

This painting shows the capture of Major John Andre, who was carrying the papers that proved that Arnold was a traitor.

On September 22, in a meeting with John Andre, Arnold explained how the Americans planned to surrender the fort to the British. After he left Arnold, Andre was captured with papers that revealed Arnold was helping the enemy.

The papers were sent to Washington, who was traveling to West Point.

When Arnold learned that Washington was on his way, he fled. Washington was shocked and disappointed to hear that a man he had greatly admired had committed treason. Arnold made his way to New York City. Andre was not so lucky. **General Nathanael Greene** conducted Andre's court-martial and determined his guilt. He was hanged as a spy on October 2.

After committing treason, Arnold became a British commander. He continued to lead British troops until 1781, including expeditions into Virginia and Connecticut.

LATER YEARS: In December 1781 Arnold moved his family to England where they stayed for several years. They then moved to New Brunswick, in Canada, where Arnold became a partner with his son and a former British officer. The men established a trading company and traveled to the West Indies once again. But Arnold was accused of starting a warehouse fire to claim the insurance money. He sued for slander and won the case. Once again, he moved to England.

In 1797 Arnold asked the Upper Canadian government to grant his family 50,000 acres in return for the service he had given. The government at first denied his request. But, in 1799, he was granted 13,400 acres.

Arnold was miserable in his last years. He stayed in England but was not given a military command. In his last days, Arnold suffered from ill health. He died on June 14, 1801 and was buried in London.

WHY DID BENEDICT ARNOLD COMMIT TREASON? Although no one really knows for certain, most writers agree that Arnold felt he had been treated badly in return for his service to America. He had been passed over several times for promotion, and he always felt he did not get the rewards he deserved for his military command. He felt he had been insulted and his honor challenged. Many believe that when he turned against his country he was seeking revenge.

Because of his treason, Arnold's heroics on the battlefield were quickly forgotten. Even though he had been one of Washington's most able officers, he is remembered for one act alone. His name is now a synonym for treachery. To be a "Benedict Arnold" is to be a traitor.

WORLD WIDE WEB SITES:

http://www.nps.gov/archive/sara/s-arnold.htm
http://www.ushistory.org/ValleyForge/served/arnold.html

Crispus Attucks

1723(?)-1770

African-American Patriot

First Person Killed at the Boston Massacre

CRISPUS ATTUCKS WAS BORN around 1723. He was born a slave in Massachusetts, and there is no record of his exact birthday. No one is exactly sure about his background and heritage. Some sources say that his father was Prince Younger, an African slave. Some say his mother was Nancy Attucks, a member of the Natick Indian tribe.

CRISPUS ATTUCKS GREW UP as a slave on a farm in Framingham, Massachusetts, historians believe. Sometime around the age of 27 he escaped and became a sailor. He probably spent 20 years as a merchant seaman on whaling ships.

THE FIRST HERO OF THE AMERICAN REVOLUTION: In the 1770s, most of the area that is now the eastern United States was a colony of England. That means that the people were ruled by England. They paid taxes to the British government and were ruled by a king, George III.

Some of the colonists accepted English rule; others resented it. The British government had imposed stiff taxes on everyday items—like newspapers and even playing cards. The angry colonists rebelled.

In March 1770, Attucks was living in Boston. The colony was in an uproar at the British government's actions. British troops were stationed in the city to keep order. In this atmosphere of political and social turmoil, Attucks became one of the first heroes of what would become the Revolutionary War.

THE BOSTON MASSACRE: On the evening of March 5, 1770, a rumor began to fly around Boston. A British soldier had supposedly struck a young barber's apprentice. Armed only with snowballs and sticks, a group of citizens confronted the soldiers. With Attucks at the head of the crowd, they marched to the Boston Customs House.

The soldiers fired into the crowd. When the smoke cleared, Crispus Attucks and three others lay dead. Eventually five men—Attucks, Samuel Gray, James Caldwell, Samuel Maverick, and Patrick Carr—died of their wounds.

The engraving by Paul Revere, depicting the Boston Massacre, where Crispus Attucks died.

The people of Boston were furious. They claimed that Attucks and the other men were martyrs in the cause of independence. Attucks and Caldwell were given funerals attended by thousands of Boston's citizens. Despite racist laws that prevented blacks from being buried in white cemeteries, Attucks was buried in the Old Granary Burial Ground.

Patriots like **Samuel Adams** called their murder "The Boston Massacre." It became a rallying cry in the years leading up to the Revolutionary War (1775-1781).

Attucks became known to history as the "first to defy, the first to die" in the cause of liberty. **John Adams**, who became the second President of the United States, reluctantly defended the British soldiers at their murder trial.

HIS LEGACY: Attucks is remembered as one of the first heroes of the American Revolution. There is a monument in Boston Common that commemorates Attucks and his companions. The inscription says: "On that night, the foundation of American independence was laid." **Paul Revere** made a famous engraving of the incident. That engraving rallied colonists to the revolutionary cause.

Hours to the Gates of this City many Thouſands of our brave Brethren in the Country, deeply affected with our Diſtreſſes, and to whom we are greatly obliged on this Occaſion—No one knows where this would have ended, and what important Conſequences even to the whole Britiſh Empire might have followed, which our Modera-tion & Loyalty upon ſo trying an Occaſion, and our Faith in the Commander's Aſſurances have happily prevented.

Laſt Thurſday, agreeable to a general Requeſt of the Inhabitants, and by the Conſent of Parents and Friends, were carried to their *Grave* in Succeſſion, the Bodies of *Samuel Gray, Samuel Maverick, James Caldwell,* and *Criſpus Attucks*, the unhappy Victims who fell in the bloody Maſſacre of the Monday Evening preceeding!

On this Occaſion moſt of the Shops in Town were ſhut, all the Bells were ordered to toll a ſolemn Peal, as were alſo thoſe in the neighboring Towns of Charleſtown Roxbury, &c. The Proceſſion began to move between the Hours of 4 and 5 in the Afternoon; two of the un-fortunate Sufferers, viz. Meſſ. *James Caldwell* and *Criſpus Attucks*, who were Strangers, borne from Faneuil-Hall,

1770 newspaper column about the Boston Massacre. The coffins in the illustration bear the initials of the four men killed: Samuel Gray, Samuel Maverick, James Caldwell, and Crispus Attucks.

Attucks is also remembered as the first black to become a patriotic hero for African-Americans. That he became a martyr for liberty, when, as a black man, he was denied it, makes his sacrifice all the more meaningful.

Booker T. Washington wrote this about him in 1898: "When in 1776, the Negro was asked to decide between British oppression and American independence, we find him choosing the better part. Crispus Attucks, a Negro, was the first to shed his blood on State Street, Boston, that the white American might enjoy liberty forever, though his race remained in slavery."

Nearly 100 years later, Attucks's biographer James Neyland summed up his importance for our era. "He is one of the most important figures in African-American history, not for what he did for his own race, but for what he did for all oppressed people everywhere. He is a reminder that the African-American heritage is not only African but American and it is a heritage that begins with the beginning of America."

WORLD WIDE WEB SITES:

http://www.africawithin.com/bios/crispus_attucks.htm
http://www.memory.loc.gov/ammem/today/mar05.html
http://www.pbs.org/wgbh/aia/part2/2p24.html

Benjamin Franklin

1706-1790

American Patriot, Statesman, Printer, and Inventor Member of the Continental Congress, Co-Author of the Declaration of Independence, Ambassador to France, and Delegate to the Constitutional Convention

BENJAMIN FRANKLIN WAS BORN on January 17, 1706, in Boston, Massachusetts. At that time, Massachusetts was a colony of Britain. His parents were Josiah and Abiah Franklin. Josiah was a soap and candle maker. Abiah took care of a household of 17 children.

Ben had seven sisters and nine brothers. His sisters were named Elizabeth, Hannah, Anne, Mary, Sarah, Lydia, and Jane. His brothers were Samuel, Josiah, John, Peter, and James. Four other brothers died as infants.

BENJAMIN FRANKLIN GREW UP in a large and lively family. He was a curious, outgoing boy. He had a natural inventiveness, too. He loved to swim, and spent hours at the sport. To improve his stroke, he created a pair of wooden swim paddles. He strapped them to his hands, and paddled in the water around Boston.

BENJAMIN FRANKLIN WENT TO SCHOOL at Latin School in Boston for one year. His father sent him to the school hoping Ben would become a preacher. But it was very expensive. So Ben was sent to another school. It was called "Mr. George Brownell's school for writing and arithmetic." Ben attended for two years, then left formal schooling for good. His father had decided it was time for him to work.

STARTING TO WORK: Ben started working for his father at the age of 10. He helped out in the soap and candle business. When he was 12, his father wanted him to become an apprentice. Ben wanted to be a sailor. But Ben's father had lost a son, Josiah, who drowned at sea. He forbade it.

Ben's father wanted him to became an apprentice to his brother James, to learn to be a printer. Ben didn't like the idea. He knew that he'd learn the business quickly. In Franklin's time, a person had to spend years as an apprentice. An apprentice was in many ways a servant, tied to his master. Ben didn't want to spend years at one thing. He wanted to learn, and do, many things.

Franklin as a printer.

LEARNING THE PRINTER'S TRADE: Despite Ben's wishes, he became James's apprentice. He worked hard, and learned all about printing.

Ben spent his free time, and all his money, on books and reading. He enjoyed books on all topics. He read about vegetarianism (a diet that doesn't include meat). He decided it would be a healthful, and cheap, way to eat. Ben was always frugal with money, too. He became a vegetarian, then talked his brother into giving him the money he'd normally spend on meat for Ben's meals.

At that time, many printers were also newspaper owners. Ben wanted to write for his brother's paper. But James wasn't interested in his articles. So Ben sent pieces he's written to the paper, using the pseudonym "Silence Dogood." A pseudonym (SOO-doe-nim) is a name an author chooses to write as, instead of his or her own.

Not knowing it was Ben's work, James printed the articles. When he found out the truth, he was furious. They argued, and Ben knew it was time for him to leave. He decided to run away. That was the only way he could escape spending years as James's apprentice.

MOVING TO PHILADELPHIA: At the age of 17, Franklin set out, alone, for Philadelphia. He found work with a printer, and soon was on his way. Within a few years, he bought his own press. Next, he bought a newspaper. It became a great success.

NEWSPAPERMAN: Franklin's newspaper was the *Pennsylvania Gazette*. It was full of lively, well-written stories. It brought a lot of attention to Franklin. He became the official printer for the colonies of Pennsylvania, New Jersey, and Delaware. That meant that he was responsible for printing government documents and money. Over the next several years, Franklin purchased papers in other parts of the colonies. He became a successful, wealthy, man.

POOR RICHARD'S ALMANAC: In 1732, Franklin began publishing the work for which he is most famous: *Poor Richard's Almanac*. At that time, most households had an almanac on hand. They came out every year, and contained information on holidays, weather, sunrises and sunsets, tides, and other data of general interest.

But Franklin's Almanac was special. It contained witty sayings and predictions for the coming year. Famous phrases of Franklin's, like "a penny saved is a penny earned," first appeared in his Almanac. "Poor Richard" was Richard Saunders, another of Franklin's pseudonyms. Franklin published *Poor Richard's Almanac* for 25 years.

CITIZEN, INVENTOR, STATESMAN: By the time he was 42, Franklin had made his fortune. He decided to devote the rest of his life to other things. Over the next 40 years, this tireless, curious man distinguished himself as a citizen, inventor, and statesman.

As a citizen of Philadelphia, he created the city's first fire department, lending library, and postal service. As an inventor, he created the lightning rod, the Franklin stove, and bifocals. As a statesman, he helped bring about the birth of a new nation, the United States of America.

CREATING MANY FIRSTS FOR THE PEOPLE OF PHILADELPHIA: Franklin was dedicated to improving the life of the people of Philadelphia. In the 1700s, there was no fire department in the city. Franklin started the first. There was also no fire insurance a homeowner could purchase to replace a home that had burned down. Franklin started the first fire insurance company in the colonies.

In the 1700s, libraries were private. There was no such thing as a public lending library. Franklin loved books and reading. He thought that books should be available to all people. So he started the first lending library in the colonies. He also created a postal system and became the first Postmaster of Philadelphia.

SCIENTIST AND INVENTOR: Franklin was fascinated by science. He studied nature and developed theories about hurricanes, the gulf stream, and other natural phenomena. Like many people of his day, he was particularly interested in electricity. Franklin theorized that lightning was a form of electricity. How he proved that led to his first major invention.

To test his theory, Franklin flew a kite in a thunderstorm. The kite had a pointed piece of metal at the top, connected to a key at the bottom of the kite string. When lightning struck the kite, the electrical charge traveled down the string to the key.

When Franklin touched the key, he got a shock. He knew that meant he'd proved his theory. Lightning was a form of electric current. Franklin published his theories, and they made him a famous man, all over the world.

THE LIGHTNING ROD: Using the knowledge from his experiment, Franklin invented the lightning rod. It was a metal rod placed on the roof of a building. It worked by drawing the electrical current from lightning away from the building and channeling it into the ground, making the current harmless. Lightning rods based on Franklin's original design are still in use today.

THE FRANKLIN STOVE: Another of his important inventions was the Franklin Stove. In Franklin's time, most homes were heated by fireplaces. Franklin's invention was an iron stove that produced more heat, cost less to run, and was more efficient than a regular fireplace. Like lightning rods, Franklin stoves are still in use today.

BIFOCALS: Franklin loved to read, and as he got older, he couldn't see as well. He needed two pairs of glasses: one for reading, and one for seeing at a distance. But he didn't like having two pairs. So he invented "bifocals." He had a glass maker cut the two pairs apart, then put them back together, with the lense for reading on the bottom, and the one for distance on top. Bifocals, too, are still used today.

Franklin didn't believe he should profit from his inventions. He never applied for a patent for any of them. Instead, he chose to share his inventions with the world.

THE SEEDS OF REVOLUTION—THE FRENCH AND INDIAN WAR: From 1754 to 1763, the British and French fought for control of North America. The conflict was called the French and Indian War. The British called a meeting to discuss their strategy against the French in 1754. The meeting, called the Albany Congress, would be crucial to the colonies. Franklin, a delegate to the Congress, created a plan. It called for a president (named by the King) and delegates chosen by the colonial assemblies.

Franklin's plan included several ideas that became central to the ideas behind the Revolutionary War. He proposed a union of colonies that would control their own defense, trade, and settlement. They would have the right to raise taxes and develop the western lands. The individual colonies weren't interested in Franklin's plan at the time. But it laid the groundwork for what would come later.

TRAVELING TO ENGLAND: In 1757, the leaders of Pennsylvania sent Franklin to England. They wanted him to develop trade agreements between the colony and the British. Franklin would remain overseas for most of the next 18 years.

THE REVOLUTIONARY WAR: By the time Franklin left Pennsylvania, trouble was brewing between the colonies and Britain. At

Franklin created this, considered the first American political cartoon, to warn the colonies to "join or die" in the fight by the British against the French in the French and Indian War. It shows a segmented snake, "S.C., N.C., V., M., R., N.J., N.Y., N.E.", representing South Carolina, North Carolina, Virginia, Maryland, Rhode Island, New Jersey, New York, and New England.

that time, the colonies were governed by England and King George III. Most American colonists believed that the colonies should have their own government, a government that they controlled. During his years in England, Franklin met the most important leaders of Europe. He kept a close eye on the developing political situation between England and his home land.

FOUNDING FATHER: Franklin headed home to Philadelphia in 1775. By the time he landed, the Revolutionary War had begun. Over the next 15 years, Franklin would serve as one of the Founding Fathers of his country.

In 1775, he was elected to the Second **CONTINENTAL CONGRESS**. As part of those duties, he helped write the **DECLARATION OF INDEPENDENCE.** Approved on July 4th, 1776, the Declaration outlined the ideas behind the Revolution. It was written in large part by **Thomas Jefferson**, but Franklin contributed his own ideas and wisdom to the document.

Next, Franklin was sent to France. The new United States needed France to provide money and military force in the war against England. Franklin did a splendid job. He won the aid and support of the French for the U.S. That aid was crucial in winning the war against England.

When the Revolutionary War ended in 1781, the U.S. called on Franklin once again. In 1783, Franklin, along with **John Adams** and

The Signing of the Declaration of Independence. John Adams is the figure at the far left. Thomas Jefferson is second from the right. Next to Jefferson is Benjamin Franklin.

Franklin's life as a diplomat in France, 1778.

John Jay, drafted the **TREATY OF PARIS**. The document defined the end of the Revolutionary War, the peace between England and the United States, and the new boundaries of the new country. The United States now stretched from the Atlantic Ocean west to the Mississippi River, and from the Canadian border south to Florida.

When he returned home, Franklin was named head of the Pennsylvania government. In 1788, at the age of 82, he performed his final service to the nation, as a delegate to the Constitutional Convention. He contributed to the writing of the **U.S. CONSTITUTION**, and, after it was written, argued passionately that the members pass it. The Constitution was passed, and Franklin signed it, on September 17, 1787.

Franklin is the only person to sign the four major documents establishing the United States. His signature appears on the Declaration of Independence (1776), The Treaty of Alliance with France (1778), The Treaty of Peace (1783), and the Constitution (1787).

LATER YEARS: At the end of the Constitutional Convention, Franklin returned home and finished his famous *Autobiography*. He moved into the Philadelphia home of his daughter, Sarah. He died there on April 17, 1790, at the age of 84.

BENJAMIN FRANKLIN'S HOME AND FAMILY: Franklin married Deborah Read in September 1730. They had two children, Francis and Sarah. Francis died as a child. They also raised a son, William, whom Franklin had with another woman. William was a Loyalist during the war, and moved to England permanently in 1782.

HIS LEGACY: Franklin was one of the most popular and famous men of his time. He brought his special inventive gifts to devices of great practicality and institutions for the common good, and his genius to the creation of a great nation.

WORLD WIDE WEB SITES:

http://sln.fi.edu/franklin/birthday
http://www.english.udel.edu/lemay/franklin
http://www.pbs.org/benfranklin/13_inquiring_little.html

Nathanael Greene

1742-1786

American Patriot and Military Leader

NATHANAEL GREENE WAS BORN on August 7, 1742, at Potowomut in Warwick, Rhode Island. His parents were Nathanael and Mary Mott Greene. His father owned several iron founderies.

Greene's ancestors had been part of the migration from England to Massachusetts in 1635. But because they were Quakers, they suffered religious persecution there. They moved to Rhode Island so they could worship as they wished.

NATHANAEL GREENE GREW UP in a family with Quaker values. Sometimes his own views were different from the Quakers'. As a young man, he was especially interested in military science and tactics. Quakers are pacifists—they don't believe in war. Greene's interest in the military caused some concern in his Quaker community. That would continue as he began an important military career.

NATHANAEL GREENE WENT TO SCHOOL at home and studied with tutors. He was a good student, and he loved to read. He bought books whenever he could.

IRON MAKER: Greene began to work for his father's iron-making foundries as a young adult. In 1770, he took over the family's iron foundry in Coventry, Rhode Island.

POLITICS AND MILITARY SERVICE: Around the same time, Greene got involved in politics. From 1770 to 1772, Greene he served in the Rhode Island Assembly. During that time, many colonists were angered by new taxes, and tighter control, by the British government.

Still interested in the military, Greene helped form a military unit called the Kentish Guards. In May 1775, he was made a brigadier general in the Rhode Island army. In June 1775, he became a general in the Continental Army.

Greene led troops in Boston during the British siege of that city in 1775 and 1776. When the British finally left Boston in 1776, Greene was put in charge of the city.

LEADING TROOPS IN BATTLE: In 1776, Greene was introduced to **George Washington**, and they became lifelong friends. He served under Washington for years.

Greene took command of troops on Long Island in 1776. He became ill, and could not take part in that battle. But soon he was fighting with Washington at the battles of Trenton, Brandywine, and Germantown. With Washington, he also braved the terrible winter of 1777-1778 at Valley Forge.

Washington made Greene the Quartermaster of the army in 1778. The Quartermaster is responsible for supplying food, arms, and other needs to soldiers. While still commanding troops, Greene took on his new responsibilities and did an excellent job.

In 1778, Greene led troops in the battles of Monmouth and Rhode Island. In 1780, he was commander of West Point. There, he headed the court-martial that convicted the British spy John Andre and revealed **Benedict Arnold** as a traitor.

THE CAROLINA CAMPAIGN: Greene was next involved in a series of battles in the south, known as the Carolina Campaign. He reorganized the army, and helped by a group of excellent officers, fought the British at Guilford Couthouse, Hobkirks Hill, and Eutaw Springs.

In January 1781, at Cowpens, South Carolina, Greene forced British General Cornwallis to divide his troops, then defeated them. The British retreated to Charleston. Cornwallis surrendered to Washington in October 1781, at Yorktown, Virginia.

Greene remained in service to his country until the British left Charleston in December 1782. The Americans took control over North and South Carolina, and nearby Georgia.

In August 1783, Greene traveled north to Princeton, New Jersey, where Congress was meeting. He met with Washington and other leaders. They expressed their heartfelt thanks to the war hero.

Statue of General Greene.

RETIREMENT: When the war was over, Greene had many debts. He had borrowed heavily to supply his men with food and military provisions during the course of the war. He had to spend his own fortune to repay those debts.

But the people of Georgia were so grateful for his aid in war time, that they gave Greene a plantation there. He lived at his home in Georgia from 1785 to 1786. He had a sudden stroke and died on June 19, 1786. He was 44 years old.

MARRIAGE AND FAMILY: Greene married Catharine Littlefield in July 1774. They had five children: George Washington, Martha Washington, Cornelia Lott, Nathanael Ray, and Louisa Catherine.

HIS LEGACY: Greene is remembered as a bold and able military leader. His strategy in the Carolina Campaign was widely admired, as was his commitment and loyalty to the cause of revolution.

WORLD WIDE WEB SITES:

http://lcweb2.loc.gov/ammem/today/aug07.html
http://www.ushistory.org/valleyforge/served/greene.html

Nathan Hale

1755-1776

American Patriot and Revolutionary War Hero

NATHAN HALE WAS BORN on June 6, 1755, in Coventry, Connecticut. His parents were Richard and Elizabeth Strong Hale. Richard was a successful farmer. Elizabeth was a homemaker devoted to raising her 12 children. Nathan was the sixth of those 12 children, with seven brothers and four sisters. Six of the Hale sons served in the Revolutionary War.

NATHAN HALE GREW UP in the countryside of Coventry. He was an excellent athlete, and enjoyed swimming and fishing.

NATHAN HALE WENT TO SCHOOL at home. He studied with a local minister named Joseph Huntington. Nathan was an outstanding student, and in 1769, at the age of 14, went to Yale College. He was a successful student, and belonged to a literary society. He also excelled in sports.

A SCHOOL TEACHER: After graduating from Yale in 1773, Hale took a job as a school teacher. He taught in East Haddam and New London, Connecticut.

THE REVOLUTIONARY WAR BEGINS: News of the battles of Lexington and Concord reached Connecticut in 1775. Hale made a passionate speech at the local town meeting. "Let us march immediately," he said. "And never lay down our arms until we obtain our independence."

Inspired by the events, Hale joined the Continental Army in July 1775. He entered the war as a lieutenant and served in Boston. In January 1776, he was promoted to captain. Hale served in the campaign in New York under Major Thomas Knowlton.

TAKING AN ASSIGNMENT AS A SPY: At this point, the war was not going well for the Patriots. General **George Washington** needed a spy to go behind British enemy lines and find out about their troop movements.

Washington asked Hale's commander, Major Knowlton, to find a volunteer for the spying mission. Knowlton asked all of his captains. Only Hale stepped forward to volunteer. When a friend

Nathan Hale just before his execution.

protested that Hale risked death in taking the assignment, Hale stood firm. "I wish to be useful, and every kind of service, necessary to the public good, becomes honorable by being necessary," he said.

Disguised as a Dutch school teacher, Hale set off on his mission. He traveled behind enemy lines on Long Island, and got the information he needed. On September 21, 1776, he was returning to the Patriot camp in New York when he was captured by the British.

Hale was taken before General Howe, head of the British troops in New York. British soldiers searched Hale and found sketches and other military information. When asked to explain himself, Hale gave his name, rank, and purpose of his mission.

Howe condemned Hale as a spy, without a trial. Charging him with treason, he sentenced Hale to be executed the next day.

EXECUTION AND A FAMOUS SPEECH: On the morning of Sunday, September 22, 1776, Hale stood on the gallows. He gave a speech, concluding with words that have rung down through history:

"I regret that I have but one life to lose for my country."

He was only 21 years old.

HIS LEGACY: Nathan Hale is remembered for his bravery and patriotism. His courage, and his stirring final words, have made him one of the best-known heroes in American history.

WORLD WIDE WEB SITES:

http://www.americaslibrary.gov/cgi-bin/page.cgi/jb/revolut/hale_1
http://www.connecticutsar.org/patriots.hale_nathan.htm
http://www.ct.gov/ctportal/cwp/

Alexander Hamilton

1755-1804

West-Indian Born American Patriot and Politician

First Secretary of the Treasury

ALEXANDER HAMILTON WAS BORN on January 11, 1755, on the island of Nevis in the British West Indies. His father was James Hamilton and his mother was Rachel Fawcett Lavien. Alexander had a brother named James. His parents did not marry, and his father left the family when Alexander was 10.

ALEXANDER HAMILTON GREW UP on Nevis and the island of St. Croix, also in the West Indies. His mother died when he was 13. After that, he and his brother lived in the home of a family friend, Edward Stevens.

ALEXANDER HAMILTON WENT TO SCHOOL first in St. Croix. After graduating from his school in St. Croix, he got a job as a clerk for a financial company. He was a bright and hardworking young man. He was an outstanding writer, too. He wrote a description of a hurricane on St. Croix that showed his intelligence and talent. It drew a lot of positive attention to young Alexander.

Edward Stevens thought Alexander would benefit from college. So he paid for Alexander to attend Columbia University in 1773. (It was called King's College at the time.)

Hamilton was living in New York when it was a center of political activity. After the **FRENCH AND INDIAN WAR**, Britain had imposed taxes on their colonies in the New World. It was part of an effort by English leaders to put the colonies under tighter control. They charged high taxes on products that people in America needed, like sugar, paper, and tea. Many colonists felt that it was not fair for England to charge them taxes without giving them a say in government.

Some colonists, known as Loyalists, wanted to work out their differences and remain part of England. But many others, known as Patriots, wanted to break away from England and form a new country. Hamilton became committed to the cause of the Patriots. He used his powerful and convincing skills as a writer. He published political pamphlets promoting the cause.

THE REVOLUTIONARY WAR BEGINS: When war broke out, Hamilton joined a New York militia. He was made a captain and fought in the battles of Long Island, White Plains, and Trenton.

SERVING UNDER GEORGE WASHINGTON IN THE REVOLUTIONARY WAR: Soon, the able young soldier came to the attention of General **George Washington.** Washington made Hamilton a lieutenant colonel on his staff.

Hamilton continued to lead troops in the field, and to serve Washington. But he was a headstrong young man, and that led him into quarrels all his life. He had a quarrel with Washington and resigned from his staff. But by the time of Yorktown and victory, the quarrel was forgotten. Washington would remain an important influence throughout Hamilton's career.

AFTER THE WAR: Hamilton returned to New York after the war and studied to become a lawyer. He soon became a successful attorney. But Hamilton's greatest interest was in politics.

SERVING IN CONGRESS: In 1782, Hamilton was elected to the **CONTINENTAL CONGRESS**. He served for two years, offering his own deeply held ideas about the shape the new government should take.

In 1784, Hamilton helped to found the Bank of New York. He was always interested in how money could be used to stabilize government. He brought his experience in banking to further aid his country.

CONSTITUTIONAL CONVENTION: Hamilton was elected to the Constitutional Convention in 1787. Once the Constitution was completed, the states had to ratify it. Hamilton passionately encouraged its passage. He saw it as an important step to form a strong central government. That was a point of major importance to him.

BELIEF IN A STRONG CENTRAL GOVERNMENT—*THE FEDERALIST*: Hamilton, along with **James Madison** and **John Jay**, wrote a series of essays called *The Federalist.* In those essays, they promoted their ideal of a strong central government, and the passage of the Constitution. The Constitution was ratified by the states.

Hamilton also had other ideas that made him very different from his fellow Americans. He believed that people were generally motivated by self-interest and greed. He didn't have faith in his fellow Americans as basically good and honorable people. Instead, he distrusted the common people, believing they weren't capable of the important decisions basic to self-government.

FIRST U.S. SECRETARY OF THE TREASURY: George Washington was elected the first President of the United States in 1789. He chose Hamilton to be the first Secretary of the Treasury. He was an inspired choice. Few people in the country knew more about the importance of money to strong government than Hamilton.

Statue of Hamilton in Washington, D.C.

Hamilton wrote a series of essays outlining his ideas. He presented his ideas about how to pay off the debt of the Revolutionary

John Adams, Gouvenor Morris, Hamilton, and Thomas Jefferson, while serving in the Continental Congress.

War, build the government's treasury, raise taxes, and budget for the needs of the new nation. He also argued that the new country's economy should be based on manufacturing as well as farming. His ideas were accepted, and they helped create a strong financial foundation for the country.

INFLUENTIAL POLITICAL FIGURE: Hamilton retired from office in 1795. He again served his nation as a major general in the army in 1798. He also stayed active in politics. He was often at odds with his former political friends, and, over the years, angered many of them. When **John Adams** was President, Hamilton wrote an attack on him that led to a deep hostility between them.

He and **Thomas Jefferson** had a very different view of the country and its people. Hamilton wanted a strong central government, and he didn't trust the common people. Jefferson believed in strong states rights, and he championed the basic honesty and nobility of individuals. They argued over these issues for years. Yet when Jefferson and Aaron Burr were tied in the presidential election of 1800, Hamilton threw his support behind Jefferson.

A DUEL WITH A POLITICAL RIVAL: Hamilton's most notorious political enemy was Burr. They were political rivals for years, but matters took a serious turn in 1804. At that time, Burr was the Vice President of the United States. As his term was ending, he ran for governor of New York. Hamilton opposed his candidacy. He was quoted in a newspaper saying damaging things about Burr's character. That infuriated the Vice President. Burr challenged Hamilton to a duel.

Hamilton had lost his son in a duel in 1801. But he felt that he had to defend his honor. Hamilton and Burr met in New Jersey on July 11, 1804. Hamilton shot into the air. Burr shot Hamilton, and he died on July 12. He was 49 years old.

MARRIAGE AND FAMILY: Hamilton married Elizabeth Schuyler in 1780. She was from a wealthy family and the daughter of a General. They had eight children: Philip, Angelica, Alexander, James Alexander, John, William, Eliza, and Philip. The eldest Philip died in a duel in 1801. The youngest Philip was named for him.

HIS LEGACY: Hamilton was a brilliant man with many gifts. Yet he was also a man of ambition, capable of political infighting and intrigue. His work on behalf of the federal banking system helped to strengthen the United States. But his life was cut short by his sometimes reckless and unwise words. All these aspects of his personality have contributed to his legacy as one of the founders of the nation.

WORLD WIDE WEB SITES:

http://www.alexanderhamiltonexhibition.org/
http://www.americaslibrary.gov/cgi-bin/page.cgi/jb/nation/hamburr_1
http://www.let.rug.nl/usa/B/hamilton/
http://xroads.virginia.edu/~CAP/ham/hamilton.html

John Hancock

1737-1793

American Patriot, Statesman, and Merchant First President of the Continental Congress and First Governor of Massachusetts

JOHN HANCOCK WAS BORN on January 12, 1737, in Braintree, Massachusetts. His parents were John and Mary Hancock. His father was a minister and his mother was a homemaker.

JOHN HANCOCK GREW UP in his family home in Braintree. When he was seven, his father died. John was raised by his uncle Thomas, who was unmarried. Thomas Hancock was also the wealthiest merchant in New England. (A "merchant" is involved in trading goods.) John would benefit from his wealth and experience.

JOHN HANCOCK WENT TO SCHOOL at Boston Latin School and Harvard. After he graduated from college, he went to work in his uncle's business.

FIRST JOBS: At that time Boston was one of the busiest ports in North America. Hancock learned about the merchant business in Boston, then, in 1760, traveled to England to lcarn about trade there.

In England, Hancock was at the center of the greatest world power of his day. He saw George III crowned king. He met with important businessmen and political figures. Full of this knowledge, Hancock returned home to Boston in 1761. He was made a partner in his uncle's company two years later.

INHERITING A FORTUNE: In 1764, Hancock's uncle died suddenly. John inherited the company and his uncle's fortune.

At this point, Boston was a center of political activity. After the **FRENCH AND INDIAN WAR**, Britain had imposed taxes on their colonies in the New World. It was part of an effort by English leaders to put the colonies under tighter control. They charged high taxes on products that people in America needed, like sugar, paper, and tea. Many colonists felt that it was not fair for England to charge them taxes without giving them a say in government.

Some colonists, known as Loyalists, wanted to work out their differences and remain part of England. But many others, known as Patriots, wanted to break away from England and form a new country. Hancock was a confirmed Patriot.

In 1768, one of Hancock's cargo ships, the *Liberty*, was seized by British officials. They suspected Hancock of smuggling. Hancock had them removed from the boat. He was later sued over the incident. **John Adams** defended him in court, and the suit was dropped.

The incident made Hancock a hero in the eyes of some Bostonians. He was elected to a position on the Massachusetts General Court. In 1770, he spoke out again against the British after **THE BOSTON MASSACRE**. He was part of a committee demanding that the governor remove British troops from Boston.

After the British Parliament enacted **THE TEA ACT** in 1773, Hancock spoke out again. As a merchant and a Patriot, he condemned the Act.

REVOLUTIONARY POLITICS: In 1775, Hancock and **Samuel Adams** ran afoul of the British government again. On April 18, 1775, they were rescued by Paul Revere during his famous ride. The British authorities wanted Adams and Hancock arrested for plotting against them.

By this point, the British knew they were facing armed rebellion. To try and keep the peace, General Gage, head of the British army in Massachusetts, made an offer of "amnesty"—freedom against prosecution—to those Patriots involved in the uprisings so far. But he was so angry with Hancock and Adams that he denied them both amnesty.

CONTINENTAL CONGRESS: Hancock was elected president of the Second Continental Congress in 1775. As head of that group, he oversaw the debate that led to the **DECLARATION OF**

A painting showing John Hancock adding his distinctive signature to the Declaration of Independence.

INDEPENDENCE. It was a document that would be associated with his name throughout history.

DECLARATION OF INDEPENDENCE: The Declaration outlined the reasons behind the Revolutionary War. It was written mainly by **Thomas Jefferson**, with help from **John Adams** and **Benjamin Franklin**. In simple, powerful language, it describes what the colonists thought about their rights as individuals and as citizens. It states that all men are born equal and free. They have the right to revolt against those who will not give them freedom. On July 4, 1776, the Continental Congress approved the Declaration of Independence.

THE FAMOUS SIGNATURE: John Hancock was the first delegate to sign the Declaration. He did it in with great flourish. So famous was his signature, that to this day people ask for a "John Hancock" when asking for a signature. He also signed it in large letters. This has led to a famous, but untrue, legend: that Hancock said he would use a signature large enough "that George III could see it without his glasses."

Hancock remained president of the Continental Congress for two years. He wanted to be named head of the Continental Army. When the Congress chose **George Washington** instead, Hancock was disappointed. He resigned as president of the Congress in 1777 and returned to Boston.

GOVERNOR OF MASSACHUSETTS: Hancock became the first governor of Massachusetts after the Revolutionary War. He served as governor for nine terms. He helped to write the Massachusetts state constitution. He also rallied his fellow statesmen to ratify the **U.S. CONSTITUTION** in 1788.

MARRIAGE AND FAMILY: Hancock married Dorothy Quincy in August 1775. They had two children, but, sadly, both died as infants. Hancock, who had been in poor health for years, was still governor when he died on October 8, 1793. He was 56 years old.

HIS LEGACY: Hancock is known as a loyal patriot who served his country honorably in the American Revolution. His signature is world-famous, a tribute to his importance in championing the freedoms that were the goals and consequences of the Revolution.

WORLD WIDE WEB SITES:

http://www.americaslibrary.gov/cgi-bin/page.cgi/jb/colonial/hancock
http://www.ushistory.org/declaration/signers/hancock.htm

Patrick Henry

1736-1799

American Patriot, Orator, and Statesman

Famous for His Speech Stating

"Give Me Liberty or Give Me Death!"

PATRICK HENRY WAS BORN on May 29, 1736, in Hanover County, Virginia. His parents were John and Sarah Henry. John had been born in Scotland and had immigrated to Virginia. He was a successful farmer. Sarah was a homemaker. Patrick had an older brother named William.

PATRICK HENRY WENT TO SCHOOL at home. His father taught him Latin and other subjects.

FIRST JOBS: Henry's father set him up in a business, but it went broke. Henry married in 1754, and he tried to make a living as a farmer on land that had come to him with his marriage. When that failed, Henry decided to study law.

BECOMING A LAWYER: In 1760, Henry traveled to Williamsburg, Virginia. That was the center of law and politics in the colony. He appeared before a panel of lawyers and was given a test of his legal knowledge. He passed, and became a lawyer.

A FIERY ORATOR: Henry established his talent as a lawyer and orator in 1763. That year, he argued a case known as "The Parson's Cause." The British Privy Council had overturned a ruling by the Virginia Assembly regarding the pay of ministers.

In court, Henry raged against the British government. He said that a King who overturned a just law, made by a representative government, was a "tyrant." Further, he said that such a King had given up "the allegiance of his subjects." The jury agreed, and Henry became a famous man.

THE VIRGINIA HOUSE OF BURGESSES: In 1764, Henry was elected to the House of Burgesses, the oldest representative group in the American colonies. He served with pride and patriotic fervor during a time of growing unrest.

GROWING POLITICAL UNREST: After the **FRENCH AND INDIAN WAR** (1754-1763), Britain had imposed taxes on the colonies. It was part of an effort by English leaders to put the colonies under tighter control. They charged high taxes on products that people in America needed, like sugar, paper, and tea. Many colonists felt that it was not fair for England to charge them taxes without giving them a say in government.

Some colonists, known as Loyalists, wanted to work out their differences and remain part of England. But many others, known as Patriots, wanted to break away from England and form a new country. Henry was a confirmed Patriot.

THE STAMP ACT: This Act of Parliament, passed in 1765, stated that most documents, such as contracts, newspapers, and pamphlets, had to be written on special paper bearing a stamp from the British government.

The colonists were forced to purchase the stamped paper for most of their documents, because documents on plain paper had no legal standing. The American colonists were suspicious of the tax because many thought that the money paid remained in the pockets of the "Stamp Men" who sold the paper to them.

HENRY'S REACTION: One of Henry's famous speeches took place on May 30, 1765, in reaction to the Stamp Act. Once again, Henry compared King George III to a tyrant. "Caesar had his Brutus, Charles the First his Cromwell, and George the III . . ." At that point in his speech, several members of the House began to cry "Treason!" Henry had dared to compare George III to Caesar and Charles the First, two tyrants toppled by their own people. It was a risky display, but it established Henry as a powerful orator and firm believer in self-government.

FAMOUS SPEECH: In March 1775, Henry gave a speech in St. John's Church in Richmond, Virginia. He was defending the

Henry giving his famous speech regarding the Stamp Act at the Virginia House of Burgesses, 1765.

colonists' right to arm themselves. He began by describing the growing agitation of the colonists against British rule.

> "Gentlemen may cry peace, peace. But there is no peace. The war is actually begun!"

In closing, he said:

> "I know not what course others may take. But as for me, give me liberty or give me death!"

The words roused the people of the colonies. It also made Henry a leading figure among those urging war with Britain. Henry joined the Virginia Committee of Correspondence, allying himself with **Samuel Adams** and other like-minded Patriots.

THE CONTINENTAL CONGRESS: In 1774, Henry represented Virginia at the First Continental Congress. He served in both the First and Second Continental Congresses. In that role, he was at the center of the movement to break with Britain.

THE REVOLUTIONARY WAR: After war was declared, Henry returned to Virginia. He recruited 6,000 Virginians to fight in the Continental Army. He also raised a militia to protect the state.

GOVERNOR OF VIRGINIA: In 1776, Virginia became a state, and Henry was named its first governor. He served in that position until 1780, and again from 1784 to 1785.

OBJECTIONS TO THE CONSTITUTION: After the war was won, Henry stayed involved in the creation of the new United States of America. He was elected to the Constitutional Convention, but did not serve. In fact, he was a critic of the **CONSTITUTION**. He thought that it gave too much power to the central government, and too little to the states. So, he fought against Federalists, like **Alexander Hamilton**, who believed a strong central government was necessary.

Henry also fought for the **BILL OF RIGHTS**. He saw them as one way of championing the rights of individual Americans against a powerful federal government. Although he had been opposed to

James Madison's Federalist policies, he backed him in passing those first 10 amendments to the Constitution.

Once the Bill of Rights was adopted, Henry dropped his opposition to the Constitution. It became the governing document uniting all the former colonies as one nation.

LATER YEARS: In his later years, Henry was still a popular politician. **President George Washington** offered him the job of Secretary of State. But Henry refused. **President John Adams** wanted him to be Ambassador to France. But Henry refused that job, too. He was even elected as Virginia's governor again, but refused that as well.

Patrick Henry died on June 6, 1799, at the age of 63. He was mourned throughout the nation as a great Patriot and leader.

MARRIAGE AND FAMILY: Henry was married twice. He married his first wife, Sarah Shelton, in 1754. They had six children. Sarah died in 1775. Henry married Dorothea Dandridge in 1778. They had eleven children.

HIS LEGACY: Patrick Henry's fiery speeches rallied the colonists to the cause of revolution. He firmly believed in self-government, and he served his state and nation as its champion. He is remembered as a staunch Patriot and symbol of the struggle for liberty.

WORLD WIDE WEB SITES:

http://www.history.org/Almanack/people/bios/biohen.
http://www.ushistory.org/declaration/related/henry.htm

John Jay

1745-1829

American Patriot, Diplomat, Writer, and Jurist
Negotiated the Peace Treaty
Ending the Revolutionary War
First Chief Justice of the Supreme Court

JOHN JAY WAS BORN on December 12, 1745, in New York City. His parents were Peter and Mary Van Cortlandt Jay. Peter was a successful merchant whose ancestors had settled in New York in the 1600s. Mary was descended from a family that traced its heritage to early Dutch settlers. John was one of ten children, but only seven survived to adulthood.

JOHN JAY GREW UP in a very close family. He was very religious, and he loved to read.

JOHN JAY WENT TO SCHOOL at home and studied with tutors. He went to King's College (later Columbia University) at age 15. He studied law and graduated in 1764.

A CAREER IN LAW: Jay got a job as a law clerk, then became a lawyer himself in 1768. He started a law firm in 1768 with Robert Livingstone. He also became involved in politics.

THE COMING OF THE REVOLUTIONARY WAR: In the 1760s and 1770s, Britain began to impose taxes on their colonies in the New World. It was part of an effort by English leaders to put the colonies under tighter control, and to pay for the costs of the **FRENCH AND INDIAN WAR**. They charged high taxes on products that people in America needed, like sugar, paper, and tea. Many colonists felt that it was not fair for England to charge them taxes without giving them a say in government.

Some colonists, known as Loyalists, wanted to work out their differences and remain part of England. But many others, known as Patriots, wanted to break away from England and form a new country.

Unlike the Patriots, Jay wasn't sure that the colonies should break with Britain. At first, he suggested a peaceful resolution rather than war.

THE CONTINENTAL CONGRESS: Jay was a representative from New York to the First and Second Continental Congresses. He continued to be a moderate in his political thinking, but when the

U.S. declared war on Britain, he became a Patriot. He served as the President of the Second Continental Congress, while continuing a leading role in New York politics.

NEW YORK: Jay served as a delegate to the convention that created the state constitution for New York in 1777. He was chosen to be the first chief justice of the New York Supreme Court in 1778.

DIPLOMAT TO SPAIN: In 1779, Jay was chosen to be the United States diplomat to Spain. His job was to win the support of the Spanish government for the American cause. The U.S. was hoping that Spain would recognize its status as a new nation. They also hoped that Spain would send them money and arms to fight the British.

Jay spent three years trying to win Spain's support, but failed. By 1782, the War for Independence was won. Jay was called to France to help **Benjamin Franklin** and **John Adams** negotiate peace with Britain.

THE TREATY OF PARIS: Jay worked with Franklin, Adams, and representatives of the British government. Finally, in September 1783, the treaty ending the Revolutionary War was finished. Called the Treaty of Paris, the document outlined several important issues. Britain officially recognized the former colonies as the United States of America. It also established the boundaries of the U.S. The new United States stretched from the Atlantic Ocean west to the Mississippi River, and from the Canadian border south to Florida.

SECRETARY OF FOREIGN AFFAIRS: When Jay returned to the U.S., he found he'd been made Secretary of Foreign Affairs. At this time, the U.S. was under the **ARTICLES OF CONFEDERATION**. Jay served from 1784 to 1789 in the post.

As Secretary, he was responsible for negotiating treaties, as he had done with the Treaty of Paris. But he found it very difficult, because he felt the Articles lacked force. He became convinced that the new nation needed a strong central government to protect itself. He became a Federalist, and contributed to *The Federalist*, with **Alexander Hamilton** and **James Madison**. As the debate over the Constitution continued, he strived to make his fellow Americans aware of how foreign policy would be effected by a strong federal government.

SUPREME COURT JUSTICE: After the Constitution was accepted, Jay was given another important post in the new government. **President George Washington** named him the first Chief Justice of the Supreme Court. He guided the Court in its earliest years, from 1789 to 1794.

THE JAY TREATY: In 1794, Washington called on Jay again to negotiate a treaty. There were still many serious issues between the U.S. and Britain. The agreements outlined in the Treaty of Paris had been violated. Laws about trade, boundaries, and the impressment of sailors had been broken. Jay went to London and negotiated a new treaty, called the "Jay Treaty," to resolve the problems. But the treaty didn't end the problems. It turned out to be very controversial, and many Americans were angry with Jay.

A painting depicting several of the early Chief Justices of the Supreme Court. Jay is at the top left.

GOVERNOR OF NEW YORK: Jay returned to the U.S. in 1795. Although he was a controversial figure, he learned that he had been elected Governor of New York. He served as Governor for two terms, until 1801.

RETIREMENT FROM POLITICS: Jay retired from politics in 1801 and moved to a large estate in Bedford, Westchester County, New York. He lived there for 28 years, and still stayed active in politics. In his later years, he became involved in the abolitionist cause. He also became president of the American Bible Society. Jay died on May 17, 1829, at the age of 83.

MARRIAGE AND FAMILY: Jay married Sarah Livingstone, the daughter of the governor of New Jersey, in April 1774. They had seven children. Sarah was sickly in later life, and she died shortly after they moved to the Bedford home.

HIS LEGACY: John Jay is remembered as a Patriot who served his country in many ways. As a delegate, diplomat, writer, and jurist, he used his varied experience to form the new nation's laws, treaties, and Constitution.

WORLD WIDE WEB SITES:

http://www.columbia.edu/cu/lweb/digital/jay/biography.html
http://www.ushistory.org/Declaraiton/related/Jay.htm

Thomas Jefferson

1743-1826

American Patriot and Statesman

"The Father of the Declaration of Independence"

Third President of the United States

THOMAS JEFFERSON WAS BORN on April 13, 1743, in Goochland, Virginia. He was born on his family's plantation, called Shadwell. His parents were Peter and Jane Jefferson. Peter was a planter and Jane was a homemaker. Thomas was the third of ten children, with four boys and six girls. Only eight lived to be adults. His surviving sisters were named Jane, Mary, Elizabeth, Martha, Lucy, and Anna. His brother was named Randolph.

THOMAS JEFFERSON GREW UP on Shadwell. As a boy, he loved to hunt, fish, and ride horses. His family was wealthy, and their plantation was worked by slaves. Jefferson's father died when he was 14, and he inherited Shadwell.

THOMAS JEFFERSON WENT TO SCHOOL when he was nine. He attended a local boarding school. There, he studied Latin, Greek, and French. When he was 14, he went to a boarding school in Charlottesville.

Jefferson went to the College of William and Mary when he was 16. After two years, he began to study law. He became very close to his law teacher, George Wythe. He said Wythe was like a "second father."

Jefferson's learning wasn't limited to school. Intelligent and artistic, he was a man of spirit, energy, and many interests. Jefferson loved music, and he learned to play the violin when he was young. He loved architecture, and he designed his own home, Monticello (mon-tah-CHELL-oh). He loved nature, and he developed types of fruits and vegetables still planted today.

POLITICAL CAREER: Jefferson finished studying law in 1767. He began to practice law in Williamsburg, which was then the capital of Virginia. He became interested in politics and began to visit the legislature—called the House of Burgesses—to hear debates. In 1769, Jefferson was elected to the House of Burgesses in Virginia.

MARRIAGE AND FAMILY: Jefferson met his future wife, Martha, in 1770. She was a lively and charming woman and the two shared a love of music. They married in 1772.

Thomas and Martha Jefferson had six children, but only two, Patsy and Mary, lived to be adults. A son died soon after birth. Three daughters also died in infancy. Martha died shortly after the birth of their last child, in 1782. Jefferson never remarried.

THE REVOLUTIONARY WAR:. In the 1770s, most of the area that is now the eastern United States were colonies of England. That means that thc people were ruled by England. They paid taxes to the British government and were ruled by a king, George III.

Some of the colonists were happy being part of England. Some were not. They believed that the colonies should have their own government, a government that they controlled. The people who wanted a separate government began to talk about breaking away from England. These were the people who began the American Revolutionary War.

Thomas Jefferson entered politics just as this revolutionary feeling was sweeping the country. He believed that the colonies should be free to determine their own government. He was a great writer, and he used that skill to write one of the most important documents in U.S. history.

THE DECLARATION OF INDEPENDENCE: In 1775, Jefferson was a delegate to the **SECOND CONTINENTAL CONGRESS**. That was the elected political group that represented the colonies. They chose Jefferson, **John Adams**, and **Ben Franklin** to write the Declaration. Jefferson was its main author.

The Declaration is made up of two parts. In the first section, it sets out the reasons why the colonists had the right to revolt against their king. The second part is a long listing of the grievances of the colonists. In this part, Jefferson outlined what George III had done. Jefferson describes how he had interfered with the representative governments of the colonies, taken away their civil rights, quartered troops in their homes, taxed them, and restricted trade, all without their consent.

But it is Jefferson's statement outlining the natural rights of the people that still inspire those who seek freedom around the world.

"We hold these Truths to be self-evident, that all Men are created equal, that they are endowed, by their Creator, with certain unalienable Rights, that among these are Life, Liberty, and the Pursuit of Happiness.—That to secure these Rights, Governments are instituted among Men, deriving their just Powers from the Consent of the Governed, that whenever any Form of Government becomes destructive of these Ends, it is the Right of the People to alter or to abolish it, and to institute new Government, laying its Foundation on such Principles, and organizing its Powers in such Form, as to them shall seem most likely to effect their Safety and Happiness."

IN CONGRESS, JULY 4, 1776.

The unanimous Declaration of the thirteen united States of America,

When in the Course of human events it becomes necessary for one people to dissolve the political bands which have connected them with another, and to assume among the powers of the earth, the separate and equal station to which the Laws of Nature and of Nature's God entitle them, a decent respect to the opinions of mankind requires that they should declare the causes which impel them to the separation. — We hold these truths to be self-evident, that all men are created equal, that they are endowed by their Creator with certain unalienable Rights, that among these are Life, Liberty and the pursuit of Happiness. — That to secure these rights, Governments are instituted among Men, deriving their just powers from the consent of the governed, — That whenever any Form of Government becomes destructive of these ends, it is the Right of the People to alter or to abolish it, and to institute new Government, laying its foundation on such principles and organizing its powers in such form, as to them shall seem most likely to effect their Safety and Happiness. Prudence, indeed, will dictate that Governments long established should not be changed for light and transient causes; and accordingly all experience hath shewn, that mankind are more disposed to suffer, while evils are sufferable, than to right themselves by abolishing the forms to which they are accustomed. But when a long train of abuses and usurpations, pursuing invariably the same Object evinces a design to reduce them under absolute Despotism, it is their right, it is their duty, to throw off such Government, and to provide new Guards for their future security. — Such has been the patient sufferance of these Colonies; and such is now the necessity which constrains them to alter their former Systems of Government. The history of the present King of Great Britain is a history of repeated injuries and usurpations, all having in direct object the establishment of an absolute Tyranny over these States. To prove this, let Facts be submitted to a candid world. — He has refused his Assent to Laws, the most wholesome and necessary for the public good. — He has forbidden his Governors to pass Laws of immediate and pressing importance, unless suspended in their operation till his Assent should be obtained; and when so suspended, he has utterly neglected to attend to them. — He has refused to pass other Laws for the accommodation of large districts of people, unless those people would relinquish the right of Representation in the Legislature, a right inestimable to them and formidable to tyrants only. — He has called together legislative bodies at places unusual, uncomfortable, and distant from the depository of their public Records, for the sole purpose of fatiguing them into compliance with his measures. — He has dissolved Representative Houses repeatedly, for opposing with manly firmness his invasions on the rights of the people. — He has refused for a long time, after such dissolutions, to cause others to be elected; whereby the Legislative powers, incapable of Annihilation, have returned to the People at large for their exercise; the State remaining in the mean time exposed to all the dangers of invasion from without, and convulsions within. — He has endeavoured to prevent the population of these States; for that purpose obstructing the Laws for Naturalization of Foreigners; refusing to pass others to encourage their migrations hither, and raising the conditions of new Appropriations of Lands. — He has obstructed the Administration of Justice, by refusing his Assent to Laws for establishing Judiciary powers. — He has made Judges dependent on his Will alone, for the tenure of their offices, and the amount and payment of their salaries. — He has erected a multitude of New Offices, and sent hither swarms of Officers to harrass our people, and eat out their substance. — He has kept among us, in times of peace, Standing Armies without the Consent of our legislatures. — He has affected to render the Military independent of and superior to the Civil power. — He has combined with others to subject us to a jurisdiction foreign to our constitution, and unacknowledged by our laws; giving his Assent to their Acts of pretended Legislation: — For Quartering large bodies of armed troops among us: — For protecting them, by a mock Trial, from punishment for any Murders which they should commit on the Inhabitants of these States: — For cutting off our Trade with all parts of the world: — For imposing Taxes on us without our Consent: — For depriving us in many cases, of the benefits of Trial by Jury: — For transporting us beyond Seas to be tried for pretended offences — For abolishing the free System of English Laws in a neighbouring Province, establishing therein an Arbitrary government, and enlarging its Boundaries so as to render it at once an example and fit instrument for introducing the same absolute rule into these Colonies: — For taking away our Charters, abolishing our most valuable Laws, and altering fundamentally the Forms of our Governments: — For suspending our own Legislatures, and declaring themselves invested with power to legislate for us in all cases whatsoever. — He has abdicated Government here, by declaring us out of his Protection and waging War against us. — He has plundered our seas, ravaged our Coasts, burnt our towns, and destroyed the lives of our people. — He is at this time transporting large Armies of foreign Mercenaries to compleat the works of death, desolation and tyranny, already begun with circumstances of Cruelty & perfidy scarcely paralleled in the most barbarous ages, and totally unworthy the Head of a civilized nation. — He has constrained our fellow Citizens taken Captive on the high Seas to bear Arms against their Country, to become the executioners of their friends and Brethren, or to fall themselves by their Hands. — He has excited domestic insurrections amongst us, and has endeavoured to bring on the inhabitants of our frontiers, the merciless Indian Savages, whose known rule of warfare, is an undistinguished destruction of all ages, sexes and conditions. In every stage of these Oppressions We have Petitioned for Redress in the most humble terms: Our repeated Petitions have been answered only by repeated injury. A Prince, whose character is thus marked by every act which may define a Tyrant, is unfit to be the ruler of a free people. Nor have We been wanting in attentions to our British brethren. We have warned them from time to time of attempts by their legislature to extend an unwarrantable jurisdiction over us. We have reminded them of the circumstances of our emigration and settlement here. We have appealed to their native justice and magnanimity, and we have conjured them by the ties of our common kindred to disavow these usurpations, which, would inevitably interrupt our connections and correspondence. They too have been deaf to the voice of justice and of consanguinity. We must, therefore, acquiesce in the necessity, which denounces our Separation, and hold them, as we hold the rest of mankind, Enemies in War, in Peace Friends. —

We, therefore, the Representatives of the united States of America, in General Congress, Assembled, appealing to the Supreme Judge of the world for the rectitude of our intentions, do, in the Name, and by Authority of the good People of these Colonies, solemnly publish and declare, That these United Colonies are, and of Right ought to be Free and Independent States; that they are Absolved from all Allegiance to the British Crown, and that all political connection between them and the State of Great Britain, is and ought to be totally dissolved; and that as Free and Independent States, they have full Power to levy War, conclude Peace, contract Alliances, establish Commerce, and to do all other Acts and Things which Independent States may of right do. — And for the support of this Declaration, with a firm reliance on the protection of divine Providence, we mutually pledge to each other our Lives, our Fortunes and our sacred Honor.

John Hancock

Button Gwinnett
Lyman Hall
Geo Walton
Wm Hooper
Joseph Hewes
John Penn
Edward Rutledge
Thos Heyward Junr.
Thomas Lynch Junr.
Arthur Middleton
Samuel Chase
Wm. Paca
Thos. Stone
Charles Carroll of Carrollton
George Wythe
Richard Henry Lee
Th Jefferson
Benja. Harrison
Thos Nelson jr.
Francis Lightfoot Lee
Carter Braxton
Robt Morris
Benjamin Rush
Benja. Franklin
John Morton
Geo Clymer
Jas. Smith
Geo. Taylor
James Wilson
Geo. Ross
Caesar Rodney
Geo Read
Tho M:Kean
Wm Floyd
Phil. Livingston
Frans. Lewis
Lewis Morris
Richd. Stockton
Jno Witherspoon
Fras. Hopkinson
John Hart
Abra Clark
Josiah Bartlett
Wm Whipple
Saml Adams
John Adams
Robt Treat Paine
Elbridge Gerry
Step. Hopkins
William Ellery
Roger Sherman
Sam el Huntington
Wm Williams
Oliver Wolcott
Matthew Thornton

Jefferson wrote later that he had not felt that it was his purpose to "invent new ideas." Rather, he wanted "to place before mankind the common sense of the subject, in terms so plain and firm as to command their assent. It was intended to be an expression of the American mind."

In words that still ring with power and clarity, he fulfilled those goals.

On July 4, 1776, the Continental Congress accepted the Declaration. The United States was born. Now a war would be fought to determine whether the new nation would remain free.

During the Revolutionary War, Jefferson served in the Virginia legislature and as Governor of Virginia. As Governor, Jefferson worked on an issue very important to him. He wrote the Bill for Establishing Religious Freedom. It said that all people should be free to worship as they liked. He always thought that bill was one of his greatest achievements.

The U.S. defeated the British in 1781, and the war was over. Jefferson's life took a sad turn after the war. His beloved wife, Martha, died after the birth of their sixth child in 1782. Jefferson was terribly sad. His daughter Patsy remembered that her father paced the floors all night.

At the urging of his friends, Jefferson accepted the job as representative to the new U.S. Congress in 1783. He helped to develop the system of money used in the U.S. to this day. He also developed the system by which territories became states in the new nation.

MINISTER TO FRANCE: In 1784, Jefferson went to France. The U.S. needed to form trading ties with other nations. Jefferson worked on trade agreements between the U.S. and countries in Europe. He spent five years in France. There, in addition to his work on trade, he enjoyed the art, architecture, and music of the country. He studied their farming and brought home ideas for his own crops and animals.

SECRETARY OF STATE: In 1789, **George Washington** was elected the first President of the United States. He formed his Cabinet, which is a group of the President's closest advisors. He chose Jefferson to be his Secretary of State.

As Secretary of State, Jefferson advised Washington on how to handle problems with other countries. He helped Washington with issues like trade. When war broke out between England and France, he advised Washington that the U.S. should not get involved.

Around this time, the first political parties began to form. These groups shared similar ideas on how government should work. Washington and **John Adams** were "Federalists." That means that they favored a strong central government. They were opposed by the Democratic-Republicans. Thomas Jefferson was a Democratic-Republican. He believed that a strong central government was a bad idea. He thought it limited the power of the states.

VICE PRESIDENT: After Washington served two terms, he retired from politics. In the election of 1796, Jefferson ran for President against John Adams. Today, candidates for President and Vice President are from the same party. In 1796, all candidates for President ran against each other, and the one getting the most votes became President, while the second-place finisher became Vice President. In 1796, Adams won the election and became President. Jefferson got the second highest number of votes. He became Vice President.

Jefferson and Adams were political opponents and rivals. In 1800, they ran against each other again for President. Adams lost to Jefferson, who became the third President of the United States.

THE ELECTORAL COLLEGE AND JEFFERSON'S ELECTION: Jefferson's election to the Presidency was determined by the House of Representatives. That is because Jefferson didn't get a majority of electoral votes.

Americans vote for President and Vice President in a different way than they do for any other elected official. The rules for the election of a President and Vice President are outlined in the Constitution.

The President and the Vice President are *not* elected by direct vote of the people. Instead, they are elected by members of the Electoral College. When a voter casts a vote for a presidential candidate, he or she is really voting for an "elector." That is someone who is pledged to vote for one of the presidential candidates. After the presidential election, the electors meet and cast their ballots for the candidates they are pledged to. If a candidate does not get a majority of the votes cast by the electors, the House of Representatives votes to decide who will be President. That's how Jefferson was elected.

Only twice in U.S. history has the House determined the Presidency. The first time was in 1801 for Jefferson, and the second was in 1825 for John Quincy Adams.

PRESIDENT OF THE UNITED STATES: As President, Jefferson worked to cut taxes and government spending. Throughout his two terms as President, Jefferson was very popular with the people. He is best remembered for the Louisiana Purchase, the addition of lands that doubled the size of the U.S.

Jefferson's daughter, Patsy, who often served as hostess when he was President.

THE LOUISIANA PURCHASE: In 1803, Jefferson organized the purchase of a huge amount of territory from France. It was called the Louisiana Purchase. The territory ranged from the Mississippi River to the Rocky Mountains, and from the Canadian border to Texas. It cost the U.S. $15 million, about three cents an acre.

Jefferson hired Meriwether Lewis and William Clark to explore the land. They journeyed for two years through the territory, finally reaching the Pacific Ocean in 1805. They returned and reported to Jefferson on the vast new portion of the U.S.

Jefferson ran for President again in 1804. He won reelection by a wide majority of votes. During his second term, England and France again went to war. During this war, British ships would sometimes stop American ships and force their sailors into the British Navy. This system, called "impressment," was like slavery. Jefferson fought to end it by stopping all trading with England and France. It was a very unpopular decision, and Jefferson later ended the trade stoppage, called an "embargo."

U.S. ships were also attacked by pirates along the Barbary Coast of North Africa. These pirates stole goods from American ships. The U.S. went to war against one of the North African states, called Tripoli. The U.S. won the war, and the ships were safe once more.

Jefferson's daughters lived with him during most of his presidency. In fact, the first baby born in the White House was Jefferson's grandson, James Madison Randolph. He was Patsy's seventh child.

RETIREMENT TO MONTICELLO: In 1808, after two terms as President, Jefferson retired to his beloved home, Monticello. "All my wishes end, where I hope my days will end, at Monticello," he said. His retirement was anything but quiet and relaxing. He continued

Jefferson's home, Monticello.

to write about government, and he wrote thousands of letters. His letters to John Adams are especially important. The two former political rivals became friends again and wrote to each other often. They wrote about politics, science, and philosophy.

Jefferson's active mind was still fascinated by many things. He invented new farm tools and developed new plants. He was a great lover and collector of books. When the congressional library burned down during the War of 1812, he sold his library to the U.S. government. It became the core of what is now the Library of Congress.

In 1819, Jefferson founded the University of Virginia. He designed everything, from the buildings to the courses for the students. He also hired the teachers. The first 40 students began classes in 1825.

Jefferson lived a long and active life. He died on July 4, 1826, the 50th anniversary of the Declaration. His great friend, John Adams, died on the same day.

HIS LEGACY: Jefferson wanted to be remembered for three things, which are engraved on his tombstone: "Author of the Declaration of Independence, of the Statute of Virginia for religious freedom, and father of the University of Virginia."

WORLD WIDE WEB SITES:

http://www.ipl.org/ref/POTUS
http://www.monticello.org
http://www.nps.thje
http://www.whitehouse.gov/WH/kids/html/kidshome.html

Marquis de Lafayette
1757-1834
French Officer Who Served in the American Revolution

THE MARQUIS de LAFAYETTE WAS BORN on September 6, 1757, in Auvergne, France. His full name was Marie Joseph Paul Yves Roche Gilbert du Motier.

Before Lafayette was two years old his father died. He had been a colonel in the French army, and died while serving in the Seven Year's War (1756-1763) between England and France. When he was twelve, Lafayette's mother died, and a few weeks later, his grandfather died.

Lafayette's family was from the nobility. So with the passing of his father and grandfather, he was left a very wealthy orphan. He inherited the title of Marquis and a large fortune.

LAFAYETTE WENT TO SCHOOL at the College of Louis le Grand for two years between 1768 and 1770. After the deaths of his mother and grandfather, he entered the Royal Army at the age of 14. By the time he was 16 years old he was a captain in the French cavalry.

MARRIAGE: Lafayette married Marie Adrienne Francoise de Noailles when he was 16. She, too, was from a noble family. In fact, she was related to the king. Marie was from one of the wealthiest families in France, so when she and Lafayette married they were very wealthy.

LEARNING ABOUT AMERICA: One evening in 1775 Lafayette was having dinner with the Duke of Gloucester (the brother of George III), when he learned of the struggle in the American colonies. Like many young soldiers in France, Lafayette was sympathetic to the colonists' struggle for liberty. Fighting the British in America would be an adventure. It would also be a chance to revenge France's losses to England in the Seven Years' War. Lafayette decided to go to America.

However, King Louis XVI of France was *not* sympathetic with the American war. He was not willing to give Lafayette permission to travel there. Lafayette defied the king, however, and in 1777 he made plans to board a ship and secretly sail to the American colonies.

Before he set sail, however, Lafayette was arrested at Bordeaux. But Lafayette escaped his captors in a disguise, and boarded the ship in Spain. Finally, he sailed to America and landed safely in South Carolina. He hurried on to Philadelphia, then the capitol of the colonies.

LAFAYETTE, AT YOUR SERVICE: Lafayette presented himself to the **CONTINENTAL CONGRESS**. He said he was willing to serve under two conditions: that he would receive no pay and would act as a volunteer. On July 31, 1777, Congress accepted his offer. They also declared that because of Lafayette's important family connections he should be given the rank of major general. The next day he met with **George Washington**, the Commander-in-Chief of the Continental Army.

A FRENCHMAN IN THE AMERICAN REVOLUTION: At 19 years old, Lafayette was the youngest commissioned officer in the Army. As he served under Washington, Lafayette fought in several battles including Brandywine (1777), Monmouth (1778) and the Rhode Island expedition (1778). He wintered with Washington and the army at Valley Forge.

In October 1778 Lafayette received permission to return to France. When he reached home, Lafayette devoted his energy to persuading the French government to send military supplies and soldiers to the colonies to help in their fight for independence.

He was very successful. On March 19, 1780, Lafayette set sail for Boston with six French ships and 12 battalions of soldiers. This help from the French gave new hope to the American cause. With the French troops, Washington made plans for battle. He hoped

Lafayette and George Washington visit the suffering troops during the hard winter at Valley Forge, 1777.

this might be the additional strength that was needed to finally defeat the British.

In April 1780, Washington sent Lafayette to Virginia to fight with the American troops against **Benedict Arnold.** The traitor Arnold was then in command of British troops. Lafayette bought clothes and equipment for the Americans with his own money. But they were still ill-equipped, and were forced to retreat.

Lafayette was charged with the defense of Virginia. He served there until the Battle of Yorktown in October 1781. With victory assured, Lafayette ended his military career in the United States.

BACK HOME IN FRANCE: Lafayette returned to Paris in December 1781. He was given many honors for his service in America. He was also made commander of the Paris National Guard, a position he held for the next ten years. He became active in politics, and worked closely with ambassadors **Benjamin Franklin** and **Thomas Jefferson** on behalf of American interests. He also took part in the movement to abolish slavery.

In 1784 Lafayette returned to America as the guest of George Washington. He stayed at Mount Vernon and traveled through the country from Virginia to Massachusetts. This was the last time these two friends were together.

Lafayette remained active in the military. In 1789 he saved the royal family from a Paris mob during the French Revolution. A year later he was promoted to Lieutenant General but resigned shortly thereafter. In 1792, when France declared war on Austria, he took command of the army. When Lafayette was replaced as commander, he left France for Belgium.

In Belgium, the Austrians captured Lafayette. They turned him over to the Prussians, who held him prisoner until 1797. Lafayette spent four years in a horrible prison, where he was treated with cruelty. With help and support from both the English and the Americans, Lafayette was finally set free. He returned to France in 1800 to find his fortune ruined.

LATER YEARS: Lafayette retired to La Grange, in Brie, his home outside Paris. During this time, Napoleon tried to gain his support and offered him a senatorship, the Legion of Honor, and the position of minister to the United States. Lafayette declined them all. He also declined President Jefferson's offer to appoint him governor of Louisiana in 1805. Lafayette lived quietly at La Grange for several years.

In 1824 Lafayette accepted an invitation from **President James Monroe** to visit the United States again. Over fourteen months, he traveled around the country and visited all 24 states and the major cities. Huge audiences packed the halls where Lafayette appeared and enthusiastically greeted and honored him. He celebrated his 68th birthday, September 6, 1825, at the White House, where President John Quincy Adams delivered a moving speech to the old war hero.

While Lafayette was in America, Congress voted to pay him back the money he had spent during the Revolution. He was also given 24,000 acres of land in Louisiana. All these tributes were in recognition of his devoted service to the American cause for independence.

During his last years, Lafayette continued to work for representative government. He remained a member of the French Chamber of Deputies until his death in 1834. He was given a magnificent funeral and was buried alongside his wife near Paris. Lafayette left one son, whom he had named George Washington after his dear American friend, and two daughters, Anastasie and Virginie.

HIS LEGACY: Lafayette's love of liberty and belief in representative government caused him to leave his homeland and serve in the American struggle for independence. His courage and loyalty made him one of the most beloved heroes of the revolution. Lafayette's contribution to the nation was recognized in July 2002, when the United States Congress voted to make him an honorary U.S. citizen.

WORLD WIDE WEB SITES:

http://www.history.org/Almanack/people/bios/biolafayette.cfm
http://www.ushistory.org/Valleyforge/served/lafayette.html

Richard Henry Lee

1732-1794

American Patriot and Statesman
Introduced Resolution Declaring American Independence

RICHARD HENRY LEE WAS BORN on January 20, 1732, at Stratford, the Lee family home in Westmoreland County, Virginia. His parents were Thomas and Hannah Ludwell Lee. Thomas was a wealthy plantation owner. Richard Henry was the seventh of eleven children. Three of his brothers, Francis Lightfoot, William, and Arthur, would, like Richard Henry, go on to play important roles in the Revolutionary War.

RICHARD HENRY LEE WENT TO SCHOOL at home for several years. After studying with private tutors, he went to England. There, he studied at Wakefield Academy in Yorkshire. He returned to Virginia in 1751.

JUSTICE OF THE PEACE: Lee's first job was as a justice of the peace (a local judge). He got the position in 1757.

VIRGINIA HOUSE OF BURGESSES: That same year, Lee began his political career as a member of the House of Burgesses. Soon, he was giving fiery speeches in favor of causes that some found controversial.

The first bill Lee presented to the House was regarding slavery, which he hated. He proposed requiring "so heavy a duty on the importation of slaves as to put an end to that iniquitous and disgraceful traffic within the colony of Virginia." He claimed that Africans "were equally entitled to liberty and freedom by the great law of nature."

By 1765, the British government was imposing taxes that many colonists opposed. One of the most hated was the **STAMP ACT.** This Act of Parliament, passed in 1765, made it mandatory that most documents, such as contracts, newspapers, and pamphlets, had to be written on special paper bearing a stamp from the British government. The colonists were forced to purchase the stamped paper for most of their documents, because documents on plain paper had no legal standing.

In response to the Stamp Act, Lee organized a group to protest the tax. He helped write a document called "The Westmoreland Resolves." It promised "danger and disgrace" to any who agreed to pay the tax. The "Resolves" were signed by four Lees: Richard, Thomas, Francis Lightfoot, and William. They were also signed by four of **George Washington's** brothers.

Lee engaged in other acts of resistance, too. He rallied support for the boycott of British goods as a way of fighting taxes. He grew his own grapes to make his own wine. He used his own looms to weave his own cloth. And he was a tireless speaker promoting the cause of revolution throughout Virginia.

THE COMMITTEE OF CORRESPONDENCE: In 1772, Lee, like **Samuel Adams**, helped to form Committees of Correspondence. These important groups shared information about resistance to the British among the colonies. The British authorities were furious.

CONTINENTAL CONGRESS: Lee was one of the most active members of the First and Second Continental Congresses. In 1774, he was part of a seven-man delegation to the First Congress, in Philadelphia. He became an ally and friend of **Samuel and John Adams**, as the colonies wrestled with the question of British taxation and tyranny.

Lee served on many committees in the Congress. With John Adams and Edward Rutledge, he was part of a committee that placed **George Washington** in command of the Continental Army.

THE DECLARATION OF INDEPENDENCE: Lee's next, and most famous appointment, was to the committee that created the "Declaration of Rights of the Colonies." It was the motion that led to the Declaration of Independence. On June 7, 1776, Lee presented the bill containing these now-famous words to the Congress:

"That these united Colonies are, and ought to be, free and independent States, that they are absolved from all allegiance from the British crown, and that all political connection between America and the State of Great Britain is, and ought to be, totally dissolved."

These words appear in the final section of the Declaration of Independence, which was ratified on July 4, 1776, and signed by two Lees, Richard Henry, and his brother Francis Lightfoot.

SERVICE DURING THE WAR: Lee remained active in the Continental Congress from 1774 to 1780. He served on committees to negotiate treaties between the new nation and foreign governments. He also headed the committee that ratified the **ARTICLES OF CONFEDERATION**. He also served for one year as the President of the Congress.

When the Revolutionary War ended, Lee continued to serve his country. He returned to the Continental Congress again in 1784, and served until 1787. Yet when the Constitutional Convention convened, Lee refused to be a delegate. This staunch Patriot was a fervent supporter of states' rights, and feared the power of a strong central government.

OPPOSING THE CONSTITUTION: Lee was an outspoken anti-Federalist. He thought that a strong central government would threaten the power of the individual states. He wrote an anti-Federalist essay, "Letters from the Federal Farmer." He stated his fears of the unrestrained powers of a President and Senate as given in the Constitution. He did, however, accept it in the end.

FIRST STATE SENATOR FROM VIRGINIA: In 1789, Lee was elected the first U.S. Senator from Virginia. He served for three years, during which he fought for the **BILL OF RIGHTS**. He believed those first 10 amendments to the Constitution would guarantee individual liberties.

RETIREMENT: In 1794, Lee became ill and left the Senate. He retired to his estate, Chantilly. He died there on June 19, 1794, at the age of 62.

MARRIAGE AND FAMILY: Lee married Anne Aylett on December 3, 1757. After her death in 1768, Lee married a widow named Anne Pinkard.

HIS LEGACY: Lee is remembered as a passionate Patriot who served the cause of revolution in the House of Burgesses and the Continental Congress. His stirring words rallied many to the Patriot cause, and appear as part of one of the most famous documents in American history.

WORLD WIDE WEB SITES:

http://www.stratfordhall.org/richardh.html
http://www.ushistory.org/Declaration/signers/rhlee.htm

Dolley Madison

1768-1849

American Patriot and First Lady

DOLLEY MADISON WAS BORN on May 20, 1768, in New Garden, North Carolina. Her name at birth was Dolley Payne. Some sources spell her name Dolly. Other sources claim that Dolley was a nickname, short for Dorothy or Dorothea. But these sources are incorrect. Historians have found that Dolley appears on her official birth certificate.

Dolley's parents were John Payne, Jr., and Mary Coles Payne. They came from Virginia, but they were visiting relatives in North Carolina at the time of Dolley's birth. Dolley was the third-oldest of their eight children. Her brothers and sisters were Walter, William Temple, Isaac, Lucy, Anna, Mary, and John.

DOLLEY MADISON GREW UP at Scotchtown, her family's plantation in rural Virginia. At that time, Virginia was one of 13 American colonies that were ruled by the king of England. When Dolley was eight years old, American leaders decided to separate from England and form a new country. The colonies declared their independence from British rule on July 4, 1776. But England did not give up so easily. The two sides went to war.

The Revolutionary War ended in victory for the Americans in 1783. The world recognized the United States of America as an independent nation. A short time later, Dolley's parents decided to move the family to Philadelphia, Pennsylvania. They sold their plantation, freed their slaves, and bought a house in the city. Dolley's father went into the starch business.

At first, Dolley enjoyed life in the big city. Many exciting things took place in Philadelphia after the end of the war. In 1787, for example, political leaders gathered there for the Constitutional Convention. **George Washington**, **Benjamin Franklin**, **James Madison**, and many other prominent men attended this meeting. They drafted the Constitution and formed a national government for the United States.

DOLLEY MADISON WENT TO SCHOOL at home. She mostly learned domestic skills like sewing, cooking, and good manners.

HARDSHIP AND TRAGEDY: The move to Philadelphia did not turn out well for Dolley's family. Her father was not a very good businessman. In 1789, his shop went out of business and he lost all his money. He died a short time later. The family struggled to make ends meet. Dolley's mother was forced to rent out rooms in their house.

By this time, Dolley had grown into a beautiful young woman. She accepted a marriage proposal from a successful lawyer, John Todd, Jr. They were married on January 7, 1790. Dolley gave birth to two sons in the next three years.

In 1793, an epidemic of yellow fever swept through Philadelphia. Many people became sick and died. The disease took the lives of Dolley's husband and youngest son. Dolley became ill too, but she eventually got well.

MARRIES JAMES MADISON: In 1794, a friend introduced Dolley to James Madison. Madison was known as one of the great political minds of his time. He helped draft the **U.S. CONSTITUTION**. In fact, he was the main person responsible for adding the **BILL OF RIGHTS** to the historic document.

The first 10 amendments to the Constitution make up the Bill of Rights. They are important because they protect the individual liberties of American citizens. They guarantee that the American people have freedom of speech, freedom of religion, and other rights.

Dolley married James Madison on September 15, 1794. He decided to retire from politics. They moved to Montpelier, his family's 5,000 acre estate in Orange County, Virginia. By all accounts, they lived there happily for the next six years.

In 1801, **Thomas Jefferson** was elected as the third President of the United States. He asked James Madison to join his cabinet as the Secretary of State. Madison was pleased to accept this important job. He became the nation's highest-ranking diplomat.

SETS SOCIAL STANDARDS IN WASHINGTON: Dolley and her husband moved to Washington, D.C. The U.S. capital had just moved there from Philadelphia the year before. Most of the government buildings were not yet finished. It was a small town surrounded by forests and swamps.

Dolley had no official duties as the wife of the Secretary of State. But she became the center of the social scene in Washington, D.C. Since President Jefferson's wife had died, Dolley often served as his hostess. She ignored the formal rules of entertaining used by English royalty. She created a new, informal style that better matched the founding ideas of the new country.

Jefferson left office in 1809. James Madison was elected as the fourth President of the United States. Dolley officially became First Lady of the nation. She was perfect for the role. Everyone said that she was friendly, charming, caring, generous, tactful, and well-mannered. She was a gracious hostess who made everyone feel welcome. Dolley was known for serving delicious food to her guests. Her most popular dish was ice cream, which was new at that time.

Dolley was also very fashionable. Women across America tried to copy her style of dress. When the White House was finished, Dolley took charge of decorating it. She chose furniture, dishes, silverware, and other items for the President's home. Dolley's decorating style was simple but elegant. She was careful not to make the White House seem too fancy. She wanted ordinary Americans to feel comfortable there.

When Washington, D.C. was set afire by the British during the War of 1812, Dolley Madison saved many important documents and other valuables from the White House.

SHOWING COURAGE IN WARTIME: In 1812, President Madison declared war against England. He was angry that England had tried to stop the United States from trading with France. He also hoped to gain some British territory by going to war.

The War of 1812 lasted for three years. Most of the battles took place at sea. But in 1814, British soldiers attacked several U.S. cities on the Atlantic Ocean. On August 24, they attacked Washington, D.C. President Madison was out of town that day. He sent word for his wife to flee the city.

Before she left, Dolley took the time to gather items of national or historic significance. She collected secret government papers and other valuables. She also took a full-length portrait of George Washington. Dolley packed these items into a wagon. She left all of her personal belongings behind.

British troops arrived in Washington two hours after Dolley left. They destroyed the city. They burned down the White House and the U.S. Capitol. The things that Dolley took with her were saved for future generations of Americans. Many people praised the First Lady's courage and quick thinking.

LATER YEARS: James Madison left office in 1817. Dolley and her husband returned to Montpelier, their home in Virginia. They lived there together for the next 20 years.

Over time, the Madisons started to run out of money. Dolley's son, John Payne Todd, was the main cause of their financial problems. He drifted between jobs and spent lots of money on drinking and gambling. He could not pay his debts and eventually went to jail. But Dolley loved him and always tried to help him get out of trouble.

James Madison spent the final years of his life organizing his papers. He had saved many letters and other writings from his long political career. These papers provided an insider's view on many significant historical events, including the Constitutional Convention. He wanted Dolley to publish the papers after his death.

Dolley Madison's home in Washington, D.C.

When her husband died in 1836, Dolley sold a batch of his papers to the Library of Congress for $30,000. This money allowed her to live comfortably for a few years. But her son continued to have financial problems. She eventually had to sell Montpelier to pay his debts.

After her husband's death, Dolley moved back to Washington, D.C. She lived with her niece, Anna Payne. Once again, she became the center of the social scene in the capital. Her many years in public life made her a respected and honored figure. Nearly every important person who came to town stopped in to visit her. President Andrew Jackson described Dolley as a "national institution."

Dolley Madison died at her home in Washington on July 12, 1849. Many prominent people attended her funeral, including the

President, cabinet officers, members of Congress, Supreme Court justices, and military leaders.

DOLLEY MADISON'S HOME AND FAMILY: Dolley Madison had two sons from her first marriage, John Payne Todd and William Temple Todd. Only John Payne Todd survived to adulthood. She did not have any children from her marriage to James Madison. Dolley and her second husband had homes in Montpelier, Virginia, and Washington, D.C.

HER LEGACY: Dolley Madison remains one of the most popular First Ladies. In 1999, her image appeared on a silver dollar. It was the first American coin ever to depict a First Lady. In 2005, the University of Virginia created a digital library to give the American people access to 700 of her personal letters.

WORLD WIDE WEB SITES:

http://www.whitehouse.gov/history/firstladies/dm4.html
http://www.vcdh.virginia.edu/madison/overview

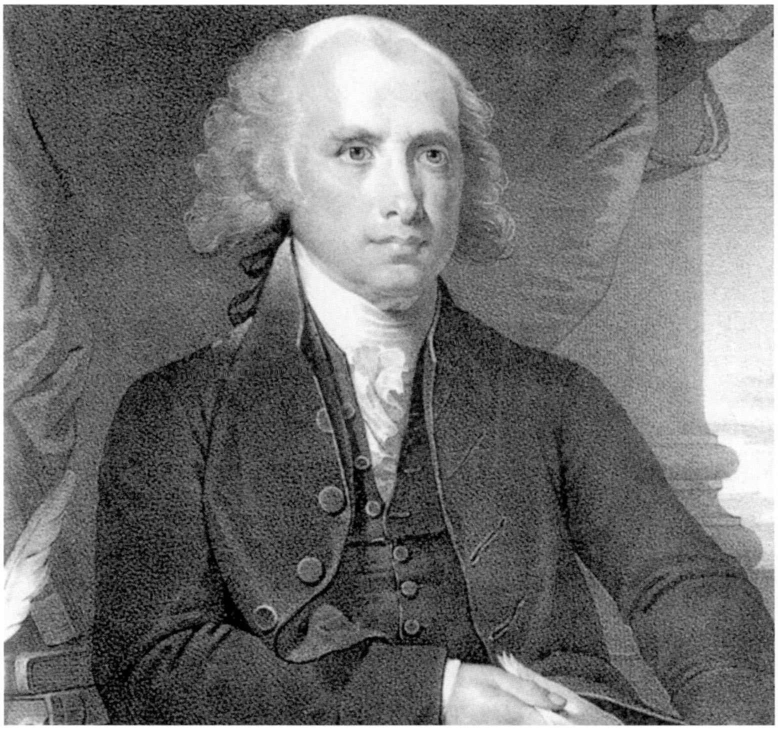

James Madison

1751-1836

American Patriot and Statesman

Fourth President of the United States

"The Father of the Constitution"

JAMES MADISON WAS BORN on March 16, 1751, in Port Conway, Virginia. His father, James Madison, was a planter. His mother, Nelly Rose Conway Madison, was a homemaker. James was the oldest of twelve children. Two children died in infancy. He had six brothers and four sisters who lived to be adults. His brothers were named Francis, Ambrose, Catlett, William, Reuben, and Eli. His sisters were named Nelly, Sarah, Elizabeth, and Frances.

JAMES MADISON GREW UP on the family plantation, called Montpelier. His great-great-grandfather, a ship carpenter from England, settled in Virginia in 1653 and started a tobacco farm. His grandfather and father moved west into present-day Orange County, Virginia. They built the family plantation to 6,000 acres. The chief crops were grains and tobacco, which were farmed by slaves.

JAMES MADISON WENT TO SCHOOL at a boarding school 70 miles away from his home when he was 11 years old. Before that, he was taught to read and write by his mother and grandmother. At boarding school, he learned English, mathematics, French and Spanish. Later he studied Latin, philosophy and astronomy.

When he was 18, Madison went to the College of New Jersey (now Princeton University). He completed the four-year course in only two years and graduated in 1771. After graduation, he returned home and continued his studies, especially in law. He also taught his younger brothers and sisters.

THE REVOLUTIONARY WAR: In the 1770s, most of the area that is now the eastern United States was a colony of England. That means that the people were ruled by England. They paid taxes to the British government and were ruled by a king, George III.

Some of the colonists were happy being part of England. Some were not. They believed that the colonies should have their own government, a government they controlled. The people who wanted a separate government began to talk about breaking away from England. These were the people who began the American Revolutionary War.

BECOMING INVOLVED IN POLITICS: As the Revolutionary War started, Madison enlisted in the military. Later, he had to drop out due to poor health. In 1776 Madison was elected as a delegate to the Virginia Revolutionary Convention. He was 25 years old. He helped pass a resolution to issue the **DECLARATION OF INDEPENDENCE.**

In 1779, Madison was elected to the Continental Congress. Even though he was one of its youngest members, he became its most effective legislator and debater. When the war ended in 1781, Madison turned his attention to the creation of the new nation. He became one of the principal writers of the plan for the new national government, the **U.S. CONSTITUTION.**

WRITING THE CONSTITUTION: James Madison was the principal author of the Constitution. It created a form of government that was the first of its kind in the world.

The U.S. Constitution divides power between three branches. The Executive Branch is made up of the President and his Cabinet. The Legislative branch is made up of the House of Representatives and the Senate. They make the laws of the country. The Judicial

Branch is made up of the U.S. Court system, including the nine-member Supreme Court.

After the Constitution was written, it had to be "ratified"—voted on—by all the states. Madison wanted to convince the country to adopt the new Constitution. Along with **Alexander Hamilton** and **John Jay**, he wrote many articles, called the Federalist Papers. In the articles he tried to persuade people to vote for the new Constitution. Finally, in 1788, enough states had voted to ratify the Constitution to guarantee that it would pass. Madison had succeeded, and the Constitution was accepted by the American people.

THE BILL OF RIGHTS: Madison also wrote the first ten amendments, or additions, to the Constitution. These are known as the Bill of Rights. The Bill of Rights guarantees specific freedoms to all Americans. Some of the major rights we enjoy—like freedom of speech and religion—are outlined in the Bill of Rights.

SECRETARY OF STATE: In 1801 **Thomas Jefferson** appointed James Madison Secretary of State. The Secretary of State helps the President solve problems with other countries.

In 1803, Jefferson organized the purchase of a huge amount of territory from France. It was called the Louisiana Purchase. The territory ranged from the Mississippi River to the Rocky Mountains, and from the Canadian border to Texas. As Secretary of State, Madison helped negotiate the purchase.

MARRIAGE AND FAMILY: Madison was still a bachelor at age 43. Then Senator Aaron Burr introduced him to Dolley Payne Todd. Dolley was 26 years old. She was a widow. Her husband and one of

The White House, painted after the War of 1812.

her two children had died of yellow fever. James and Dolley fell in love and were married on September 15, 1797. They did not have children.

PRESIDENT OF THE UNITED STATES: With the help of his friend, Thomas Jefferson, Madison ran for, and was elected President in 1808.

The years of Madison's Presidency were hard times for America. France and Great Britain were at war. America did not take sides in the war. This means that America was neutral. Even so, both Britain and France kept capturing American ships. Britain also forced American sailors into their Navy. Finally, Madison asked Congress to declare war on Britain. This war is known as the War of 1812.

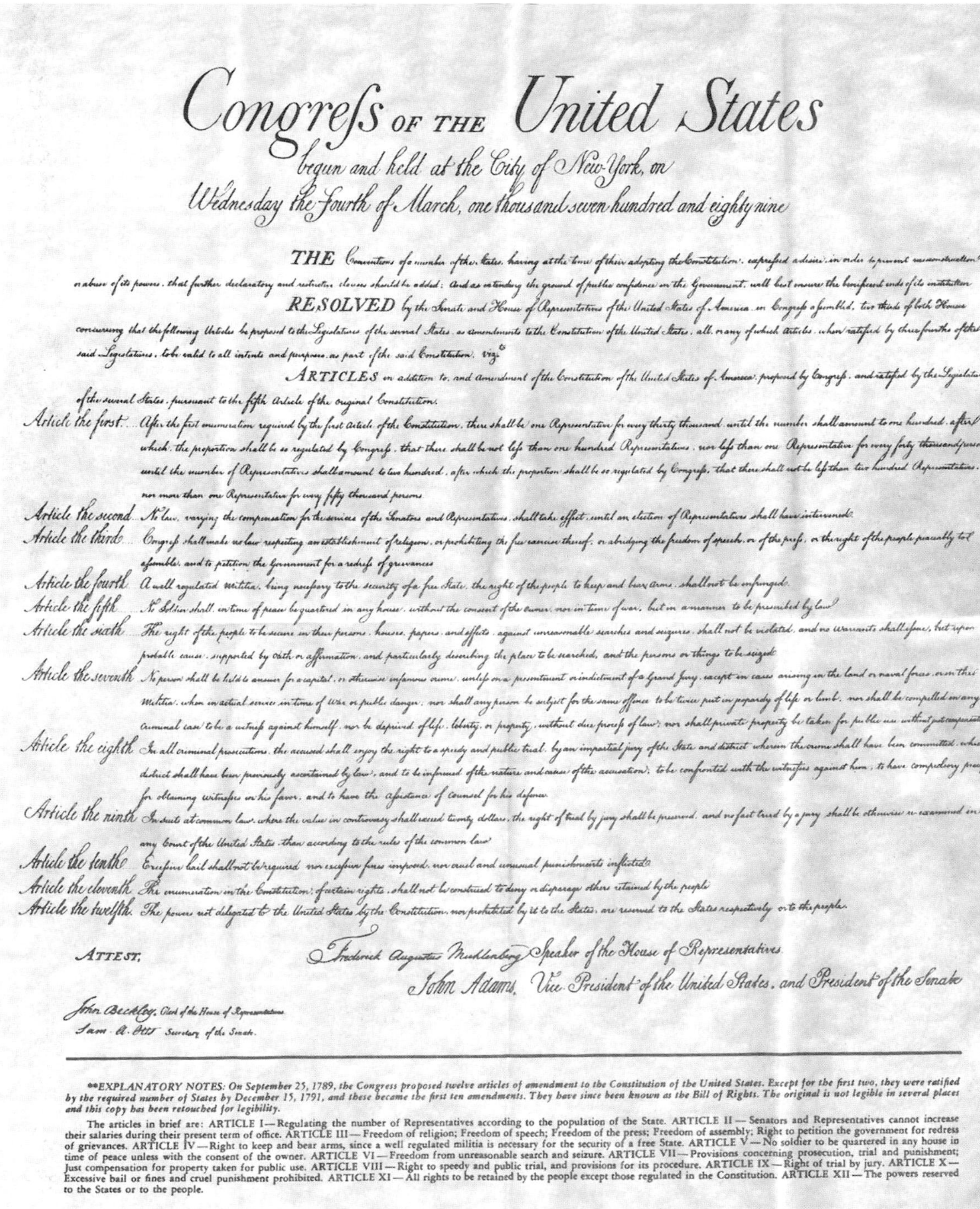

Congress OF THE United States

begun and held at the City of New-York, on Wednesday the fourth of March, one thousand seven hundred and eighty nine

THE Conventions of a number of the States, having at the time of their adopting the Constitution, expressed a desire, in order to prevent misconstruction or abuse of its powers, that further declaratory and restrictive clauses should be added: And as extending the ground of public confidence in the Government, will best ensure the beneficent ends of its institution

RESOLVED by the Senate and House of Representatives of the United States of America, in Congress assembled, two thirds of both Houses concurring, that the following Articles be proposed to the Legislatures of the several States, as amendments to the Constitution of the United States, all, or any of which Articles, when ratified by three fourths of the said Legislatures, to be valid to all intents and purposes, as part of the said Constitution; viz.

ARTICLES in addition to, and Amendment of the Constitution of the United States of America, proposed by Congress, and ratified by the Legislatures of the several States, pursuant to the fifth Article of the original Constitution.

Article the first. ... After the first enumeration required by the first Article of the Constitution, there shall be one Representative for every thirty thousand, until the number shall amount to one hundred, after which, the proportion shall be so regulated by Congress, that there shall be not less than one hundred Representatives, nor less than one Representative for every forty thousand persons, until the number of Representatives shall amount to two hundred, after which the proportion shall be so regulated by Congress, that there shall not be less than two hundred Representatives, nor more than one Representative for every fifty thousand persons.

Article the second. ... No law, varying the compensation for the services of the Senators and Representatives, shall take effect, until an election of Representatives shall have intervened.

Article the third. ... Congress shall make no law respecting an establishment of religion, or prohibiting the free exercise thereof; or abridging the freedom of speech, or of the press, or the right of the people peaceably to assemble, and to petition the Government for a redress of grievances.

Article the fourth. ... A well regulated militia, being necessary to the security of a free State, the right of the people to keep and bear arms, shall not be infringed.

Article the fifth. ... No Soldier shall, in time of peace be quartered in any house, without the consent of the owner, nor in time of war, but in a manner to be prescribed by law.

Article the sixth. ... The right of the people to be secure in their persons, houses, papers, and effects, against unreasonable searches and seizures, shall not be violated, and no warrants shall issue, but upon probable cause, supported by oath or affirmation, and particularly describing the place to be searched, and the persons or things to be seized.

Article the seventh. ... No person shall be held to answer for a capital, or otherwise infamous crime, unless on a presentment or indictment of a Grand Jury, except in cases arising in the land or naval forces, or in the Militia, when in actual service in time of War or public danger; nor shall any person be subject for the same offence to be twice put in jeopardy of life or limb; nor shall be compelled in any criminal case, to be a witness against himself, nor be deprived of life, liberty, or property, without due process of law; nor shall private property be taken for public use without just compensation.

Article the eighth. ... In all criminal prosecutions, the accused shall enjoy the right to a speedy and public trial, by an impartial jury of the State and district wherein the crime shall have been committed, which district shall have been previously ascertained by law, and to be informed of the nature and cause of the accusation; to be confronted with the witnesses against him; to have compulsory process for obtaining witnesses in his favor, and to have the assistance of counsel for his defence.

Article the ninth. ... In suits at common law, where the value in controversy shall exceed twenty dollars, the right of trial by jury shall be preserved, and no fact tried by a jury shall be otherwise re-examined in any Court of the United States, than according to the rules of the common law.

Article the tenth. ... Excessive bail shall not be required, nor excessive fines imposed, nor cruel and unusual punishments inflicted.

Article the eleventh. ... The enumeration in the Constitution, of certain rights, shall not be construed to deny or disparage others retained by the people.

Article the twelfth. ... The powers not delegated to the United States by the Constitution, nor prohibited by it to the States, are reserved to the States respectively, or to the people.

ATTEST,

Frederick Augustus Muhlenberg Speaker of the House of Representatives.
John Adams, Vice-President of the United States, and President of the Senate.

John Beckley, Clerk of the House of Representatives.
Sam. A. Otis Secretary of the Senate.

**EXPLANATORY NOTES: *On September 25, 1789, the Congress proposed twelve articles of amendment to the Constitution of the United States. Except for the first two, they were ratified by the required number of States by December 15, 1791, and these became the first ten amendments. They have since been known as the Bill of Rights. The original is not legible in several places and this copy has been retouched for legibility.*

The articles in brief are: ARTICLE I—Regulating the number of Representatives according to the population of the State. ARTICLE II—Senators and Representatives cannot increase their salaries during their present term of office. ARTICLE III—Freedom of religion; Freedom of speech; Freedom of the press; Freedom of assembly; Right to petition the government for redress of grievances. ARTICLE IV—Right to keep and bear arms, since a well regulated militia is necessary for the security of a free State. ARTICLE V—No soldier to be quartered in any house in time of peace unless with the consent of the owner. ARTICLE VI—Freedom from unreasonable search and seizure. ARTICLE VII—Provisions concerning prosecution, trial and punishment; Just compensation for property taken for public use. ARTICLE VIII—Right to speedy and public trial, and provisions for its procedure. ARTICLE IX—Right of trial by jury. ARTICLE X—Excessive bail or fines and cruel punishment prohibited. ARTICLE XI—All rights to be retained by the people except those regulated in the Constitution. ARTICLE XII—The powers reserved to the States or to the people.

The Bill of Rights.

THE WAR OF 1812: As the war began in 1812, Madison ran for reelection and won, despite strong opposition from members of the Federalist Party. They did not want to go to war with Great Britain, and they didn't support Madison's stand.

At first, the war did not go well for the United States. In 1814 the British captured Washington, D.C., and set it on fire. Dolley Madison barely escaped before the invaders. She took a wagon loaded with many belongings from the President's House, including a portrait of George Washington.

During the invasion of Washington, James Madison took command of the defending American army. He is the only President to ever personally command an army while in office. Later, the Americans won victories in Baltimore and New York. This forced the British to sign a peace treaty in 1814.

HOW THE WHITE HOUSE GOT ITS NAME: The Madisons had to live in another house, called the Octagon House, while the President's House was repaired after the fire. The President's House was painted white to cover over the scorch marks left from the fire. That's how the President's House camc to be called the "White House."

Dolley Madison was one of the most popular hostesses in Washington. She served pink ice cream at the White House. Known for her stylishness, she had a large collection of shoes and turbans. She set many fashion trends in Washington as the First Lady. When she bought a pet macaw—a kind of parrot—many fashionable ladies did so, too.

RETIREMENT TO VIRGINIA: In 1817, after serving two terms as President, Madison returned to his family home at Montpelier. There he developed scientific farming methods that are still used.

Madison helped found the University of Virginia with Thomas Jefferson. He became its second president after Jefferson's death. He also continued to write articles on government until his death.

James Madison lived a long life. He died on June 28, 1836, at the age of 85. Dolley moved back to Washington, D.C., where she lived until her death in 1849.

HIS LEGACY: Madison is remembered as the author of the Constitution and the Bill of Rights. His work on behalf of the document and its passage have made him an honored Founding Father of the nation he helped to form.

WORLD WIDE WEB SITES:

http://www.ipl.org/ref/POTUS
http://www.whitehouse.gov/WH/kids/html/kidshome.html

John Marshall

1755-1835

American Patriot and Jurist

Fourth Chief Justice of the Supreme Court

JOHN MARSHALL WAS BORN on September 24, 1755, in Fauquier County, Virginia. His parents were Thomas and Mary Keith Marshall. Thomas was a successful surveyor who also sold land. Mary was a homemaker and mother of 15. John was the oldest in the family.

JOHN MARSHALL GREW UP in the frontier territory, in a log cabin. Very early on, he showed a keen intelligence and fascination with the law. He used to visit the local courts when he was a young man.

JOHN MARSHALL WENT TO SCHOOL at home. He was educated by private tutors. Also, his father had a large library. He encouraged his son to read history and poetry.

THE COMING OF THE REVOLUTIONARY WAR: In the 1760s and 1770s, Britain began to impose taxes on their colonies in the New World. It was part of an effort by English leaders to put the colonies under tighter control, and to pay for the costs of the **FRENCH AND INDIAN WAR**. They charged high taxes on products that people in America needed, like sugar, paper, and tea. Many colonists felt that it was not fair for England to charge them taxes without giving them a say in government.

Some colonists, known as Loyalists, wanted to work out their differences and remain part of England. But many others, known as Patriots, wanted to break away from England and form a new country. Marshall was a firm believer in the Patriot cause.

Marshall as a young man.

In 1775, when he was 20, Marshall joined the 3rd Virginia Regiment, ready to fight in the Revolutionary War. He served first as a lieutenant, then as a captain in the Continental Army. He reported to General **George Washington**, and served bravely at Brandywine, Germantown, and Monmouth. He spent the winter of 1777 to 1778 at Valley Forge, with Washington and the army.

While serving as an officer, Marshall also served as a "judge advocate." In that job, he offered legal support for members of the Army.

STUDYING LAW: In 1780, Marshall began to formally study law. He attended the College of William and Mary and studied under George Wythe. He began to practice law that same year.

A SUCCESSFUL LAWYER: Marshall became a successful lawyer, and practiced in Fauquier County and Richmond. He continued to practice while he served his country in several government positions.

VIRGINIA ASSEMBLY: Marshall served in the Virginia Assembly from 1782 to 1791. When the war ended and the debate over the Constitution began, he became involved in that historical document.

THE U. S. CONSTITUTION: In 1788, Marshall served at the state convention where ratification (approval) of the Constitution was debated. Marshall was a great champion of the Constitution, and spoke eloquently for it. He also made his own political opinions clear.

At that time, the leaders of the new nation were dividing up into two major groups. On one side were the Federalists. Their group included **George Washington**, **John Adams**, **Alexander Hamilton,** and Marshall. The Federalists believed in a strong central government. The other side, known as the Democratic-Republicans, included **Thomas Jefferson**. They believed in the states retaining power, rather than a strong central government.

As a Federalist, Marshall also believed in a strong federal judiciary. The Constitution divides power among three branches. The Executive Branch is made up of the President and the Cabinet. The Legislative Branch, or Congress, is made up of the House of Representatives and the Senate. The Judicial Branch is made up of the U.S. Court system, including the Supreme Court.

The Constitution was ratified by the states, and Marshall went back to life as a lawyer and member of the Virginia Assembly. During this time, George Washington, now President, offered Marshall several positions in his government, including Secretary of State and Minister to France. But Marshall refused. He did serve in the House of Representatives, but only from 1799 to 1800.

SERVING IN THE ADAMS ADMINISTRATION: In 1800 President John Adams offered Marshall the position of Secretary of State. He accepted. He served from June 1800 to March 1801.

In 1801, Adams appointed Marshall to be Chief Justice of the Supreme Court. He would go on to be one of the finest judges in American history.

CHIEF JUSTICE OF THE SUPREME COURT: Marshall served on the Supreme Court for 34 years, longer than almost any other Justice. His impact on the Court and on American law was enormous.

The Supreme Court is made up of nine justices and is headed by the Chief Justice. The Court hears cases involving the Constitution. The justices determine whether laws or decisions made in lower state or federal courts are true to the meaning of the Constitution and the rights it guarantees.

A painting depicting several of the early Chief Justices of the Supreme Court. Marshall is in the middle, on the left.

Marshall took part in more than 1,000 decisions, and he wrote more than 500 opinions. Some of these were the most important cases ever argued before the court.

Marshall's opinions over the years helped to establish several groundbreaking precedents. One of these was the concept of "judicial review." That concept defined the power of the Supreme Court to declare any Congressional action invalid, if the Court ruled it unconstitutional.

Under Marshall, the Court also ruled that it had the power to reverse a decision of a state court. He established the Court as the final authority in disputes between the states and the federal government.

While serving as Chief Justice, Marshall was asked to write a biography of George Washington. Marshall went on to write a five-volume biography of the man he admired so much. It was a great success.

MARRIAGE AND FAMILY: Marshall married Mary Ambler in 1783. They had ten children, but only six lived to be adults. Mary was quite sickly in her later years, and died in 1831. Marshall continued to serve as Chief Justice until 1835. Following a stagecoach accident, his health declined, and he died on July 6, 1835.

HIS LEGACY: John Marshall is considered the most important Chief Justice in history. He helped to create and define the judicial branch of government, as he led the Supreme Court through its early years. The wisdom and sound judgment of his decisions helped determine the powers of the Court, and his influence is evident to this day.

WORLD WIDE WEB SITES:

http://www.lva.lib.va.us/whoweare/marshall.index.htm
http://www.oyez.org/justices/john_marshall
http://www.ushistory.org/valleyforge/served/marshall.html

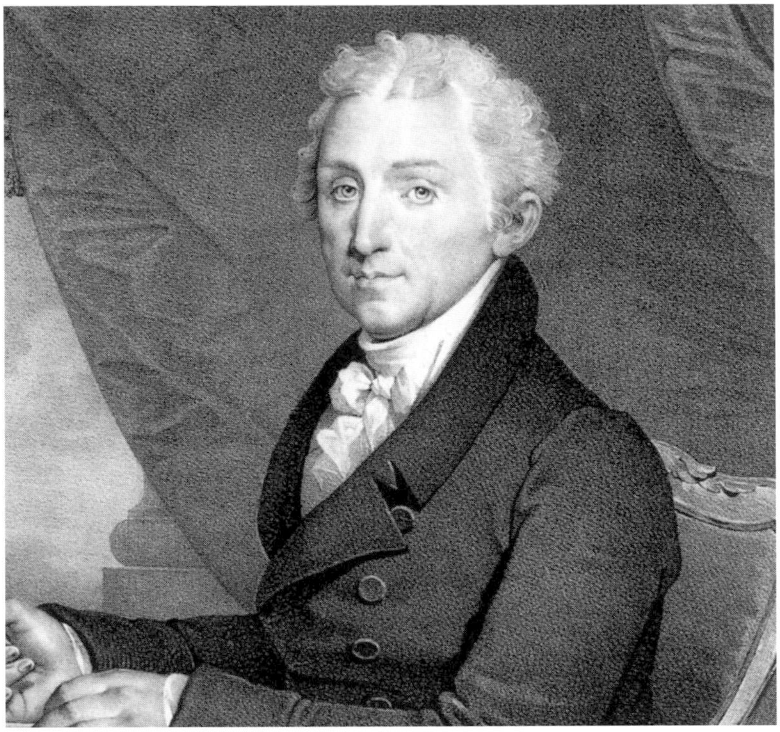

James Monroe

1758-1831

American Patriot and Statesman

Fifth President of the United States

"Last of the Cocked Hats"

JAMES MONROE WAS BORN on April 28, 1758, in Westmoreland County, Virginia. His parents were Spence and Elizabeth Monroe. Spence was a planter and Elizabeth was a homemaker. James was the oldest of five children. He had three brothers and one sister. His brothers' names were Andrew, Spence, and Joseph, and his sister's name was Elizabeth.

JAMES MONROE GREW UP in the country in Virginia. His father had a small farm, and James enjoyed playing in the fields.

JAMES MONROE WENT TO SCHOOL at a private school run by a man named Parson Campbell. James was an excellent student. He did especially well in Latin and math. When James was just 16, he went to the College of William and Mary. But his college years were cut short by the Revolutionary War.

THE REVOLUTIONARY WAR: In the 1770s, most of the area that is now the eastern United States were colonies of England. That means that the people were ruled by England. They paid taxes to the British government and were ruled by a king, George III.

Some of the colonists were happy being part of England. Some were not. They believed that the colonies should have their own government, a government that they controlled. The people who wanted a separate government began to talk about breaking away from England. These were the people who began the American Revolutionary War.

Monroe was just 18 when he left college and joined the army. He fought in several of the major battles in the war. In 1777, he was an aide to one of **George Washington's** generals. Monroe was a brave soldier. In the Battle of Trenton, he was seriously wounded. In 1778, he was given a group of soldiers to command. He was just 20 years old. He served in the army until 1780.

STUDENT OF THOMAS JEFFERSON: In 1780, Monroe began to study law with **Thomas Jefferson.** Jefferson thought his new pupil was very bright and able. He encouraged Monroe to enter politics. Monroe did, and he served his country in many different posts from 1781 to 1825.

ENTERING POLITICS: In 1781, the U.S. defeated the British and became a new, free nation. Monroe became a member of the Virginia legislature. Two years later, he was elected to the Congress of the Confederation. That was the political group that ran the country while the **U.S. CONSTITUTION** was being written.

MARRIAGE AND FAMILY: Monroe met his future wife, Elizabeth Kortright, in 1783, while he was working with the Congress. They fell in love and married in March 1786. They had three children, two girls and a boy. Their daughters were named Eliza and Maria. Their son died when he was a baby.

From 1790 to 1794, Monroe served as the U.S. Senator from Virginia. In 1794, during the presidency of George Washington, he was Minister to France. Two years later, he returned home. He was then elected Governor of Virginia, a post he served in from 1799 to 1802.

Monroe's wife, Elizabeth Monroe.

LIFE AS A DIPLOMAT: In 1803, Monroe's good friend Jefferson was President. Jefferson chose Monroe to go to France and work out the Louisiana Purchase. Monroe had worked in foreign countries before. Working with other heads of government, he developed his ability as a diplomat.

In the Louisiana Purchase, the U.S. bought from France a huge amount of land. The territory ranged from the Mississippi River to the

Rocky Mountains, and from the Canadian border to Texas. The price was $15 million, less than three cents an acre.

Monroe was known as a skilled diplomat. He had done an excellent job for the U.S. The Louisiana Purchase doubled the size of the new country. It also showed Monroe as a man who was hard-working, intelligent, and able.

Jefferson next sent Monroe to England and Spain. There, he worked on treaties between the U.S. and those nations. In 1807, he returned to the U.S. Back in Virginia, he once again served in the legislature and as governor.

In 1811, **President James Madison** chose Monroe to be Secretary of State. As Secretary of State, Monroe advised Madison on how to handle problems with other countries. This was especially important during the War of 1812, when the U.S. went to war against England. England was the major naval power at that time. They would not allow U.S. ships to sail the oceans freely. As the war went on, Madison also made Monroe Secretary of War.

The U.S. won the war in 1814. Monroe, honored by his country as a man of honesty and dedicated service, accepted the urging of his friends and ran for President. In 1816, he was elected.

PRESIDENT OF THE UNITED STATES: President Monroe's first four years were known as the "Era of Good Feeling." It was a time of prosperity in the country.

Monroe had worked in government for a long time when he became President. He had helped form the Democratic-Republican party of Jefferson. But over the years, he had seen a lot of fighting between members of rival political parties. He saw how political

Monroe as President.

rivalries could stop the progress of a nation. As President, he worked for more cooperation between the parties.

Monroe had excellent advisors in his Cabinet. John Quincy Adams, the son of the **John Adams**, was one of the finest. Adams was Monroe's Secretary of State. He worked with Great Britain to settle the border of Canada and the U.S. He signed a treaty with Spain that expanded the border of the southern U.S. He also worked out the purchase of Florida from Spain.

When Monroe ran for reelection in 1820, he won by one of the biggest margins in history. During his second term Monroe developed the policy for which he is best known, the Monroe Doctrine.

THE MONROE DOCTRINE: The Monroe Doctrine stated that the U.S. would not allow European countries to develop colonies in North or South America. The U.S. didn't want Spain, England, or other European nations interfering with the countries of the New World. The Monroe Doctrine was a declaration of freedom for the new nations of the Americas.

MONROVIA: Liberia was an African nation formed in the 1820s as a home for freed slaves. The people of Liberia named their capital, Monrovia, after James Monroe, in 1822.

RETIREMENT FROM POLITICS: In 1825, Monroe retired from politics. After a lifetime given to public service, he returned to his farm in Virginia. There, he spent his last years writing. He had to sell much of his land after his retirement, because his political positions had not paid him very much.

Elizabeth Monroe died in 1830. Soon after, Monroe moved to New York to live with his daughter, Maria. He died there on July 4, 1831, at the age of 73. He shares the death date of July 4 with two other heroes of his era, John Adams and Thomas Jefferson.

HIS LEGACY: As the "last of the cocked hats," Monroe was the last of the Revolutionary War heroes to serve as President of the United States. He is remembered for serving with distinction as a soldier, statesman, and political leader.

WORLD WIDE SITES:

http:www.artcom.com/museums/vs/gl22401-58.htm
http://www.ipl.org/ref/POTUS
http://www.whitehouse.gov/WH/kids/html/kidshome.html

Thomas Paine
1737-1809
English-born American Patriot and Writer
Author of *Common Sense* and Other Works Supporting the American Revolution

THOMAS PAINE WAS BORN on January 29, 1737, in Thetford, England. His parents were Joseph and Mary Paine. His father was a Quaker and made corsets for a living.

THOMAS PAINE WENT TO SCHOOL at a local school for about seven years. At that time, children rarely received even that much education.

APPRENTICESHIP: Thomas's family was poor, and his father needed his help.

So at the age of 13, he left school and began as an apprentice in his father's shop. But he hated the work. Soon, he was planning his escape.

RUNNING AWAY: When he was 16, Thomas ran away from home. He worked as a sailor on a British "privateer." That's a private ship hired to disrupt commercial shipping, usually during war time. This was during the Seven-Year's War between England and France. (It was called the **FRENCH AND INDIAN WAR** in the colonies.) But Thomas didn't like the work, and soon returned home.

RETURN TO ENGLAND AND POVERTY: Paine settled in London, and got work making corsets. He also taught school briefly. Then, Paine got a job as a tax collector. He made very little money at his job. He wrote a letter requesting that he and other tax collectors get a raise. His bosses didn't like it; Paine was fired.

COMING TO THE NEW WORLD: Paine had met the famous **Benjamin Franklin** in London, and Franklin encouraged him to move to America. With Franklin's help, Paine traveled to Philadelphia in November 1774, and found work with a printer, Robert Aiken.

Aiken was the publisher of the *Pennsylvania Magazine*. Soon, Paine was writing essays that were so popular that the number of subscribers grew from 600 to 1,500 in just a few months.

A POWERFUL WRITER: Paine wrote powerful essays in a plain style. In simple but lively language, he made his message known on many major issues of the day. He wrote about the evils of slavery. He also condemned the British policies in the colonies.

COMMON SENSE: In January 1776, Paine published his most influential piece, *Common Sense*. He used his powerful prose to outline the argument for war with Britain. It was a sensation. Soon, there were more than a half a million copies in print in the colonies. Newspapers and magazines published sections, too.

Paine urged a revolutionary way of thinking about government. He believed that governments by kings and a rich aristocracy were corrupt and wrong. That form of government didn't value common people, or grant them power. Paine believed that only independence and a new government was right for Americans.

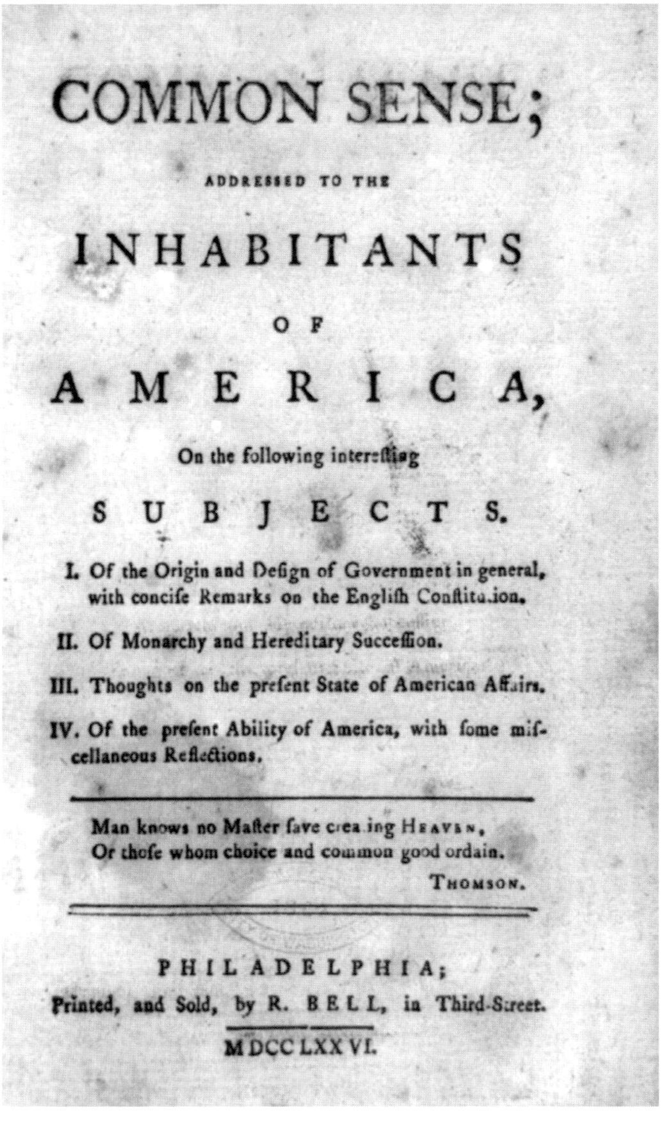
COMMON SENSE;
ADDRESSED TO THE
INHABITANTS
OF
AMERICA,
On the following intereſting
SUBJECTS.
I. Of the Origin and Deſign of Government in general, with conciſe Remarks on the Engliſh Conſtitution.
II. Of Monarchy and Hereditary Succeſſion.
III. Thoughts on the preſent State of American Affairs.
IV. Of the preſent Ability of America, with ſome miſcellaneous Reflections.

Man knows no Maſter ſave creating Heaven,
Or thoſe whom choice and common good ordain.
Thomson.

PHILADELPHIA;
Printed, and Sold, by R. BELL, in Third-Street.
MDCCLXXVI.

THE REVOLUTIONARY WAR: Paine joined the army in July 1776. He served as an aide to **General Nathanael Greene.** He also kept writing, sending news from the war front. Paine was a popular writer, throughout the colonies, among the troops and the generals, too.

THE AMERICAN CRISIS: By the end of 1776, things were looking grim for the American forces. The British had taken New York. **George Washington** was in retreat. Paine was with Washington's troops as they retreated across New Jersey. With all that in mind, he wrote one of the best-known pieces of the era, "The American Crisis, Number 1." It begins:

> "These are the times that try men's souls. The summer soldier and the sunshine patriot will, in this crisis, shrink from the service of their country. But he that stands in now, deserves the love and thanks of man and woman. . . . The harder the conflict, the more glorious the triumph."

Paine's new pamphlet spread throughout the colonies like wildfire. According to another writer of the time, it was "read in every camp." Its first line became a battle cry.

Washington had his troops listen to Paine's new essay on Christmas Eve, 1776. His words rallied the weary troops. Armed with new strength, the army fought on, rowing across the Delaware and surprising the British.

THE AMERICAN'S TRIUMPH: Throughout the war, Paine continued to publish his *Crisis* essays. On the eighth anniversary of the battle of Lexington and Concord, April 19, 1783, he wrote his final *Crisis* piece. In it, he said:

> "'The times that tried men's souls' are over. And the greatest and completest revolution the world ever knew, gloriously and happily accomplished."

In addition to his writing on behalf of the Revolution, Paine also served as a clerk in the Pennsylvania Assembly. In that role, he helped to draft laws of the new state, including a law that abolished slavery.

AFTER THE REVOLUTION: In 1784, Paine moved to New York. The state had given him 300 acres in recognition of his services to the new nation.

Paine had always been interested in science and invention. After the war he tried to develop a smokeless candle and an iron bridge.

RETURN TO EUROPE: Paine left America in 1787, to work on his bridge project. He thought he would be away just one year. But his stay lasted 15 years. Just as he had been a central figure in the American Revolution, so would he be in the French Revolution.

THE FRENCH REVOLUTION: Paine was invited to France by two old friends from the American Revolution, **Marquis de Lafayette** and **Thomas Jefferson.** At that time, France still had a king, Louis XVI. He was famous for his extravagant living. France's rulers were known for being corrupt and neglecting the people. The poor and starving rose up against the king and their rulers.

Paine wrote a vigorous defense of the French Revolution, published in England as *Rights of Man*. He was charged with libel in England and fled to France, where he witnessed the revolution.

The French Revolution had little in common with the American Revolution. A small group of politicians seized control of the government. It became a chaotic blood bath. The new leaders executed members of the monarchy, aristocracy, and their political enemies. Among the thousands killed were King Louis XVI and his wife, Marie Antoinette. Paine was thrown into prison and nearly lost his life, too. **James Monroe**, then America's ambassador to France, arranged his release in 1794.

Paine wrote his next work, *The Age of Reason*, from 1794 to 1795. It was a very controversial work, because he attacked the organized Christian faiths. He believed in God, and that all men were equal in the sight of God. But he rejected many of the ideas of Christianity. Paine lost many followers over the work.

RETURNING TO AMERICA: Paine returned to America in 1802. He was welcomed by **President Thomas Jefferson**, but shunned by other friends from the Revolutionary War.

LAST YEARS: Paine spent his last years on his farm in New York. He died on June 8, 1809.

MARRIAGE AND FAMILY: Paine was married twice. His first wife was named Mary Lambert. They were married in 1759 until Mary's death one year later. Paine married Elizabeth Olive in 1771. They separated in 1774. He had no children.

HIS LEGACY: Thomas Paine's powerful words rallied Americans to the cause of revolution. In *Common Sense*, he outlined their goals, and in *The American Crisis*, he instilled patriotism and fire into weary soldiers and citizens alike. In 1805, **John Adams** said: "I know not whether any man in the world has had more influence on its inhabitants or affairs for the last thirty years than Tom Paine."

WORLD WIDE WEB SITES:

http://www.historyguide.org/intellect/paine.html
http://www.thomaspaine.org/
http://www.ushistory.org/PAINE

Molly Pitcher
(Mary Ludwig Hays McCauley)
1754-1832
American Patriot and Revolutionary War Heroine

MOLLY PITCHER was a nickname given to women who carried water to American forces during the Revolutionary War. Some soldiers drank the water. Others used it to cool off their cannons. Hundreds of different women probably carried water during different battles. The most famous of these women was Mary Ludwig Hays McCauley. She is recognized in the *History of the United States Army* as the person who started the legend of Molly Pitcher.

The woman who became known as Molly Pitcher was born on October 13, 1754, in Pennsylvania. Her name at birth was Mary

Ludwig. When she was born, Pennsylvania was one of 13 American colonies that were ruled by the king of England. Molly's parents, Hans George Ludwig and Anna Margretha Wildt, had come to America from Germany. She had one brother, Martin.

MOLLY PITCHER GREW UP on a small dairy farm. She did not receive much education. As a teenager she was sent to Carlisle, Pennsylvania, to become a servant for a doctor.

FOLLOWING HER HUSBAND TO WAR: On July 24, 1769, Molly married John Casper Hays. He died a short time later. Then Molly married William Hays, who was most likely the brother of her first husband. William worked as a barber.

Around this time, tensions between the American colonies and their English rulers erupted into war. The first shots were fired on April 19, 1775, near Lexington, Massachusetts. On July 4, 1776, leaders of the 13 colonies decided to separate from England and form a new nation. They issued the **DECLARATION OF INDEPENDENCE** to inform the king of their plans. General **George Washington** was chosen to lead the Continental Army into battle against the British forces.

Men throughout the colonies joined the fight for independence. Molly's husband enlisted in the 7th Pennsylvania Regiment of Artillery. When William went off to war, Molly lost her main source of money and protection. Like thousands of other women facing this situation, she became a "camp follower." Molly traveled with her husband's regiment and lived in the army camp. She helped out the soldiers by working as a nurse, cook, and maid.

Pitcher firing a cannon at the Battle of Monmouth, 1778.

THE BATTLE OF MONMOUTH: Molly and her husband spent the hard winter of 1777-78 in Valley Forge with Washington's army. On June 28, 1778, their regiment fought in the Battle of Monmouth in New Jersey.

The battle took place on a very hot day. Molly went out on the field to help the Americans. She carried buckets of water to exhausted troops and cared for wounded soldiers. William's role in the battle was to fire a big cannon. When he collapsed from the heat, Molly took his place. She fired the cannon for the rest of the battle. She kept going even after an enemy musket ball passed between her legs and tore a hole in her skirt. After the battle, General Washington thanked her personally for her service.

RECOGNITION FOR BRAVERY: The Revolutionary War ended when the **TREATY OF PARIS** was signed on September 3, 1783. The treaty recognized the United States of America as an independent nation. Molly gave birth to a son that year, Johanes Ludwig Hays. Sadly, her husband William died a short time later. Molly was eventually married a third time, to John (some sources say George) McCauley. Following his death in 1813, she supported herself by working as a maid and nanny.

On February 21, 1822, the General Assembly of Pennsylvania voted to grant Molly a military pension of $40 per year. A notice in the *American Volunteer* explained that she received the award "for services she rendered during the Revolutionary War. It appeared satisfactorily that this heroine had braved the hardships of the camp and dangers of the field with her husband, who was a soldier of the revolution."

Molly died on January 22, 1832, at her home in Carlisle, Pennsylvania. In 1876—the 100th anniversary of the Declaration of Independence—a special marker was placed on her grave honoring her wartime service.

MOLLY PITCHER'S HOME AND FAMILY: Molly lived in Carlisle, Pennsylvania, for most of her life. She was survived by her son and seven grandchildren.

HER LEGACY: Molly Pitcher is remembered for her courage and loyalty to the cause of the Revolutionary War. She has become a symbol of the spirit that created the nation, and defined its character.

WORLD WIDE WEB SITES:

http://www.archives.gov/publications/prologue/1999/summer/pitcher
http://www.ushistory.org/ValleyForge/youasked/070.htm

Paul Revere
1735-1818
American Patriot and Colonial Craftsman Famous for his "Midnight Ride" to Alert Boston Colonists to the British Invasion

PAUL REVERE WAS BORN on January 1, 1735 in Boston, Massachusetts. His father, Paul Revere Sr., was a French Protestant who came to the New World at the age of 13 to learn the gold and silver trades. He changed his name from "Apollos DeRevoire" to "Paul Revere" so, he said, the "bumpkins could pronounce it easier." Paul's mother was Deborah Hichborn. Paul Jr. was the third of 12 children. The family made their home in the North End section of Boston.

PAUL REVERE WENT TO SCHOOL at the North Grammar School in Boston. At age 12 he began to learn the silversmith trade as an apprentice to his father. It is believed that he also earned extra money by ringing the bells each day at nearby Old North Church.

Paul's father died in 1754. That meant that at the age of 19, he became the main supporter of his family.

LIFE AS A SILVERSMITH: Paul practiced the trade he had learned from his father—working with gold and silver. For more than 40 years his silvershop was the center of his life. He made everything from simple spoons to complicated tea sets. He hired other journeymen and apprentices to help him.

When Revere was 21 years old he volunteered to fight in the **FRENCH AND INDIAN WAR.** After only six months he returned to Boston.

MARRIAGE AND FAMILY: Revere married Sarah Orne in 1757 when he was 22 years old. Together they had eight children. When Sarah died in 1773, Paul married Rachel Walker. They, too, had eight children together.

AMERICAN CRAFTSMAN: Before the American Revolution the country was in an economic depression. Revere began to make extra money by engraving copper plate for printing. He also drew illustrations for books and magazines, business cards, political cartoons, bookplates, and menus for taverns.

Between 1768 and 1775 Revere also advertised himself to be a dentist. He cleaned teeth and wired in false teeth made from walrus ivory or animal teeth.

Revere's home in Boston's North End.

Business records from this period show that Revere's shop was a very active place. As the master of the shop he was responsible for the quality of the work that was produced. He had a steady hand and a good eye for design. He became known as one of America's finest craftsman.

Silver pieces made by Paul Revere, Sr. and Paul Revere, Jr. are marked with the family name (Revere) in a rectangle, or "P.R." in crude capital letters in a rectangle. Some beautiful silver pieces made by the Reveres can still be seen today in museums.

THE COMING OF THE REVOLUTION: In the 1760s and 1770s, Britain began to impose taxes on their colonies in the New World. It was part of an effort by English leaders to put the colonies under tighter control, and to pay for the costs of the French and Indian War. They charged high taxes on products that people in America needed, like sugar, paper, and tea. Many colonists felt that it was not fair for England to charge them taxes without giving them a say in government.

Some colonists, known as Loyalists, wanted to work out their differences and remain part of England. But many others, known as Patriots, wanted to break away from England and form a new country.

AMERICAN PATRIOT: Revere was a fierce Patriot and active in the call for independence. He became a member of several Patriot organizations, including the Committees of Correspondence and the **SONS OF LIBERTY.** Because he was an excellent horseback rider, he rode many miles carrying messages between Patriot groups in Boston, New York, and Philadelphia.

THE BOSTON MASSACRE: On the evening of March 5, 1770, a rumor began to fly around Boston. A British soldier had supposedly struck a young barber's apprentice. Armed only with snowballs and sticks, a group of citizens confronted the soldiers. With **Crispus Attucks** at the head of the crowd, they marched to the Boston Customs House.

The soldiers fired into the crowd. When the smoke cleared, Attucks and three others lay dead. Eventually five men—Attucks, Samuel Gray, James Caldwell, Samuel Maverick, and Patrick Carr—died of their wounds.

The people of Boston were furious. They claimed that Attucks and the other men were martyrs in the cause of independence. **Samuel Adams** called their murder "The Boston Massacre." It became another rallying cry of the patriots. Revere made a famous engraving of the incident. It was circulated throughout the colonies.

TEA ACT: The Tea Act was passed in 1773. The East India Company was a large importer/exporter of tea. The tea was stored in English warehouses and shipped to America. In order to sell more tea to the colonists and help out the East India Company, the British government permitted the company to recover the duties it paid to the government before shipping the tea across the sea. In America, East India could sell the tea at a much reduced price to

Revere's engraving of the Boston Massacre.

the Americans. This allowed them to undersell the colonial tea merchants. The colonists were angry, and took action.

THE BOSTON TEA PARTY: On the evening of December 16, 1773, three tea-laden British ships sitting in Boston Harbor received a surprise visit. Paul Revere and a group of his followers in the Sons of Liberty dressed up like Mohawk Indians in war paint and feathers. They boarded the ships and dumped 342 chests of tea into the water.

The British were furious. They closed the Port of Boston completely. Parliament then passed **THE COERCIVE ACTS**, which angered the colonists even more. The spark that led to the American Revolution was lit.

PAUL REVERE ON HORSEBACK: Revere mounted his horse and rode to New York to tell other members of the Sons of Liberty what had happened in Boston. When the Port of Boston was closed in 1774, he carried the protest and call for help to New York and Philadelphia on horseback. He rode to Philadelphia carrying information about the colonists plan to respond to the Coercive Acts.

Revere was then named the official courier for the Massachusetts Provincial Assembly to Congress. As he rode across the countryside, he became a familiar sight. Soon his name began appearing in newspapers in London.

In December 1774, the British decided to move valuable ammunition from the arsenal at Fort William and Mary in New Hamphire. Revere galloped off to warn the colonial militia. He then rode to Portsmouth to call the New Hampshire Patriots into action. Although Revere didn't take part in the colonists' raid on the Fort, he is given credit for supplying the information that led to the first aggressive act of the colonists against the British in the American Revolution. The powder and gunshot they took from the Fort was later used to protect the Continental soldiers as they retreated at Bunker Hill.

THE RIDE OF PAUL REVERE: On April 16th, 1775, Revere rode to Lexington to warn the patriots to move their military stores from Concord. It was on this ride that he made his plan for alerting the colonial military about the coming of the British troops. If the British were coming by water, two lanterns would be hung in the Old North Church steeple. If they were coming by land, only one lantern would be lit.

Old North Church in Boston, where the lanterns were hung warning of the British invasion, 1775.

Revere's second, most famous, ride to Lexington was on the night of April 18th, 1775. Patriot leader Dr. Joseph Warren sent for Revere, and told him to warn **Samuel Adams** and **John Hancock** that the British were on their way to capture them.

Revere rowed across the Charles River in the dark and then mounted a work horse to reach Lexington to warn Adams and Hancock. Along the way, Revere stopped by each house, warning them of the British soldiers' approach. He then set off to warn the Patriots at Concord.

Revere was joined in his journey by two other riders, William Dawes and Dr. Samuel Prescott. On the way to Concord, they were stopped by British scouts. Prescott and Dawes were released, but the scouts kept Revere for a while, finally letting him go. They kept his horse, however, and Paul had to make his way to Lexington on foot. Even so, he carried a trunk of valuable papers and documents that Hancock and Adams had left behind in their rush to leave.

DURING THE REVOLUTION: Although Revere wanted to fight in the Revolution, he didn't receive a command in the Continental Army right away. He stayed in Boston and began designing and printing the first Continental money. He also designed the first official seal for the colonies and the state seal.

Revere was named a lieutenant colonel in the Massachusetts Artillery. In 1778, he was made commander at Castle Island in Boston Harbor. He took part in expeditions in Rhode Island and Massachusetts. His military career ended with an expedition to Maine.

AFTER THE REVOLUTION: After the war, Revere expanded his business interests. He ran a small hardware store that sold things he had imported from England.

In 1788 he opened a foundry that made the bolts, spikes and nails needed by shipyards. He also made the brass fittings for the

A painting of Revere on his famous midnight ride.

U.S.S. *Constitution,* the first ship built for the U.S. navy in 1794. The foundry produced cannons and cast bells. One of Paul Revere's largest bells still rings in Boston's King's Chapel today.

In 1801, Revere opened the first copper rolling mill in North America. From this mill the copper for the hull of the U.S.S. *Constitution* was made, as was the copper for the dome of the Massachusetts State House.

Revere was active in the Freemason society and held several offices. He also served as the first president of the Massachusetts Charitable Mechanics Association, a group of artisans and businessmen who worked to improve working conditions in their trades.

LAST YEARS: Revere retired in 1811 at the age of 76. He left his copper business to his sons and grandsons. Paul Revere died on

May 10, 1818 of natural causes. He was 83 years old. He was buried in Boston at the Granary Burying Ground.

HIS LEGACY: Paul Revere is remembered as a talented craftsman, an energetic Patriot, and a well-respected leader among the people of Boston. Today there are two famous portraits of him in the Boston Museum of Fine Arts. The finest collection of his silver creations are housed there as well. His home in Boston's North End also receives thousands of visitors each year.

For many years, he was best known to generations of school children for his exploits as described in Henry Wadsworth Longfellow's 1863 poem, "Paul Revere's Ride." Today, as the full story of his patriotism and courage on behalf of the Revolution is better known, his reputation continues to grow.

WORLD WIDE WEB SITES:

http://oncampus.richmond.edu/academics/as/education/projects/webunits/

http://www.paulreverehouse.org/bio/

Betsy Ross
1752-1836
American Patriot and Businesswoman Believed to Be the Person Who Sewed the First American Flag

BETSY ROSS WAS BORN on January 1, 1752, in Philadelphia, Pennsylvania. Her name at birth was Elizabeth Griscom. At the time she was born, Pennsylvania was one of 13 American colonies that were ruled by the king of England. Betsy was the eighth of 17 children born to Samuel and Rebecca Griscom. Her father was a successful carpenter. He helped build a tower to hold the Liberty Bell at Philadelphia's Independence Hall.

BETSY ROSS GREW UP in Philadelphia. Her family belonged to a religious group called the Society of Friends or Quakers. As a child, Betsy was expected to wear plain clothing and follow strict rules.

BETSY ROSS WENT TO SCHOOL in Philadelphia at a school run by the Society of Friends. She learned to read and write and showed a great talent for needlework. When she finished school, Betsy served as an apprentice to a local upholsterer. She learned to do all types of sewing jobs. For example, she made and repaired curtains, bedcovers, tablecloths, rugs, umbrellas, and other fabric items.

During her time at the upholstery shop, Betsy fell in love with a fellow apprentice, John Ross. He was the son of an Episcopalian minister. Betsy's family did not approve of the relationship. Quakers were not allowed to marry people from a different faith. But Betsy wanted to be with the man she loved. On November 4, 1773, she and John ran away together. They crossed the Delaware River and got married in Gloucester, New Jersey. When the Quakers found out, Betsy was kicked out of the church and disowned by her family.

OPENING AN UPHOLSTERY BUSINESS: In 1775 Betsy and her husband opened a sewing shop on Arch Street in Philadelphia. Around this time, tensions between the American colonies and their English rulers erupted into war.

Betsy's business struggled as the war got started. Fabric was in short supply. Her husband decided to join the fight against the British. He enlisted in the Pennsylvania state militia. One night, John Ross stood guard over supplies of gunpowder on a wharf. Some of the gunpowder exploded and he was seriously injured. He died of his wounds on January 21, 1776. After John's death, Betsy supported herself by doing sewing projects for the Continental Army. She made and mended uniforms, tents, blankets, flags, and other items used by the American troops.

SEWING THE STARS AND STRIPES: In the spring of 1776, leaders of the 13 American colonies met in Philadelphia. This group, known as the **SECOND CONTINENTAL CONGRESS**, had important matters to discuss. They had to decide whether the colonies should remain loyal to the king or break away from England and form a new country.

According to legend, three members of the Continental Congress came to Betsy's upholstery shop in late May or early June. They were **George Washington**, commander of the Continental Army; Robert Morris, one of the wealthiest men in America; and George Ross, the uncle of Betsy's dead husband. They told Betsy that the Continental Congress had decided to separate from England and form an independent nation. They asked her to help them create a national flag for the new country.

Before this time, many different flags were used to represent various colonies, militias, and branches of the armed services. Some of these flags looked similar to England's national flag, the Union Jack. In order to avoid confusion and show national pride and unity, the Continental Congress wanted to create a single flag for the United States of America.

As the story goes, Washington showed Ross a sketch of a flag. It had 13 horizontal stripes and thirteen six-pointed stars arranged in a circle. Six-pointed stars were commonly used on British flags. Ross suggested using five-pointed stars instead. She showed the men that they were easy to make. She cut a folded piece of paper into this type of star in one snip. They agreed on a design using five-pointed stars. Then Ross sewed the flag in the back room of her upholstery shop.

On July 4, 1776, the Continental Congress issued the **DECLARATION OF INDEPENDENCE**. This historic document explained the reasons why the American colonies chose to separate from England. It also set out goals of liberty and equality for the new nation. Nearly a year later, on June 14, 1777, the Continental Congress formally adopted the national flag.

LOSING ANOTHER HUSBAND TO WAR: The next day, Betsy Ross married Captain Joseph Ashburn. He served in the Continental Navy during the Revolutionary War. In 1780, Ashburn was first mate on a ship that sailed to the West Indies to get supplies for the American troops. The ship was captured at sea by the British Navy. The crew was sent to prison in England. Ashburn died there on March 3, 1782.

Betsy heard the news of her husband's death from a family friend, John Claypoole. He was a navy man who had been held in the same prison. He and Betsy fell in love. They were married on May 8, 1783. The Revolutionary War officially ended two months later, with the signing of the **TREATY OF PARIS**. This treaty recognized the United States of America as an independent nation.

Claypoole left the navy when the war ended. He took a job with the U.S. Customs House in Philadelphia. He suffered from poor health, though, and died on August 3, 1817. Betsy continued working in her upholstery shop until 1827. Then she turned the

A painting of Ross showing Major Ross and Robert Morris how she cut the stars for the American flag; George Washington sits in a chair on the left.

successful business over to one of her daughters. She died on January 30, 1836, and was buried in Philadelphia.

BECOMING A PART OF HISTORY: For many years after Betsy Ross's death, only a few people knew about her role in creating the American flag. This situation began to change in 1870. One of her grandsons, William Canby, told the story to the Pennsylvania Historical Society. He presented signed statements from Betsy's daughter, granddaughter, and niece as well. They all said that Betsy had often told family members about making the flag.

An article about Betsy Ross sewing the first American flag appeared in *Harper's Monthly* magazine in 1873. The story spread quickly from there. Before long, it was presented as a fact in history textbooks. The house in Philadelphia where Ross supposedly made the flag became a historical landmark in 1887.

There is no written proof that Betsy Ross sewed the original stars and stripes. But there are many small details that support the possibility. Ross knew the members of the Continental Congress who supposedly came to her shop. She was related to George Ross by marriage, and she attended the same church as George Washington. Records show that these men and Betsy Ross were all in Philadelphia in May 1776, so the meeting could have taken place. There is also evidence that Ross had sewn flags before and was known as a flag maker. Finally, one of Ross's friends had a five-pointed star made out of folded paper with the famous upholsterer's signature on it.

Historians have found "that there is no congressional record of any secret flag committee, no official flag resolution until June of the following year, and no mention of Betsy Ross in George Washington's letters," Lindsey Galloway wrote in *U.S. News and World Report.* "But they have also found that no rival flag maker has proved to be as likely a candidate, and no other story accounts for the origins of the distinctive five-pointed stars on Old Glory."

BETSY ROSS'S HOME AND FAMILY: Betsy Ross was married three times. She had seven children. Her marriage to Joseph Ashburn produced two daughters, Zillah and Eliza. She also had five daughters from her marriage to John Claypoole: Clarissa, Susannah, Rachel, Jane, and Harriet. Only five of her children survived to adulthood.

Betsy Ross's house in Philadelphia.

HER LEGACY: Although Ross was never proven to be the creator of the first American flag, she is the legendary figure most often associated with it. For this, she has become an honored historical symbol of the Revolutionary War.

WORLD WIDE WEB SITES:

http://www.ushistory.org/betsy/flaglife.html
http://www.betsyrosshouse.org/hist_woman

Mercy Warren
1728-1814
American Patriot, Writer, and Historian

MERCY WARREN WAS BORN on September 14, 1728, in West Barnstable, Massachusetts. Her name at birth was Mercy Otis. At the time she was born, Massachusetts was one of 13 American colonies that were ruled by the king of England. Mercy's father, James Otis, Sr., was a prosperous lawyer and merchant. Her mother, Mary Allyne Otis, was a homemaker. Mercy was the third-oldest of 13 children in her family.

MERCY WARREN GREW UP in a comfortable home. Her family had lived in Massachusetts for generations. In fact, some of her mother's relatives had arrived on the *Mayflower* with the Pilgrims in 1620.

MERCY WARREN WENT TO SCHOOL at home. Like most other girls of her time, she did not have a formal education. Girls were expected to become wives and mothers. Mercy mostly learned cooking, sewing, good manners, and other skills she would need in these roles.

In the meantime, her two older brothers studied with a tutor. They learned math, science, history, and other subjects to prepare for college. Mercy found this situation unfair. She convinced her brothers' tutor, the Reverend Jonathan Russell, to let her read the books in his large library. Her favorite book was Sir Walter Raleigh's *History of the World.*

Later in her life, Mercy fought to improve educational opportunities for women. In a letter to her friend **Abigail Adams**, she wrote that any "Deficiency [in women's understanding of the world] lies not so much in Inferior Contexture of Female Intellects as in the different Education bestow'd on the Sexes." Mercy believed that women were as smart as men. She argued that educating women would benefit the whole society.

A GATHERINGS OF REVOLUTIONARIES: On November 14, 1754, Mercy married James Warren. He was a successful farmer and merchant. They lived in a large home in Plymouth, Massachusetts.

In 1765 James Warren was elected to the Massachusetts House of Representatives. He and Mercy became friends with many other political leaders and their wives. Their social circle included people like **John and Abigail Adams**, **George and Martha**

Washington, **Thomas Jefferson**, **John Hancock**, and **Patrick Henry**. They often gathered at the Warren home to talk about important issues of the day. "By the Plymouth fireside were many political plans originated, discussed, and digested," Mercy noted.

A big topic of discussion was the growing tension between the American colonies and England. Beginning in 1764, English leaders had tried to put the colonies under tighter control. They charged high taxes on products that people in America needed, like sugar, paper, and tea. Many colonists felt that it was not fair for England to charge them taxes without giving them a say in government. As Mercy's brother, James Otis, Jr., declared: "Taxation without representation is tyranny."

Some colonists, known as Loyalists, wanted to work out their differences and remain part of England. But many others, known as Patriots, wanted to break away from England and form a new country. Mercy and her family were Patriots. They often spoke out against British rule. Their home became a meeting place for the revolutionary group known as the **SONS OF LIBERTY**.

WRITING FOR THE PATRIOT CAUSE: Mercy was a talented writer. She wrote hundreds of letters to her important friends. She also wrote poetry and plays. Mercy used her writing as a way to promote her political views. She tried to convince other people to support the Patriot cause.

In the early 1770s, Mercy wrote two plays that criticized Thomas Hutchinson. He was the colonial governor of Massachusetts. He had been appointed by the King of England. The king wanted Hutchinson to take tighter control over the colony.

Hutchinson's policies made him very unpopular among the Patriots.

Mercy made Hutchinson the villain of her plays *The Adulateur* (1772) and *The Defeat* (1773). She made him and other representatives of the British government seem dishonest and evil. She portrayed the Americans who opposed them as good and brave. Since the plays commented on political events, Mercy did not want anyone to know that she wrote them. She published them anonymously.

WAR: The tensions between England and the American colonies eventually exploded into war. On July 4, 1776, colonial leaders formally decided to separate from England and form a new nation. They issued the **DECLARATION OF INDEPENDENCE** to inform the king of their plans. General **George Washington** was chosen as commander of the Continental Army. James Warren served as the paymaster for Washington's troops. Mercy followed news of the war closely from her home in Plymouth.

The Revolutionary War officially ended on September 3, 1783, when American leaders signed a peace agreement with England. **THE TREATY OF PARIS** recognized the United States as an independent nation. For the next few years, leaders of the new country worked to write the **U.S. CONSTITUTION** and form a government. Many of Mercy's friends were involved in this task. She often wrote them letters to express her opinion.

Mercy believed that most of the power in the new nation should belong to state governments. She felt that the proposed U.S. Constitution gave too much power to the federal or national government. For this reason, she argued that the states should not approve, or "ratify," the Constitution. Mercy explained her views in a pamphlet called *Observations on the New Constitution* (1788). Once again, she published her work anonymously. Many of her prominent friends disagreed with her position. They voted to ratify the Constitution.

In 1790, Mercy published her first book under her own name. It was a collection called *Poems, Dramatic and Miscellaneous.* It included many poems and two new plays, *The Sack of Rome* and *The Ladies of Castille.* Both of these plays had female main characters who took an interest in political events of the day. Like Mercy Warren, these characters were not satisfied with traditional women's roles.

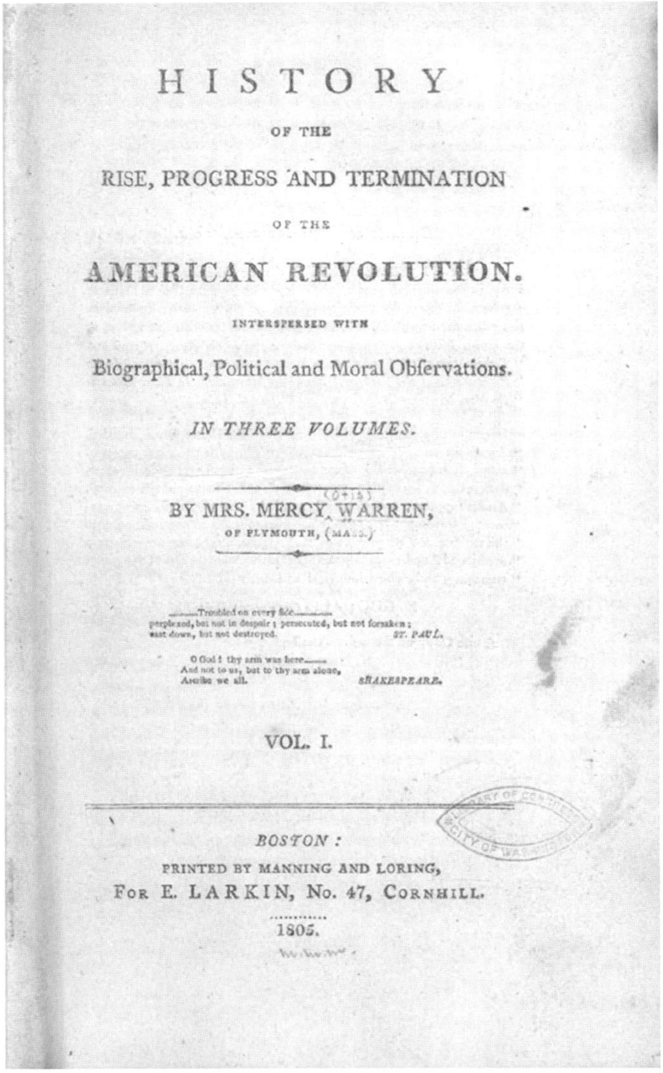
HISTORY

OF THE

RISE, PROGRESS AND TERMINATION

OF THE

AMERICAN REVOLUTION.

INTERSPERSED WITH

Biographical, Political and Moral Obfervations.

IN THREE VOLUMES.

BY MRS. MERCY WARREN,

OF PLYMOUTH, (MASS.)

——Troubled on every fide——
perplexed, but not in despair; persecuted, but not forsaken;
cast down, but not destroyed. *ST. PAUL.*

O God! thy arm was here——
And not to us, but to thy arm alone,
Ascribe we all. *SHAKESPEARE.*

VOL. I.

BOSTON:

PRINTED BY MANNING AND LORING,

FOR E. LARKIN, No. 47, CORNHILL.

1805.

A HISTORY OF THE REVOLUTION: In 1805, Mercy published a three-volume history of the Revolutionary War. It was called *History of the Rise, Progress, and Termination of the American Revolution.* She had worked on the project for 30 years. It gave readers an insider's view of the people and events of this period in history.

In her book, Mercy presented the ideas and goals behind the revolution as a good example for future generations to follow. "If peace and unanimity are cherished, and the equalization of liberty, and the equity and energy of law, maintained by harmony and justice, the present representative government may stand for ages a luminous monument of republican wisdom, virtue and integrity," she wrote. "The principles of the revolution ought ever to be the pole-star of the statesmen, respected by the rising generation."

Mercy's history led to a famous feud between her and John Adams. He was a longtime friend who served as the second president of the United States. Adams did not like the way Mercy described him in the book. They argued about it in 16 different letters. Finally, they stopped speaking to each other. They did not make up for nearly five years.

LATER YEARS: Mercy Warren died on October 19, 1814, at her home in Plymouth. By this time, she was widely considered to be the leading poet and historian of the Patriot cause. Some fans called her the "Conscience of the Revolution." Hundreds of the letters she exchanged with important people were published after her death.

MERCY WARREN'S HOME AND FAMILY: Mercy Warren and her husband had five sons: James, Winslow, Charles, Henry, and George.

HER LEGACY: According to Doris Weatherford in *American Women's History,* Mercy Otis Warren's written works "provide historians with interesting details and insightful commentary on the founding of the nation by one whose gender excluded her from the direct participation that she doubtless would have preferred." In

2002, Mercy was inducted into the National Women's Hall of Fame in Seneca Falls, New York.

WORLD WIDE WEB SITES:

http://www.masshist.org/bh/mercybio.html
http://www.pinn.net/~sunshine/whm2002/warren.html
http://www.samizdat.com/warren/generalintroduction.html

George Washington

1732-1799

American Patriot, Military Leader, and Statesman
Commander-in-Chief of the Continental Army
First President of the United States
"The Father of His Country"

GEORGE WASHINGTON WAS BORN on February 22, 1732, in Westmoreland County, Virginia. His father was Augustine Washington and his mother was Mary Washington. Augustine was a planter and Mary was a homemaker. George was the oldest of six children. He had two sisters, Elizabeth and Mildred, and three brothers, Samuel, John, and Charles. Augustine Washington also had children from an earlier marriage. His first wife, Jane Washington, died in 1728.

George had two half-brothers, Lawrence and Augustine, from that first marriage.

GEORGE WASHINGTON GREW UP on the family farm, called Ferry Farm. Augustine Washington owned a plantation that was worked by slaves. When George was seven, his family moved to a larger farm, called Mount Vernon. George loved the outdoors and especially riding his pony.

When George was just 11 years old, his father died. Soon after, his half-brother Lawrence married and became head of the plantation at Mount Vernon. George lived with his mother and sisters and brothers at Ferry Farm.

George spent a lot of time at Mount Vernon visiting Lawrence. Lawrence was in many ways like a father to George. He taught him to hunt and fish.

GEORGE WASHINGTON WENT TO SCHOOL at a local school. His teacher was a minister who taught George how to read, write, and add. George only went to school for a few years, and he never went to college. He almost joined the Navy when he was just 14. But his mother was against it. Instead, George began to work when he was 16.

BECOMING A SURVEYOR: George Washington's first job was as a surveyor. A surveyor measures land for governments and for land owners to determine the boundaries of properties. As a surveyor, Washington got a chance to travel and see the country.

Washington's first job was to survey land in the western part of Virginia. He enjoyed this work for several years. But his life

Washington as a surveyor.

changed again when he was 20 and his half-brother Lawrence died. He had been very close to Lawrence and he felt his loss deeply. A year after Lawrence died, Washington decided to become a soldier.

LIFE AS A SOLDIER: When George Washington was growing up, the United States did not yet exist. Instead, several European countries controlled parts of what is now the U.S. In the 1750s, when Washington became a soldier, the British and French were fighting over who controlled areas in what is now Ohio and Pennsylvania.

FRENCH AND INDIAN WAR: By the mid-1700s, most of the colonies in the New World were under British rule. However, there were also areas that were claimed by France, and also areas where Native American populations continued to fight British settlers and refused to acknowledge British control. The British fought several wars in order to claim the territory. The most important of these was the French and Indian War (1754-1763).

In 1754, France controlled a huge amount of land, from Quebec to New Orleans. It included most of the land west of the Appalachian Mountains to the Mississippi River. They also had forged partnerships with the Native American tribes in the Great Lakes region and Canada. The French built a series of forts, designed to limit the British movement into the area. At that time, Britain controlled the colonies stretching from Maine to Georgia, reaching inland from the Atlantic coast to the Appalachians.

As part of an army of volunteers from Virginia, George Washington fought for the British against the French. He was a brave man, especially in a battle in what is now Pittsburgh. Twice his horse was shot out from under him. He found four holes in his coat where bullets had gone through the cloth.

The British finally defeated the French, and in 1763, the Peace of Paris was signed, ending the War. Canada and all of North America east of the Mississippi River became British territory.

LIFE AS A PLANTER: In the 1760s, Washington gave up his life as a soldier and returned to Virginia. He took over Mount Vernon and became a planter. He grew tobacco, corn, and wheat.

Washington's lands were worked by slaves. After he and his wife died, all of Washington's slaves were made free.

This famous painting shows Washington crossing the Delaware River to New Jersey, December 25, 1776.

MARRIAGE AND FAMILY: George and Martha Washington married on January 6, 1759, after he had returned to Mount Vernon to become a planter. Martha had been married before but her first husband died. She had two children named John and Martha.

George and Martha never had children of their own. Washington always loved his stepchildren. He treated Martha, whose nickname was Patsy, and John, whose nickname was Jackie, as if they were his own. Sadly, Patsy died when she was just a teenager. Jackie died while serving in the Revolutionary War. Despite their losses, George and Martha were a happy, loving couple.

THE REVOLUTIONARY WAR: In the 1770s, most of the area that is now the eastern United States was a colony of England. That means that the people were ruled by England. They paid taxes to the British government and were ruled by a king, George III.

Some of the colonists were happy being part of England. Some were not. They believed that the colonies should have their own government, a government that they controlled. The people who wanted a separate government began to talk about breaking away from England. These were the people who began the American Revolutionary War.

Washington was a Patriot, and served as a delegate to the First and Second Continental Congresses. On May 10, 1775, delegates met in Philadelphia. **John Hancock** was elected president. The members had to respond to the news from Lexington and Concord. British and American soldiers had met in two battles, and there were deaths on both sides. The same day the Congress had its first meeting, **Ethan Allen** and **Benedict Arnold** took the British Fort Ticonderoga.

The Continental Congress voted to go to war with the British. **John Adams** recommended Washington as commander-in-chief of the army on June 15.

COMMANDER IN CHIEF OF THE ARMY: Washington took control of the Continental Army in July 1775 in New York. He found a group of untrained soldiers and officers. There was much to do to prepare them for war. Also, the Continental Congress continued to interfere with his decisions. In one case, they forced him to defend a position in New York that resulted in defeat and retreat.

Washington retreated with his men through New Jersey and Pennsylvania. On the night of December 25, 1776, Washington and

Washington during the harsh winter at Valley Forge, praying for his troops.

his men boarded boats and crossed the Delaware River. They surrounded the British at Trenton, and defeated them. Next, he defeated the British at Princeton, in January 1777.

Washington's next battles, at Brandywine and Germantown, ended in defeat. This was followed by the winter at Valley Forge, from late 1777 to early 1778.The outlook was bleak for the young nation. Washington's men, 11,000 in all, were tired, hungry, and close to despair. Congress hadn't sent the money for the soldiers' food, clothing, and weapons.

Some 3,000 of the soldiers had no shoes. Many died of starvation. Horses and oxen died of starvation, too. When that happened, the men had to pull the wagons themselves. Over 2,000 of the soldiers deserted that winter.

It was up to Washington to lift the mens' spirits and inspire them to continue the fight for independence. Washington was helped in his task by several European volunteers, especially **The Marquis de Lafayette**. He joined the fight for independence and offered supplies to the army, which he paid for himself. Another volunteer, Baron von Steuben, helped to drill the soldiers and ready them for battle.

The soldiers' devotion to Washington, and to the cause of independence got them through this bleak time. But at last, there was good news. France had agreed to recognize the new nation, and send soldier, weapons, and supplies.

Washington as President.

The war moved to the south, and Washington brought his forces to Yorktown, Virginia, for a final confrontation. The combined American and French forces on land and on sea, 16,000 in all, trapped

British General Charles Cornwallis at Yorktown. On October 19, 1781, Cornwallis surrendered. He and 7,247 soldiers laid down their arms. Washington had proved an able commander-in-chief.

THE NEW UNITED STATES: Washington retired to Mount Vernon for several years. But soon, he was being asked to serve his country again. In 1787, he was named president of the **CONSTITUTIONAL CONVENTION**. Over the next two years, he worked hard to help create, then to ratify the new Constitution.

FIRST PRESIDENT: Washington never wanted to be President. He said that he "had no wish but that of living and dying an honest man on my own farm." But, as before, he ran for the office for the good of his country, and won.

THE NATION'S CAPITAL CHANGES LOCATION: At the time Washington became president, New York City was the capital of the nation. So as the first President, he served from New York City. The next year, Washington and his wife, Martha, moved to Philadelphia, the new capital of the nation. Wherever they lived, Martha was known as a warm and gracious First Lady.

THE EARLY YEARS OF THE NEW NATION: In the early years of the country, many problems had to be discussed and decisions had to be made. Some people were afraid that the new government would grow too strong. It would become too powerful and individuals would lose their rights.

The country was growing. There were 13 states originally, and by the time Washington left office there were 18. What should the governments of each state be like? France was at war. Should the

U.S. get involved? These and many other problems had to be decided by the new government.

Washington gave his advice on these and many issues. He was always a man of honesty and people valued his thoughts. Washington also created the first "Cabinet." The Cabinet is a group of advisors who help the president make decisions. Washington chose great patriots like **Thomas Jefferson** to be in that first Cabinet.

In 1791, Congress established the District of Columbia as the nation's capital. It was named in honor of our first president: Washington, D.C. Washington laid the cornerstone for the U.S. Capitol building in 1793.

Presidents are elected to terms that last four years. At the end of his first term, Washington was ready to retire to Mount Vernon. But the country still wanted him as President. So, reluctantly, he ran again. He was reelected by an overwhelming majority of votes and stayed another four years. Finally, in 1797, Washington stepped down. He began the tradition of a President voluntarily retiring after two terms. That tradition was continued until President Franklin D. Roosevelt ran for a third and fourth term in 1940 and 1944.

RETIREMENT TO MOUNT VERNON: Washington was happy to retire from office. He was eager to return to Mount Vernon and to his life as a planter.

But his retirement lasted only two years. In December 1799, Washington went out on his farm on a cold, rainy day. He became very ill and couldn't swallow or breathe. Martha was at his side when he died on December 17, 1799.

The country mourned the death of their first President. General Henry Lee spoke to the Congress at Washington's death. He called him "First in war, first in peace, and first in the hearts of his countrymen."

HIS LEGACY: Washington was one of the most important figures of the Revolutionary War and early American history. He was a man of great integrity, honesty, and loyalty. He served his country faithfully, and never for personal gain. He was beloved by citizens, and by the other leaders of the new nation. Their respect for his wisdom and leadership was unequaled.

WORLD WIDE WEB SITES:

http://www.ipl.org/ref/POTUS
http://www.mountvernon.org
http://www.nps.gov/gewa/index.htm
http://www.whitehouse.gov/WH/kids/html/kidshome.html

Martha Washington
1732-1802
American Patriot and First Lady

MARTHA WASHINGTON WAS BORN on June 2, 1732, in New Kent County, Virginia. Her name at birth was Martha Dandridge. At the time she was born, Virginia was one of 13 American colonies that were ruled by the king of England. Martha's parents were John Dandridge and Frances Jones Dandridge. She was the oldest of their eight children. Martha had three brothers, John, William, and Bartholomew, and four sisters, Anna Maria, Frances, Elizabeth, and Mary.

MARTHA WASHINGTON GREW UP at Chestnut Grove, her family's plantation near Williamsburg, Virginia. She enjoyed gardening, horseback riding, and dancing.

MARTHA WASHINGTON WENT TO SCHOOL at home and at a neighboring plantation. Like other girls of this era, she mostly learned domestic skills like sewing and cooking. But her father also provided her with some formal education. Martha studied reading, writing, and math. She also developed a strong knowledge of farming and animals.

A WEALTHY WIDOW: In 1750, Martha married Daniel Parke Custis. He was a wealthy plantation owner. They lived in a mansion called White House on the Pumunkey River. Martha gave birth to four children over the next five years. Sadly, two of her children died at a young age. In 1757, Martha's husband died as well. He left a large fortune to his wife and two surviving children. They owned 17,000 acres of land that was used to grow tobacco.

MARRYING GEORGE WASHINGTON: On January 6, 1759, Martha married Colonel George Washington. He had become famous as the commander of Virginia troops in the **FRENCH AND INDIAN WAR.** She and the children went to live at his Virginia estate, called Mount Vernon. For the next few years, Martha enjoyed a peaceful existence. She spent her time taking care of her home and family.

Around 1764, relations between England and the American colonies grew strained. British rulers tried to take tighter control over the colonies. They charged high taxes on products the colonists needed, like sugar, tea, and paper. Many colonists became angry and refused to buy these products. Some suggested that the American colonies should break away from England and form a new country.

Americans who wanted to separate from England were called Patriots. Those who wanted to remain part of England and settle their differences were called Loyalists. George Washington was a Patriot. He thought the colonies might have to fight for independence. He began recruiting and training armed forces in Virginia. Martha had mixed feelings, but she supported her husband.

THE COMING OF WAR: As George Washington expected, the tensions between the American colonies and England erupted into war. He met with the **CONTINENTAL CONGRESS**. They decided to separate from England and create a new nation. On July 4, 1776, they issued the **DECLARATION OF INDEPENDENCE** to inform the king of their plans.

The Continental Congress named George Washington as the commander of the American military forces. Martha was not pleased that her husband was chosen to lead the Continental Army. She knew that it was a dangerous job that would keep him far from home. But once again, she supported him. "I am still determined to be cheerful and happy, in whatever situation may be," she wrote to a friend. "For I have also learned from experience that the greater part of our happiness or misery depends upon our dispositions, and not upon our circumstances."

During the Revolutionary War, Martha spent lots of time at army headquarters. She joined her husband in Massachusetts in 1775, New York in 1776, and New Jersey in 1777. She even spent the harsh winter of 1778 with the troops at Valley Forge. She cared for the soldiers and helped keep their spirits up. She even led a campaign to get other military wives to volunteer to help the army.

SERVES AS FIRST LADY: After eight years of fighting, George Washington's army defeated the British. The Revolutionary War officially ended on September 3, 1783, when both sides signed the

TREATY OF PARIS. This agreement recognized the United States of America as an independent nation. With the war over, George Washington resigned from the army and went home to Mount Vernon. Martha looked forward to resuming their peaceful life on the plantation.

In the meantime, American leaders worked to create the **CONSTITUTION** and form a government. They elected George Washington to serve as the first President of the United States. Washington felt that he could not turn down such an important honor. Martha accepted his decision. "I cannot blame him for having acted according to his ideas of duty in obeying the voice of his country," she wrote.

George Washington took office on April 30, 1789. Martha stepped into her new role as the President's wife. The job kept her very busy. She often found it overwhelming. Martha recognized that "many younger and gayer women would be extremely pleased" in her position. But she valued her privacy and did not like being in the public spotlight.

Even though she did not enjoy being the First Lady, Martha did her best for her husband and country. She served as the hostess of countless dinners, parties, and receptions. Critics claimed that her style of entertaining was too formal. But many people felt that Martha represented the new government well. They said that her warm hospitality made everyone feel welcome at official functions.

PROTECTS HER PRIVACY: After eight years in office, George Washington retired from public life. Martha was relieved and grateful to return to Mount Vernon with her husband. George died on December 14, 1799. In his will, he made arrangements to free all

Martha and George Washington with their children at Mount Vernon.

the African-American slaves who worked on the plantation. Martha carried out his wishes in 1800.

Martha died on May 22, 1802. During the last few weeks of her life, she burned all the letters that she and George had written to each other over the years. Many prominent people from this era saved their letters for future generations. But Martha never enjoyed public attention. Historians think that she destroyed the letters in one final attempt to protect her family's privacy.

MARTHA WASHINGTON'S HOME AND FAMILY: Martha Washington had four children from her marriage to Daniel Parke Custis. They were Daniel, Frances, John (known as Jacky), and Martha (known as Patsy). Daniel and Frances both died in childhood, and

Patsy died as a teenager. Jacky was married with children of his own when he died in 1781. During her time as First Lady, Martha helped raise her two youngest grandchildren, Eleanor Parke Custis (known as Nelly) and George Washington Parke Custis (known as Wash).

HER LEGACY: Martha Washington is remembered as a woman devoted to her country, and to the spirit of public service represented by her husband, George Washington.

WORLD WIDE WEB SITES:

http://www.whitehouse.gov/history/firstladies/mw1.html
http://www.firstladies.org/biographies/firstladies.aspx?biography=1
http://www.ushistory.org/ValleyForge/served/martha.html

Phillis Wheatley

1753?-1784

African-American Patriot and Poet

Created Religious and Patriotic Poetry

PHILLIS WHEATLEY WAS BORN around 1753 in Gambia, Africa. No one is sure of her exact birth date or her original name. When she was around seven years old, she was captured from her African home and sold into slavery. She was brought by a slave ship called *Phillis* to Boston. There, she was bought by John and Susannah Wheatley on July 11, 1761. They named her Phillis Wheatley.

PHILLIS WHEATLEY GREW UP in the Wheatley home. She was supposed to be a servant, but she was often in poor health. She was very intelligent, and learned English very quickly.

LEARNING TO READ AND WRITE: The Wheatleys discovered Phillis writing on a wall with chalk. They encouraged her to devote herself to learning. They taught her to read and write, and she thrived. She learned several languages, including Latin and Greek. She studied theology—the study of religion—and literature. She especially loved poetry.

STARTING TO WRITE POETRY: Soon Phillis began to write poetry of her own. One of her poems was published in 1767, in a Rhode Island newspaper. It was called "On Messrs. Hussey and Coffin."

Wheatley liked to write a form of poetry called an "elegy." An elegy is a poem celebrating the life and works of an individual, usually written at the individual's death. Wheatley showed her deep Christian faith and her admiration for Colonial leaders in these poems. They made her a very popular poet. Some of her work appeared as broadsides and were widely read.

Wheatley attended services at the Old South Church in Boston. When her minister, Joseph Sewall, died in 1769, she wrote an elegy commemorating his life. It was admired by many Bostonians.

In 1770, she published her most famous elegy, "On the Death of Mr. George Whitefield." Whitefield was an English minister who was well known in Colonial America. Wheatley's poem was read and celebrated in Boston and London. It caught the attention of a wealthy English admirer, the Countess of Huntingdon.

A TRIP TO LONDON: Wheatley sailed to England in 1773, hoping to meet the Countess. Although they were unable to meet, the Countess provided the money to publish Wheatley's first book of poetry.

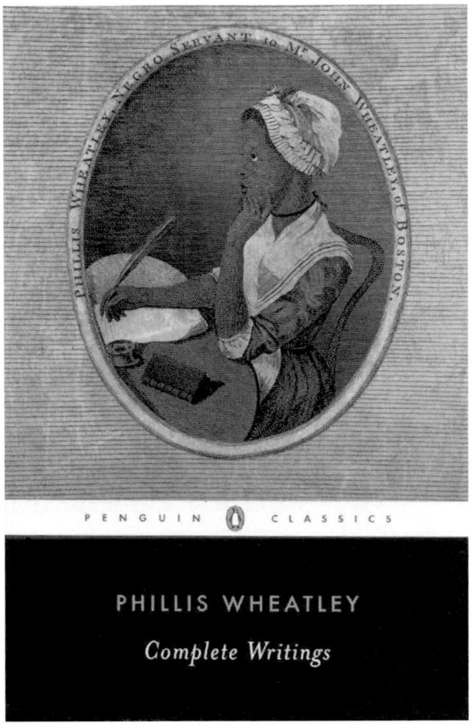

PUBLISHING HER BOOK: Wheatley's first book, *Poems on Various Subjects, Religious and Moral,* was published in 1773. It was the first book ever published by an African-American. And it was only the second book of poetry ever published by an American woman. (The first was by Anne Bradstreet, an earlier Colonial American.)

BECOMING A FREE WOMAN: When Phillis returned from England, the Wheatleys freed her. She was a free woman at last.

Wheatley continued to write poems. In 1776, the colonies declared war against England. Wheatley wrote a poem dedicated to General **George Washington**. He praised her verse and her support of the Revolutionary War. He also invited her to meet him. They did meet in 1776. Wheatley's poem on Washington was printed and distributed during the war, rallying Americans to the cause.

Wheatley was a strong supporter of the cause of independence, and liberty for all people. She also believed that slavery was a curse that Colonial Americans must confront. In one poem, she states that white people cannot "hope to find/Divine acceptance with th'Almighty mind" when "they disgrace/And hold in bondage Afric's blameless race."

Wheatley's letters also reveal her hatred of slavery. In a letter to a friend, she wrote: "In every human Breast, God has implanted a Principle, which we call Love of Freedom. It is impatient of Oppression, and pants for Deliverance."

Wheatley's last known poem was published in 1784, the year of her death. It was called "Liberty and Peace." In it, she celebrates the victory of the Revolution. She tried to find subscribers to pay for the publication of another collection of her poems, but died before she could find enough supporters. Tragically, her final manuscripts were never found.

PHILLIS WHEATLEY'S HOME AND FAMILY: Wheatley married John Peters in 1778. He was a free black man. He had a business, but it failed. The family struggled in poverty for several years. Phillis had to find work as a servant. She had three children, but, tragically, all died. Phillis Wheatley died on December 5, 1784, around the age of 30.

HER LEGACY: Wheatley is honored as the first African-American to publish a book in the U.S. Her poetry was admired for its religious and patriotic themes. She was a woman of great intelligence and poetic gifts. She used those gifts to praise God, and also to promote freedom for all.

WORLD WIDE WEB SITES:

http://americanslibrary.gov/cgi-bin/page.cgi/jb/revolut/poetslave_
http://www.pbs.org/wgbh/aia/part2/2p12/html

Symbols of the Revolutionary War

There are several symbols that are associated with the Revolutionary War, and most of them are patriotic. Their history is fascinating and tells us much about the new nation as it came into being. Symbols help people, and nations, to define themselves and to create a sense of shared identity and meaning.

The American Flag

Before the first official flag of the United States was created in 1777, the soldiers of the Continental Army carried flags representing their own colonies. Some of these became famous symbols of the revolution. One of these featured a rattlesnake and the words, "Don't Tread on Me" and was carried by soldiers from Virginia and Pennsylvania.

The very first official flag of the new United States had 13 stars and 13 stripes. The 13 stars were white, placed in a circle, on a blue field. The 13 stripes were red and white, placed in an alternating pattern.

The number "13" represented the 13 colonies. Although there is no record that states exactly what the colors mean, over the years Americans have developed traditional meanings for them. According to tradition, red stands for courage, blue for loyalty and justice, and white for liberty and purity. Also according to tradi-

Betsy Ross displays the first American flag to George Washington.

tion, it was **Betsy Ross** who sewed the first flag. While that has never been proven, she is always associated with it.

George Washington said this about the flag's symbols:

> "We take the stars from heaven, and the red from our Mother Country, separating it by white stripes, thus showing that we have separated from her, and the white stripes shall go down to posterity representing liberty."

Congress approved the first flag on June 14, 1777. This is what they wrote:

> "Resolved: that the flag of the United States be thirteen stripes, alternate red and white; that the union be thirteen stars, white in a blue field, representing a new constellation."

June 14, the date the flag was approved, is now celebrated as Flag Day.

The Eagle

In 1782, Congress declared the American bald eagle to be the national bird. Throughout history, eagles have been symbols of strength and courage. When the Congress was debating which bird to choose to represent the new nation, **Ben Franklin** nominated the wild turkey. He said that the eagle, because it steals food from other bird's nests, was "a bird of bad character." Instead, he stated that the turkey was "more respectable." But the eagle carried the day, and now appears on coins, dollar bills, stamps, and in pictures, a symbol of a proud nation.

It is interesting to note that the eagle is not really "bald," as in having no hair. Instead, it comes from the word "piebald," meaning "white."

The Liberty Bell

One of the great symbols of freedom in the U.S. is the Liberty Bell. It was commissioned by the Pennsylvania Assembly in 1751 to celebrate the 50th anniversary of **WILLIAM PENN'S** "Charter of Privileges." That list of laws and rules outlined the goals of the Quaker colony.

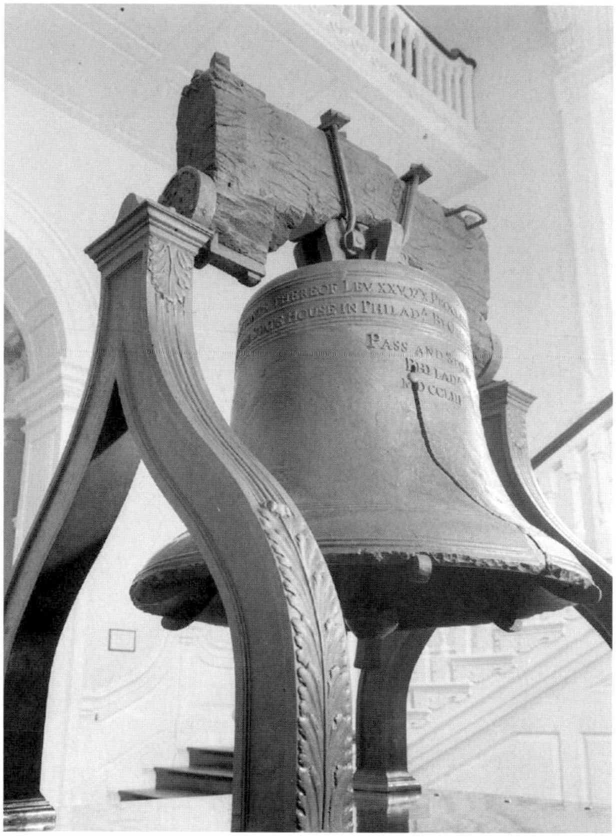

The bell was made in England and was hung in the tower of the State House on June 7, 1752. It cracked soon after it was installed in Philadelphia. A new bell was cast in 1753, using the original bell's metal.

The inscription is taken from the Bible. It states, simply and profoundly, the beliefs of the Quakers: "Proclaim liberty throughout all the land unto all the inhabitants thereof."

The Liberty Bell was rung throughout the years leading up to the Revolution. In 1765, it tolled to mark the hated **STAMP ACT**, and in 1767 to announce meetings resisting the **TOWNSHEND DUTIES**. In 1773, it was rung to bring the citizens to a meeting on the **TEA ACT**.

After the battles at Lexington and Concord, the great bell rang again, rallying the colonists of Philadelphia to the news of war. The great bell was rung on July 8, 1776, to celebrate the **DECLARATION OF INDEPENDENCE**. On that day, the Declaration was read aloud to the people of Philadelphia. As the British approached Philadelphia in 1777, the Liberty Bell was taken to Allentown, Pennsylvania for safe keeping.

The figure above has a Liberty Cap on her spear.

A small crack appeared on the bell after it was rung to celebrate **George Washington's** birthday in February 1835, and the death of **John Marshall** that same year. In 1846, it developed a more serious crack, as it was rung once again to celebrate Washington. It hasn't been rung since then, but still symbolizes the concept of liberty for Americans.

The Liberty Cap

Although it's rarely seen today, the Liberty Cap was a very popular symbol in colonial times. It was based on a cap worn in ancient Greece, sometimes called a "Phrygian" (FRIG-ee-en) cap. It was often shown in colonial art atop a **Liberty Pole** (see below). It was also often shown in the hand of a woman, a symbol of purity and freedom in colonial times. She often holds a shield or sword, and together these symbols represent the justness of the cause of the Revolution.

This is the Liberty Tree in Boston,
site of the August 1765 protest of the Stamp Act.

The Liberty Tree and the Liberty Pole

"Liberty Trees" and "Liberty Poles" were symbols of resistance to British rule and the colonists' commitment to freedom. The tree as a symbol of liberty has a long history. There is a legend that in 1687 colonial settlers in Connecticut hid their charter in an oak tree to protect it from the royal governor. This became known as the "Charter Oak," an early symbol of liberty and freedom for the colonists.

But the most famous Liberty Tree is from colonial Boston, at the time of the **STAMP ACT**. On August 14, 1765, a group of colonists (who later became the **SONS OF LIBERTY**) hung an effigy (a dummy) of Andrew Oliver from an elm tree in front of the home of Dean Elliott. Oliver was the collector of the hated Stamp Tax. The effigy was a warning to Oliver, and to the British, that the colonists wouldn't stand for the tax.

The effigy caused a sensation. A crowd gathered, and they paraded the effigy throughout Boston, set it on fire, and destroyed Andrew Oliver's stamp office. The next day, Oliver resigned.

The elm tree where the effigy was hung became a gathering place for the colonists. On September 11, 1765, the Sons of Liberty met beneath the tree, and placed a copper plate inscribed, "The Tree of Liberty." It became a center for Boston's colonial Patriots. They gathered under the tree throughout the years leading up to the Revolutionary War. When Parliament announced the Townshend Duties in 1767, tax men were once again hung in effigy in its branches. August 14th became an annual holiday, with Patriots marching from the Liberty Tree to a local tavern to celebrate.

Soon, Liberty Trees began appearing all over New England, then spread to the southern colonies. Liberty Trees began to appear on colonial flags. It became one of the most enduring symbols of revolutionary fervor in America.

The Liberty Pole's history is linked to New York City. It was a tall pole made of wood, and was put up by town leaders to celebrate the repeal of the Stamp Act. They placed the pole in front of the British soldiers' barracks. The Patriots of New York used it as a meeting place. A group of British soldiers cut it down in August 1766. The colonists raised a new one the very next day. This happened several times over the years leading up to the Revolution. Sometimes there was violence at the site of pole, leading to injury and death.

One of the worst acts of violence occurred in January 1770. British soldiers blew up the Liberty Pole, and the town erupted

Colonists putting up a Liberty Pole.

into violence. Soldiers and civilians fought for several days. When the fighting was over, the British forbade the colonists to raise another Liberty Pole.

In defiance, another Pole was raised, this time on private land. It became another rallying place for the Patriots. News of the Liberty Pole spread throughout the colonies. Other colonists raised new Poles, to the new cry of Liberty. They were especially popular in the area around New York City, in Connecticut, and New Jersey. In New England, they were sometimes raised next to a Liberty Tree, uniting the symbols of liberty and defiance.

Yankee Doodle

Another famous symbol of the Revolutionary War is Yankee Doodle. We know him from the song in which he appears:

"Yankee Doodle came to town
Riding on a pony,
Stuck a feather in his cap
And called it macaroni."

No one is quite sure about the origin of this mythic figure. But by the time of the American Revolution, he was quite well known as a spirit of freedom throughout the colonies. It's possible that he appeared for the first time in a song written by an Englishman named Richard Shuckburgh. He was a doctor who served in the **FRENCH AND INDIAN WAR** and lived in New York.

"Yankee Doodle" might have been written around 1760, and it might have been written to mock the "Yankee," or colonial soldiers. The British soldiers were more trained, and more proper, than their fellow troops. So Shuckburgh created the words that describe "Yankee Doodle," as a kind of country bumpkin. He took the tune from an old English song called "Fisher's Jig."

The song was immediately popular. Colonists liked it, and so did the British. In fact, it was played by British troops sent to America to clamp down on the unruly Patriots. The British sang it to make fun of the colonists.

The English fife and drum corps played it as the troops marched to Concord on April 19, 1775. After they were defeated, the British wearily retreated back to Boston. As they walked, a Patriot asked the commander "how he liked the tune now."

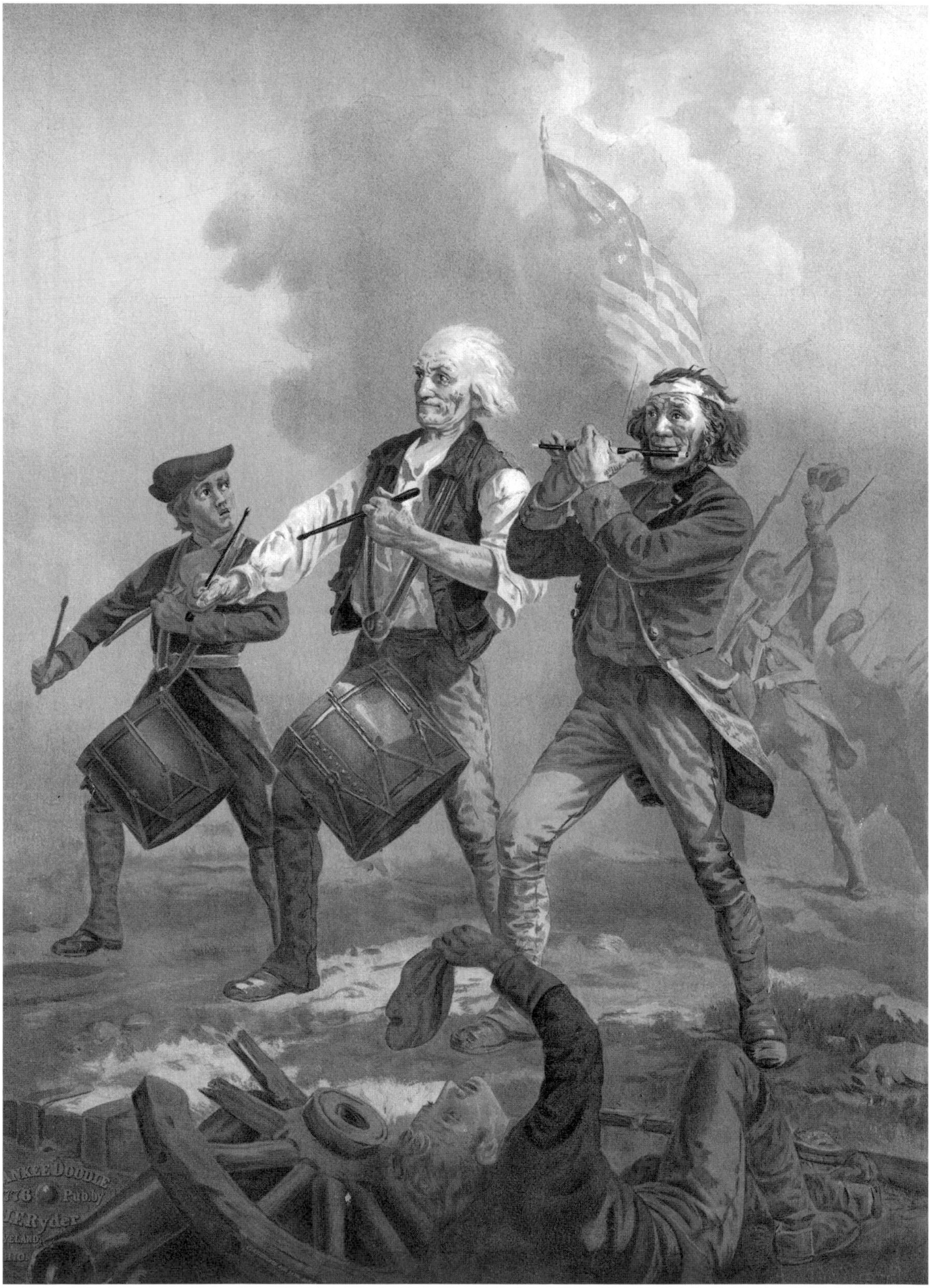
ANKEE DOODLE
776 Pub.by
J.F.Ryder
VELAND,
HIO.

Throughout the Revolutionary War, people made up many verses to the tune. Some were about war heroes, including **George Washington**. But they always maintained a light humor.

American soldiers played “Yankee Doodle” once again as the British troops surrendered their weapons at Saratoga in 1777. A British officer sadly recalled that they didn’t think much of their Yankee opponents until they were bested that day. “So it was a little mortifying to hear them play this tune, of all others, when our army marched down to surrender.”

WORLD WIDE WEB SITES:

http://kids.niehs.nih.gov/lyrics/yankee/htm
http://lcweb.z.loc.gov/ammem/today/arp19.htm

Photo and Illustration Credits

All illustrations Courtesy the Library of Congress, and:

John Adams: Courtesy of the National Park Service, Adams National Site

Thomas Jefferson: Courtesy of Monticello/Thomas Jefferson Memorial Foundation, Inc.

Construction of Jamestown Fort: National Park Service, Colonial National Historical Park

Glossary and Brief Biographies

This glossary contains terms used in the entries on Colonial America and the Revolutionary War. It includes descriptions of historical events, political terms, the parlimentary acts that led to the Revolution, and other terms that appear frequently in the entries.

The "Brief Biographies" section includes short profiles of people who were prominent in the early colonial era, and who do not have full entries in the volume. Glossary terms are bold-faced in the entries.

ARTICLES OF CONFEDERATION: The Articles of Confederation were the ruling laws of the U.S. before the **CONSTITUTION** was adopted. They were written in 1777 by the **CONTINENTAL CONGRESS**, and served as the national constitution from March 1781 until June 21, 1788, when the U.S. Constitution went into effect. There were many problems and weaknesses in the Articles, notably regarding the size and power of the federal government, the rights of the states, taxation, and boundaries of the states.

BILL OF RIGHTS: The Bill of Rights is a document that lists the first ten amendments, or additions, to the **CONSTITUTION**. The Bill of Rights guarantees specific freedoms to all Americans. Some of the major rights we enjoy—like freedom of speech and religion—are outlined in the Bill of Rights. The principal author of the Bill of Rights was **James Madison**. It was approved and added to the Constitution in 1791.

BOSTON MASSACRE: By 1770, many citizens of Boston were angry over a series of taxes imposed on them by the British. On the evening of March 5, 1770, a rumor began to fly around Boston. A British soldier had supposedly struck a young barber's apprentice. Armed only with snowballs and sticks, a group of citizens confronted the soldiers. With **Crispus Attucks** at the head of the crowd, they marched to the Boston Customs House.

The soldiers fired into the crowd. When the smoke cleared, Attucks and three others lay dead. Eventually five men—Attucks, Samuel Gray, James Caldwell, Samuel Maverick, and Patrick Carr—died of their wounds.

The people of Boston were furious. They claimed that Attucks and the other men were martyrs in the cause of independence. Patriots like Samuel Adams called their murder "The Boston Massacre." It became a rallying cry in the years leading up to the Revolutionary War. John Adams reluctantly defended the British soldiers at their murder trial.

BOSTON TEA PARTY: Although the **TEA ACT** did not impose additional duties or taxes on the colonists, they were suspicious of Parliament's motives in passing the act. The colonists felt that the British would not stop increasing taxes and that it was time to resist as best they could. On December 16, 1773, in what was to become known as "The Boston Tea Party," a hostile group of people dumped 342 chests of tea into the harbor.

The British were infuriated. They closed the port of Boston to all trade in March 1774.

COERCIVE ACTS: The Coercive Acts were passed by Parliament in May 1774 in response to the **BOSTON TEA PARTY**, and were intended to restrict Massachusetts government. (These were also called the Intolerable Acts.) There were four points to the act. 1) The port of Boston was closed. 2) the colony's charter was revoked and town meetings were forbidden. 3) British troops were allowed to live with any colonist. 4) martial law was declared and courts were run by military judges.

CONSTITUTION OF THE UNITED STATES: The Constitution is a document that contains the plan for the national government. It was written by members of the Constitutional Convention in 1787. One of the most important authors of the Constitution was **James Madison.**

The Constitution divides power between three branches. The Executive Branch is made up of the President and the Cabinet. The Legislative branch, or Congress, is made up of the House of Representatives and the Senate. They make the laws for the country. The Judicial Branch is made up of the U.S. Court system, including the Supreme Court.

CONTINENTAL CONGRESS: The Continental Congress was the legislature of the 13 colonies from 1774 to 1789. The first Continental Congress met in 1774 to protest the Coercive Acts. They decided to refuse to import British goods. The Second Continental Congress met in May 1775. In response to the Battles of Lexington and Concord, they declared war on Britain. The Congress appointed **GEORGE WASHINGTON** Commander in Chief of the Army. On July 4, 1776, they signed the **DECLARATION OF INDEPENDENCE**. Throughout the Revolutionary War, the Congress tried to raise money for the army's support. It was dissolved after the war, and replaced with Congress outlined in the **CONSTITUTION**.

DECLARATION OF INDEPENDENCE: The Declaration outlined the reasons behind the Revolutionary War. It was written mainly by **Thomas Jefferson**, with help from **John Adams** and **Benjamin Franklin**. In simple, powerful language, it describes what the colonists thought about their rights as individuals and as citizens. It states that all men are born equal and free. They have the right to revolt against those who will not give them freedom. On July 4, 1776, the Continental Congress, which was the governing body of the colonies, accepted the Declaration of Independence. (A copy of the Declaration appears in the Appendix section.)

FRENCH AND INDIAN WAR: By the mid-1700s, most of the colonies in the New World were under British rule. However, there were also areas that were claimed by France, and also areas where Native American populations continued to fight British settlers and refused to acknowledge British control. The British fought several wars in order to claim the territory. The most important of these was the French and Indian War (1754-1763).

In 1754, France controlled a huge amount of land, from Quebec to New Orleans. It included most of the land west of the Appalachian Mountains to the Mississippi River. They also had forged partnerships with the Native American tribes in the Great Lakes region and Canada. The French built a series of forts, designed to limit the British movement into the area. At that time, Britain controlled the colonies stretching from Maine to Georgia, reaching inland from the Atlantic coast to the Appalachians. The British finally defeated the French, and in 1763, the Peace of Paris was signed, ending the War. Canada and all of North America east of the Mississippi River became British territory.

After the war, the British began to impose a series of taxes on the American colonists. They did this to pay for the costs of the war, and to exercise control over the colonists. But the taxes roused many colonists to question British rule, and were one of the main causes of the Revolutionary War.

THE INTOLERABLE ACTS: See **COERCIVE ACTS**

MAYFLOWER COMPACT: The Mayflower Compact, written in 1620, is one of the most important government documents in U.S. history. In it, the settlers who established the Plymouth Colony agreed to follow majority rule, to enact their own laws, and to cooperate for the general good of colony. Here is part of what the document says:

"We whose names are underwritten do by these Presents, solemnly and mutually in the presence of God and one another covenant and combine ourselves under into a civil Body Politick . . .and by Virtue hereof do enact such just and equal Laws . . . as shall be thought most meet and convenient for the general Good of the Colony."

These simple words created both a government for the Pilgrims, and set the precedent followed by the other colonies as they established themselves in the New World.

SONS OF LIBERTY: The Sons of Liberty was a group of men, including **Samuel Adams** and **Paul Revere**, who were adamantly opposed to British rule in the colonies. They first formed their group in response to the **STAMP ACT**. Often in secret, they met to plan the best way to protest British laws. They were the group responsible for **THE BOSTON TEA PARTY**.

STAMP ACT: This Act of Parliament, passed in 1765, made it mandatory that most documents, such as contracts, newspapers, and pamphlets, had to be written on special paper bearing a stamp from the British government.

The colonists were forced to purchase the stamped paper for most of their documents, because documents on plain paper had no legal standing. The American colonists were suspicious of the tax because many thought that the money paid remained in the pockets of the "Stamp Men" who sold the paper to them. The colonists protested so much that in 1766, the Stamp Act was repealed.

SUGAR ACT (also known as the American Revenue Act): This 1764 law revised a previous tax on sugar, molasses, and other goods imported from the French West Indies. The Sugar Act changed the way in which money was collected from the colonists, making it much harder for them to smuggle those goods into the colonies and ensuring that the colonists paid the tariffs.

TARIFFS: Tariffs are taxes on goods that are imported into the United States. That means that things that are made in other countries cost more than American-made goods. In the 1760s and 1770s, the British government created several high taxes on goods sold to colonists that caused major political problems, and even revolt against British laws. See especially **the Sugar Act, the Currency Act, the Stamp Act,** and **the Tea Act**.

TEA ACT: Probably the most famous law passed by Parliament was the Tea Act. Passage of this law, and the events that occurred after it, were the stepping stones to the Revolutionary War. The Act was passed in 1773. The East India Company was a large importer/exporter of tea . The tea was stored in English warehouses and shipped to America. In order to sell more tea to the colonists and help out the East India Company, the British government permitted the company to recover the duties it paid to the government before shipping the tea across the sea. In America, East India could sell the tea at a much reduced price to the Americans. This allowed them to undersell the colonial tea merchants.

When the first of these shipments arrived in New York and Philadelphia, the colonists forced the ships to return to England. In Charleston, the colonists refused the shipments, and left the tea to rot. In Boston, the colonists refused to allow the tea-laden ships to unload. But their shipments were unloaded, at night, at the **BOSTON TEA PARTY**.

TOWNSHEND DUTIES: The Townshend duties were enacted by the British Parliament in 1767. They forced the colonists to pay duties on glass, lead, paints, paper, and tea. Again, the colonists refused to pay the duty and protested passage of the law. By 1770, the Townshend Duties were repealed.

TREATY OF PARIS: The Treaty of Paris was the document defining the end of the Revolutionary War, the peace between England and the United States, and the new boundaries of the new country. It was drafted by **John Adams, Benjamin Franklin,** and **John Jay**. The new country stretched from the Atlantic Ocean west to the Mississippi River, and from the Canadian border south to Florida.

* * *

BRIEF BIOGRAPHIES

BERKELEY, SIR WILLIAM (1606-1677): The earliest colonial leader in Virginia was Sir William Berkeley. He came to the New World in

1642 from the south of England. He brought with him a commission signed by King Charles I, naming him Royal Governor of Virginia.

Berkeley was a Royalist, an Anglican, and a member of the English upper class. As a Royalist, he was deeply loyal to the King. As an Anglican, he had a deep faith in the Church of England. As a member of the English upper class, he created a social and political order based on the one he knew in England. That order established a small ruling upper class and a large servant class.

Over 35 years, Berkeley had a great impact on the development of Virginia. He helped write its laws, establish its commerce, and shaped the makeup of its society.

BRADFORD, WILLIAM: William Bradford (1590-1657) was the second, and best known, governor of the Plymouth colony. Born in England, Bradford had gone with the early Pilgrims to Holland, in search of religious freedom. He was aboard the *Mayflower* when in landed on Cape Cod in 1620.

In 1621, Bradford negotiated an important treaty with Massasoit, the chief of the Wampanoag. In the treaty, Massasoit granted the tribe's land to the Pilgrims. He also vowed peace between the Native peoples and the colonists. Bradford was helped in drawing up the treaty by **SQUANTO**. Squanto acted as an interpreter between Bradford and the Wampanoag. Sadly, Squanto died just a year later, while on a scouting party around Cape Cod.

Much of what we know of the early years of the Plymouth colony is from Bradford's writing. His book is titled *The History of the Plymouth Plantation, 1620-1647*. It is full of rich detail of the early Pilgrim settlement.

PENN, WILLIAM (1644-1718): William Penn was one of the most important colonists of his era. He was an English Quaker who received the land that became Pennsylvania from the English king, Charles II. It was in payment of a debt owed his late father. It was Charles II who named the new area "Pennsylvania," for the man who was its most important early leader. Penn developed its laws, society, and commerce, and also oversaw its growth. He established a colony built on the idea of harmony and love among the people.

POCAHONTAS (c. 1595-1617): Pocahontas was a member of the Powhatan tribe, daughter of its chief, Wahunsunacock. She is best known as the person who saved Captain John Smith after his capture by her tribe. She also married an English settler, John Rolfe. Sadly, she died very young, at the age of 22. But her descendents live in Virginia to this day.

SMITH, CAPTAIN JOHN (1580-1631): One of the more colorful figures in early American history, Smith was a soldier of fortune before he came to Jamestown. He helped the colonists plant crops and defend themselves against the hostile Algonquin people. But he is best known to history as the prisoner of the Indian chief Powhatan, and his rescue by the chief's daughter, **Pocahontas.**

The exact details of Smith's captivity are unknown. He was known to be a boastful man, who often exaggerated his achievements. But according to his account, he was captured by Powhatan's men and held captive for several weeks. Smith always insisted that it was Pocahantas who rescued him from death. He was eventually returned to the Jamestown colony, where he became its leader.

The colony was badly in need of leadership. They lacked food and fresh water. Some had squabbled among themselves. Others had deserted the colony. Smith set out to explore the region and find food. He also created rules for the colonists, including an order that everyone had to contribute to raising food. "He who does not work, will not eat," he declared. Due in part to Smith's contributions, Jamestown survived.

SQUANTO: Squanto (1585?-1622) was a Wampanoag who was of special help to the Pilgrims of the Plymouth Colony. He had been captured and sold into slavery by Spanish explorers when he was a young man. He escaped, and fled to England. There, he learned the language, and returned to his native land aboard an English ship in 1619, one year before the Pilgrims arrived. He returned to his tribe's area, and when the Pilgrims arrived, he was a ready and helpful friend. Thanks to his help, the colonists learned to farm, to fish, and to survive in their new land. Later, he acted as an interpreter between the settlers and the Wampanoag.

WILLIAMS, ROGER (1603?-1683): Roger Williams was a minister in Salem, Massachusetts. He was a Puritan, but some of his views were too extreme for the Bay Colony leaders. He believed in the freedom of each individual to practice his or her own religion. Because of this, he thought it was wrong for the Puritan church to have any say in the government of the colony.

Williams also believed that the colonists had no right to take the land belonging to the Native American tribes. He thought they should buy it. Because of these two beliefs, Williams was banished from the Massachusetts Bay Colony.

With his followers, he left Massachusetts and moved to the Naragansett Bay Area. There, he founded the city of Providence. In 1643, Williams went to England. He asked for a charter for the settlement. It became known as the Rhode Island and Providence Plantation.

Williams established a democratic form of government. He offered the people of the colony complete freedom of religion. He provided a very strict separation of church and government. This early settlement drew many other dissenters, including Anne Hutchinson, from Puritan New England. Williams's ideals would influence some of the central ideas behind the Revolutionary War.

WINTHROP, JOHN (1588-1649): Winthrop was the first governor of the Massachusetts Bay Colony. He had been elected governor before the Puritans left England, and was re-elected many times in the New World. The devout Winthrop famously wrote that he believed that the Puritans were founding "a City on a Hill," to inspire all.

He could be a very stern ruler—he banished both Roger Williams and Anne Hutchinson from the community. But he did bring new ideas to the governing of the colony. He thought that a small group of Puritan leaders needed the popular support of the people to govern effectively. He wanted to extend governmental power to a larger number of colonists. He and the other Puritan leaders made about 100 of the new settlers "freeman." They became part of the governing authority, adding to its success and stability.

Appendix

THE MAYFLOWER COMPACT

In the name of God, Amen. We whose names are under-written, the loyal subjects of our dread sovereign Lord, King James, by the grace of God, of Great Britain, France, and Ireland King, Defender of the Faith, etc.

Having undertaken, for the glory of God, and advancement of the Christian faith, and honor of our King and Country, a voyage to plant the first colony in the northern parts of Virginia, do by these presents solemnly and mutually, in the presence of God, and one of another, covenant and combine our selves together into a civil body politic, for our better ordering and preservation and furtherance of the ends aforesaid; and by virtue hereof to enact, constitute, and frame such just and equal laws, ordinances, acts, constitutions and offices, from time to time, as shall be thought most meet and convenient for the general good of the Colony, unto which we promise all due submission and obedience. In witness whereof we have hereunder subscribed our names at Cape Cod, the eleventh of November [New Style, November 21], in the year of the reign of our sovereign lord, King James, of England, France, and Ireland, the eighteenth, and of Scotland the fifty-fourth. Anno Dom. 1620.

John Carver
William Bradford
Edward Winslow
William Brewster
Isaac Allerton
Miles Standish
John Alden
Samuel Fuller
Edmond Margeson
Christopher Martin

William Mullins
James Chilton
John Craxton
John Billington
Richard Warren
John Howland
Steven Hopkins
Edward Tilly
John Tilly
Francis Cook
Thomas Tinker
John Rigdale
Edward Fuller
Thomas Rogers
John Turner
Francis Eaton
Moses Fletcher
Digery Priest
Thomas Williams
Gilbert Winslow
Peter Brown
Richard Bitteridge
Richard Clark
Richard Gardiner
John Allerton
Thomas English
Edward Doten
Edward Liester
John Goodman
George Soule
William White

THE CHARTER OF PRIVILEGES

28 October 1701

William Penn Proprietary and Governour of the Province of Pennsilvania and Territories thereunto belonging To all to whom these presents shall come Sendeth Greeting

Whereas King Charles the Second by his Letters Patents under the Great Seale of England beareing Date the fourth day of March in the Yeare one thousand, Six hundred and Eighty was Graciously pleased to Give and Grant unto me my heires and Assignes forever this Province of Pennsilvania with divers great powers and Jurisdictions for the well Governement thereof

And whereas the King's dearest Brother James Duke of York and Albany &c by his Deeds of Feofment under his hand and Seale duely perfected beareing date the twenty fourth day of August one thousand Six hundred Eighty and two Did Grant unto me my heires and Assignes All that Tract of Land now called the Territories of Pennsilvania together with powers and Jurisdictions for the good Government thereof

And whereas for the Encouragement of all the Freemen and Planters that might be concerned in the said Province and Territories and for the good Governement thereof I the said William Penn in the yeare one thousand Six hundred Eighty and three for me my heires and Assignes Did Grant and Confirme unto all the Freeman Planters and Adventurers therein Divers Liberties Franchises and properties as by the said Grant Entituled the Frame of the Government of the Province of Pensilvania and Territories thereunto belonging in America may Appeare which Charter or Frame being found in Some parts of it not soe Suitable to the present Circumstances of the Inhabitants was in the third Month in the yeare One thousand Seven hundred Delivered up to me by Six parts of Seaven of the Freemen of this Province and Territories in Generall Assembly mett provision being made in the said Charter for that End and purpose

And whereas I was then pleased to promise that I would restore the said Charter to them againe with necessary Alterations or in liew thereof Give them another better adapted to Answer the present Circumstances and Conditions of the said Inhabitants which they have now by theire Representatives in a Generall Assembly mett at Philadelphia requested me to Grant

Know ye therefore that for the further well being and good Governement of the said Province and Territories and in pursuance of the Rights and Powers before mencioned I the said William Penn doe Declare Grant and Confirme unto all the Freemen Planters and Adventurers and other Inhabitants in this Province and Territories these following Liberties Franchises and Priviledges soe far as in me lyeth to {be} held Enjoyed and kept by the Freemen Planters and Adventurers and other Inhabitants of and in the said Province and Territories thereunto Annexed for ever

first Because noe people can be truly happy though under the Greatest Enjoyments of Civil Liberties if Abridged of the Freedom of theire Consciences as to theire Religious Profession and Worship. And Almighty God being the only Lord of Conscience Father of Lights and Spirits and the Author as well as Object of all divine knowledge Faith and Worship who only {[can]} Enlighten the mind and perswade and Convince the understandings of people

I doe hereby Grant and Declare that noe person or persons Inhabiting in this Province or Territories who shall Confesse and Acknowledge one Almighty God the Creator upholder and Ruler of the world and professe him or themselves Obliged to live quietly under the Civill Governement shall be in any case molested or prejudiced in his or theire person or Estate because of his or theire Conscientious perswasion or practice nor be compelled to frequent or mentaine any Religious Worship place or Ministry contrary to his or theire mind or doe or Suffer any other act or thing contrary to theire Religious perswasion

And that all persons who also professe to beleive in Jesus Christ the Saviour of the world shall be capable (notwithstanding theire other perswasions and practices in point of Conscience and Religion) to Serve this Governement in any capacity both Legislatively and Executively he or they Solemnly promiseing when lawfully required Allegiance to the King as Soveraigne and fidelity to the Proprietary and Governour

And takeing the Attests as now Establisht by the law made at Newcastle in the yeare One thousand Seven hundred Intituled an Act directing the Attests of Severall Officers and Ministers as now amended and Confirmed this present Assembly

Secondly For the well Governeing of this Province and Territories there shall be an Assembly yearly Chosen by the Freemen thereof to Consist of foure persons out of each County of most note for Virtue wisdome and Ability (Or of a greater number at any time as the Governour and Assembly shall agree) upon the first day of October forever And shall Sitt on the Fourteenth day of the said Month in Philadelphia unless the Governour and Councell for the time being shall See cause to appoint another place within the said Province or Territories

Which Assembly shall have power to choose a Speaker and other theire Officers and shall be judges of the Qualifications and Elections of theire owne Members Sitt upon theire owne Adjournments, Appoint Committees prepare Bills in or to pass into Laws Impeach Criminalls and Redress Greivances and shall have all other Powers and Priviledges of an Assembly according to the Rights of the Free-borne Subjects of England and as is usuall in any of the Kings Plantations in America

And if any County or Counties shall refuse or neglect to choose theire respective Representatives as aforesaid or if chosen doe not meet to Serve in Assembly those who are soe chosen and mett shall have the full power of an Assembly in as ample manner as if all the representatives had beene chosen and mett Provided they are not less then two thirds of the whole number that ought to meet

And that the Qualifications of Electors and Elected and all other matters and things Relateing to Elections of Representatives to Serve in Assemblies though not herein perticulerly Exprest shall be and remaine as by a Law of this Government made at Newcastle in the Yeare One thousand [Seven] hundred Intituled An act to ascertaine the number of members of assembly and to Regulate the elections

Thirdly That the Freemen [in Ea]ch Respective County at the time and place of meeting for Electing [th]eire Representatives to serve in Assembly may as often as there shall be Occasion choose a Double number of persons to present to the Governour for Sheriffes and Coroners to Serve for three Yeares if they Soe long behave themselves well out of which respective Elections and Presentments the Governour shall nominate and Commissionate one for each of the said Officers the third day after Such Presentment or else the first named in Such Presentment for each Office as aforesaid shall Stand and Serve in that Office for the time before respectively Limitted

And in case of Death and Default Such Vacancies shall be Supplyed by the Governour to serve to the End of the said Terme Provided allwayes that if the said Freemen shall at any time neglect or decline to choose a person or persons for either or both the aforesaid Offices then and in Such case the persons that are or shall be in the respective Offices of Sheriffes or Coroner at the time of Election shall remaine therein untill they shall be removed by another Election as aforesaid

And that the Justices of the respective Counties shall or may nominate and present to the Governour three persons to Serve for Clerke of the Peace for the said County when there is a vacancy, one of which the Governour shall Commissionate within Tenn dayes after Such Pressentment or else the first Nominated shall Serve in the said Office dureing good behaviour

fourthly That the Laws of this Government shall be in this Stile Vizt "By the Governour with the Consent and Approbation of the Freemen in Generall Assembly mett" And shall be after Confirmation by the Governour forthwith Recorded in the Rolls Office and kept at Philadelphia unless the Governour and Assembly shall Agree to appoint another place fifthly that all Criminalls shall have the same Priviledges of Wittnesses and Councill as theire Prosecutors

Sixthly That noe person or persons shall or may at any time hereafter be obliged to answer any Complaint matter or thing whatsoever relateing to Property before the Governour and Councill or in any other place but in the Ordinary courts of Justice unless Appeales thereunto shall be hereafter by law appointed

Seventhly That noe person within this Governement shall be Licensed by the Governour to keep Ordinary Taverne or house of publick entertainment but Such who are first recommended to him under the hands of the Justices of the respective Counties Signed in open Court which Justices are and shall be hereby Impowred to Suppress and forbid any person keeping Such publick house as aforesaid upon theire Misbehaviour on such penalties as the law doth or shall Direct and to recommend others from time to time as they shall see occasion

Eighthly If any person through Temptation or Melancholly shall Destroy himselfe his Estate Reall and personall shall notwithstanding Descend to his wife and Children or Relations as if he had dyed a Naturall Death

And if any person shall be Destroyed or kill'd by casualty or Accident there shall be noe forfeiture to the Governour by reason thereof

And noe Act Law or Ordinance whatsoever shall at any time hereafter be made or done to Alter Change or Diminish the forme or Effect of this Charter or of any part or Clause therein Contrary to the True intent and meaning thereof without the Consent of the

Governour for the [time being and] six parts of Seven of the Assembly [mett]

But because the happiness of Mankind Depends So much upon the Enjoying of Libertie of theire Consciences as aforesaid I Doe hereby Solemnly Declare Promise and Grant for me my heires and Assignes that the first Article of this Charter Relateing to Liberty of Conscience and every part and Clause therein according to the True Intent and meaneing thereof shall be kept and remaine without any Alteration Inviolably for ever

And Lastly I the said William Penn Proprietary and Governour of the Province of Pensilvania and Territories thereunto, belonging for my Selfe my heires and Assignes Have Solemnly Declared Granted and Confirmed And doe hereby Solemnly Declare Grant and Confirme that neither I my heires or Assignes shall procure or doe any thing or things whereby the Liberties in this Charter contained and expressed nor any part thereof shall be Infringed or broken And if any thing shall be procured or done by any person or persons contrary to these presents it shall be held of noe force or Effect

In wittnes whereof I the said William Penn at Philadelphia in Pensilvania have unto this present Charter of Liberties Sett my hand and Broad Seale this twenty Eighth day of October in the Yeare of our Lord one thousand Seven hundred and one being the thirteenth yeare of the Reigne of King William the Third over England Scotland France and Ireland &c And in the Twenty first Yeare of my Government.

And notwithstanding the closure and Test of this present Charter as aforesaid I think fitt to add this following Provisoe thereunto as part of the same That is to say that notwithstanding any Clause or Clauses in the above mencioned Charter obligeing the Province and Territories to Joyne Together in Legislation I am Content and doe hereby Declare That if the representatives of the Province and Territories shall not hereafter Agree to Joyne togather in Legislation and that the same shall be Signifyed to me or my Deputy In open Assembly or otherwise from under the hands and Seales of the Representatives (for the time being) of the Province or Territories or the Major part of either of them any time within three yeares from the Date hereof That in Such case the Inhabitants of each o' the three Counties of this Province shall not have less then Eight persons to represent them in Assembly for the Province and the Inhabitants of the Towne of Philadelphia (when the said Towne is Incorporated) Two persons to represent them in Assembly and the Inhabitants of each County in the Territories shall have as many persons to represent them in a Distinct Assembly for the Territories as shall be requested by them as aforesaid Notwithstanding which Seperation of the Province and Territories in Respect of Legislation I doe hereby promise Grant and Declare that the Inhabitants of both Province and Territories shall Seperately Injoy all other Liberties Priviledges and Benefitts granted Joyntly to them in this Charter Any law usage or Custome of this Governement heretofore made and Practised or any law made and Passed by this Generall Assembly to the Contrary hereof Notwithstanding.

Wm Penn
Edwd: Shippen
Phineas Pemberton
Sam: Carpenter
Griffith Owen
Caleb Pusey Tho: Story

Propry and
Governours Council

THE DECLARATION OF INDEPENDENCE

IN CONGRESS, JULY 4, 1776.
THE UNANIMOUS
DECLARATION
OF THE
THIRTEEN UNITED STATES OF AMERICA.

WHEN, in the Course of human Events, it becomes necessary for one People to dissolve the Political Bands which have connected them with another, and to assume, among the Powers of the Earth, the separate and equal Station to which the Laws of Nature and of Nature's GOD entitle them, a decent Respect to the Opinions of Mankind requires that they should declare the Causes which impel them to the Separation.

We hold these Truths to be self-evident, that all Men are created equal, that they are endowed, by their CREATOR, with certain unalienable Rights, that among these are Life, Liberty, and the Pursuit of Happiness.—That to secure these Rights, Governments are instituted among Men, deriving their just Powers from the Consent of the Governed, that whenever any Form of Government becomes destructive of these Ends, it is the Right of the People to alter or to abolish it, and to institute new Government, laying its Foundation on such Principles, and organizing its Powers in such Form, as to them shall seem most likely to effect their Safety and Happiness. Prudence, indeed, will dictate, that Governments long established, should not be changed for light and transient Causes; and accordingly all Experience hath shewn, that Mankind are more disposed to suffer, while Evils are sufferable, than to right themselves by abolishing the Forms to which they are accustomed. But when a long Train of Abuses and Usurpations, pursuing invariably the same Object, evinces a Design to reduce them under absolute Despotism, it is their Right, it is their Duty, to throw off such Government, and to provide new Guards for their future Security. Such has been the patient Sufferance of these Colonies; and such is now the Necessity which constrains them to alter their former Systems of Government. The History of the present King of Great-Britain is a History of repeated Injuries and Usurpations, all having in direct Object the Establishment of an absolute Tyranny over these States. To prove this, let Facts be submitted to a candid World.

HE has refused his Assent to Laws, the most wholesome and necessary for the public Good.

HE has forbidden his Governors to pass Laws of immediate and pressing Importance, unless suspended in their Operation till his Assent should be obtained; and when so suspended, he has utterly neglected to attend to them.

HE has refused to pass other Laws for the Accommodation of large Districts of People, unless those People would relinquish the Right of Representation in the Legislature, a Right inestimable to them, and formidable to Tyranny only.

HE has called together Legislative Bodies at Places unusual, uncomfortable, and distant from the Depository of their public Records, for the sole Purpose of fatiguing them into Compliance with his Measures.

HE has dissolved Representative Houses repeatedly, for opposing with manly Firmness his Invasions on the Rights of the People.

HE has refused for a long Time, after such Dissolutions, to cause others to be elected; whereby the Legislative Powers, incapable of Annihilation, have returned to the People at large for their exercise; the State remaining, in the mean Time, exposed to all the Dangers of Invasion from without, and Convulsions within.

HE has endeavoured to prevent the Population of these States; for that Purpose obstructing the Laws for Naturalization of Foreigners; refusing to pass others to encourage their Migrations hither, and raising the Conditions of new Appropriations of Lands.

HE has obstructed the Administration of Justice, by refusing his Assent to Laws for establishing Judiciary Powers.

HE has made Judges dependent on his Will alone, for the Tenure of their Offices, and the Amount and Payment of their Salaries.

HE has erected a Multitude of new Offices, and sent hither Swarms of Officers to harrass our People, and eat out their Substance.

HE has kept among us, in Times of Peace, Standing Armies, without the Consent of our Legislatures.

HE has affected to render the Military independent of and superior to the Civil Power.

HE has combined with others to subject us to a Jurisdiction foreign to our Constitution, and unacknowledged by our Laws; giving his Assent to their Acts of pretended Legislation:

FOR quartering large Bodies of Armed Troops among us:

FOR protecting them, by a mock Trial, from Punishment for any Murders which they should commit on the Inhabitants of these States:

FOR cutting off our Trade with all Parts of the World:

FOR imposing Taxes on us without our Consent:

FOR depriving us, in many Cases, of the Benefits of Trial by Jury:

FOR transporting us beyond Seas to be tried for pretended Offences:

FOR abolishing the free System of English Laws in a neighbouring Province, establishing therein an arbitrary Government, and enlarging its Boundaries, so as to render it at once an Example and fit Instrument for introducing the same absolute Rule into these Colonies:

FOR taking away our Charters, abolishing our most valuable Laws, and altering fundamentally the Forms of our Governments:

FOR suspending our own Legislatures, and declaring themselves invested with Power to legislate for us in all Cases whatsoever.

HE has abdicated Government here, by declaring us out of his Protection, and waging War against us.

HE has plundered our Seas, ravaged our Coasts, burnt our Towns, and destroyed the Lives of our People.

HE is, at this Time, transporting large Armies of foreign Mercenaries to complete the Works of Death, Desolation, and Tyranny, already begun with Circumstances of Cruelty and Perfidy, scarcely paralleled in the most barbarous Ages, and totally unworthy the Head of a civilized Nation.

HE has constrained our Fellow-Citizens, taken Captive on the high Seas, to bear Arms against their Country, to become the Executioners of their Friends and Brethren, or to fall themselves by their Hands.

HE has excited domestic Insurrections amongst us, and has endeavoured to bring on the Inhabitants of our Frontiers, the merciless Indian Savages, whose known Rule of Warfare, is an undistinguished Destruction, of all Ages, Sexes, and Conditions.

IN every Stage of these Oppressions we have Petitioned for Redress in the most humble Terms: Our repeated Petitions have been answered only by repeated Injury. A Prince, whose Character is thus marked by every Act which may define a Tyrant, is unfit to be the Ruler of a free People.

NOR have we been wanting in Attentions to our British Brethren. We have warned them, from Time to Time, of Attempts by their Legislature to extend an unwarrantable Jurisdiction over us. We have reminded them of the Circumstances of our Emigration and Settlement here. We have appealed to their native Justice and Magnanimity, and we have conjured them by the Ties of our common Kindred to disavow these Usurpations, which would inevitably interrupt our Connexions and Correspondence. They too have been deaf to the Voice of Justice and of Consanguinity. We must, therefore, acquiesce in the Necessity, which denounces our Separation, and hold them, as we hold the Rest of Mankind, Enemies in War, in Peace Friends.

WE, therefore, the Representatives of the UNITED STATES OF AMERICA, in GENERAL CONGRESS Assembled, appealing to the Supreme Judge of the World for the Rectitude of our Intentions, do, in the Name, and by Authority of the good People of these Colonies, solemnly Publish and Declare, That these United Colonies are, and of Right ought to be, FREE AND INDEPENDENT STATES; that they are absolved from all Allegiance to the British Crown, and that all political Connexion between them and the State of Great-Britain, is, and ought to be, totally dissolved; and that as FREE AND INDEPENDENT STATES, they have full Power to levy War, conclude Peace, contract Alliances, establish Commerce, and to do all other Acts and Things which INDEPENDENT STATES may of Right do. And for the Support of this Declaration, with a firm Reliance on the Protection of DIVINE PROVIDENCE, we mutually pledge to each other our Lives, our Fortunes, and our sacred Honour.

John Hancock.
GEORGIA, Button Gwinnett, Lyman Hall, Geo. Walton.
NORTH-CAROLINA, Wm. Hooper, Joseph Hewes, John Penn.
SOUTH-CAROLINA, Edward Rutledge, Thos Heyward, junr. Thomas Lynch, junr. Arthur Middleton.
MARYLAND, Samuel Chase, Wm. Paca, Thos. Stone, Charles Carroll, of Carrollton.
VIRGINIA, George Wythe, Richard Henry Lee, Ths. Jefferson, Benja. Harrison, Thos. Nelson, jr. Francis Lightfoot Lee, Carter Braxton.
PENNSYLVANIA, Robt. Morris, Benjamin Rush, Benja. Franklin, John Morton, Geo. Clymer, Jas. Smith, Geo. Taylor, James Wilson, Geo. Ross.
DELAWARE, Caesar Rodney, Geo. Read.

NEW-YORK, Wm. Floyd, Phil. Livingston, Frank Lewis, Lewis Morris.
NEW-JERSEY, Richd. Stockton, Jno. Witherspoon, Fras. Hopkinson, John Hart, Abra. Clark.
NEW-HAMPSHIRE, Josiah Bartlett, Wm. Whipple, Matthew Thornton.
MASSACHUSETTS-BAY, Saml. Adams, John Adams, Robt. Treat Paine, Elbridge Gerry.
RHODE-ISLAND AND PROVIDENCE, &c. Step. Hopkins, William Ellery.
CONNECTICUT, Roger Sherman, Saml. Huntington, Wm. Williams, Oliver Wolcott.

IN CONGRESS, JANUARY 18, 1777.

ORDERED,
THAT an authenticated Copy of the DECLARATION OF INDEPENDENCY, with the Names of the MEMBERS of CONGRESS, subscribing the same, be sent to each of the UNITED STATES, and that they be desired to have the same put on RECORD.
By Order of CONGRESS,
JOHN HANCOCK, President.

THE CONSTITUTION OF THE UNITED STATES

We the People of the United States, in Order to form a more perfect Union, establish Justice, insure domestic Tranquility, provide for the common defence, promote the general Welfare, and secure the Blessings of Liberty to ourselves and our Posterity, do ordain and establish this Constitution for the United States of America.

Article. I.

Section. 1.

All legislative Powers herein granted shall be vested in a Congress of the United States, which shall consist of a Senate and House of Representatives.

Section. 2.

The House of Representatives shall be composed of Members chosen every second Year by the People of the several States, and the Electors in each State shall have the Qualifications requisite for Electors of the most numerous Branch of the State Legislature.

No Person shall be a Representative who shall not have attained to the Age of twenty five Years, and been seven Years a Citizen of the United States, and who shall not, when elected, be an Inhabitant of that State in which he shall be chosen.

Representatives and direct Taxes shall be apportioned among the several States which may be included within this Union, according to their respective Numbers, which shall be determined by adding to the whole Number of free Persons, including those bound to Service for a Term of Years, and excluding Indians not taxed, three fifths of all other Persons. The actual Enumeration shall be made within three Years after the first Meeting of the Congress of the United States, and within every subsequent Term of ten Years, in such Manner as they shall by Law direct. The Number of Representatives shall not exceed one for every thirty Thousand, but each State shall have at Least one Representative; and until such enumeration shall be made, the State of New Hampshire shall be entitled to chuse three, Massachusetts eight, Rhode-Island and Providence Plantations one, Connecticut five, New-York six, New Jersey four, Pennsylvania eight, Delaware one, Maryland six, Virginia ten, North Carolina five, South Carolina five, and Georgia three.

When vacancies happen in the Representation from any State, the Executive Authority thereof shall issue Writs of Election to fill such Vacancies.

The House of Representatives shall chuse their Speaker and other Officers; and shall have the sole Power of Impeachment.

Section. 3.

The Senate of the United States shall be composed of two Senators from each State, chosen by the Legislature thereof for six Years; and each Senator shall have one Vote.

Immediately after they shall be assembled in Consequence of the first Election, they shall be divided as equally as may be into three Classes. The Seats of the Senators of the first Class shall be vacated at the Expiration of the second Year, of the second Class at the Expiration of the fourth Year, and of the third Class at the Expiration of the sixth Year, so that one third may be chosen every second Year; and if Vacancies happen by Resignation, or otherwise, during the Recess of the Legislature of any State, the

Executive thereof may make temporary Appointments until the next Meeting of the Legislature, which shall then fill such Vacancies.

No Person shall be a Senator who shall not have attained to the Age of thirty Years, and been nine Years a Citizen of the United States, and who shall not, when elected, be an Inhabitant of that State for which he shall be chosen.

The Vice President of the United States shall be President of the Senate, but shall have no Vote, unless they be equally divided.

The Senate shall chuse their other Officers, and also a President pro tempore, in the Absence of the Vice President, or when he shall exercise the Office of President of the United States.

The Senate shall have the sole Power to try all Impeachments. When sitting for that Purpose, they shall be on Oath or Affirmation. When the President of the United States is tried, the Chief Justice shall preside: And no Person shall be convicted without the Concurrence of two thirds of the Members present.

Judgment in Cases of Impeachment shall not extend further than to removal from Office, and disqualification to hold and enjoy any Office of honor, Trust or Profit under the United States: but the Party convicted shall nevertheless be liable and subject to Indictment, Trial, Judgment and Punishment, according to Law.

Section. 4.

The Times, Places and Manner of holding Elections for Senators and Representatives, shall be prescribed in each State by the Legislature thereof; but the Congress may at any time by Law make or alter such Regulations, except as to the Places of chusing Senators.

The Congress shall assemble at least once in every Year, and such Meeting shall be on the first Monday in December, unless they shall by Law appoint a different Day.

Section. 5.

Each House shall be the Judge of the Elections, Returns and Qualifications of its own Members, and a Majority of each shall constitute a Quorum to do Business; but a smaller Number may adjourn from day to day, and may be authorized to compel the Attendance of absent Members, in such Manner, and under such Penalties as each House may provide.

Each House may determine the Rules of its Proceedings, punish its Members for disorderly Behaviour, and, with the Concurrence of two thirds, expel a Member.

Each House shall keep a Journal of its Proceedings, and from time to time publish the same, excepting such Parts as may in their Judgment require Secrecy; and the Yeas and Nays of the Members of either House on any question shall, at the Desire of one fifth of those Present, be entered on the Journal.

Neither House, during the Session of Congress, shall, without the Consent of the other, adjourn for more than three days, nor to any other Place than that in which the two Houses shall be sitting.

Section. 6.

The Senators and Representatives shall receive a Compensation for their Services, to be ascertained by Law, and paid out of the

Treasury of the United States. They shall in all Cases, except Treason, Felony and Breach of the Peace, be privileged from Arrest during their Attendance at the Session of their respective Houses, and in going to and returning from the same; and for any Speech or Debate in either House, they shall not be questioned in any other Place.

No Senator or Representative shall, during the Time for which he was elected, be appointed to any civil Office under the Authority of the United States, which shall have been created, or the Emoluments whereof shall have been encreased during such time; and no Person holding any Office under the United States, shall be a Member of either House during his Continuance in Office.

Section. 7.

All Bills for raising Revenue shall originate in the House of Representatives; but the Senate may propose or concur with Amendments as on other Bills.

Every Bill which shall have passed the House of Representatives and the Senate, shall, before it become a Law, be presented to the President of the United States: If he approve he shall sign it, but if not he shall return it, with his Objections to that House in which it shall have originated, who shall enter the Objections at large on their Journal, and proceed to reconsider it. If after such Reconsideration two thirds of that House shall agree to pass the Bill, it shall be sent, together with the Objections, to the other House, by which it shall likewise be reconsidered, and if approved by two thirds of that House, it shall become a Law. But in all such Cases the Votes of both Houses shall be determined by yeas and Nays, and the Names of the Persons voting for and against the Bill shall be entered on the Journal of each House respectively. If any Bill shall not be returned by the President within ten Days (Sundays excepted) after it shall have been presented to him, the Same shall be a Law, in like Manner as if he had signed it, unless the Congress by their Adjournment prevent its Return, in which Case it shall not be a Law.

Every Order, Resolution, or Vote to which the Concurrence of the Senate and House of Representatives may be necessary (except on a question of Adjournment) shall be presented to the President of the United States; and before the Same shall take Effect, shall be approved by him, or being disapproved by him, shall be repassed by two thirds of the Senate and House of Representatives, according to the Rules and Limitations prescribed in the Case of a Bill.

Section. 8.

The Congress shall have Power To lay and collect Taxes, Duties, Imposts and Excises, to pay the Debts and provide for the common Defence and general Welfare of the United States; but all Duties, Imposts and Excises shall be uniform throughout the United States;

To borrow Money on the credit of the United States;

To regulate Commerce with foreign Nations, and among the several States, and with the Indian Tribes;

To establish an uniform Rule of Naturalization, and uniform Laws on the subject of Bankruptcies throughout the United States;

To coin Money, regulate the Value thereof, and of foreign Coin, and fix the Standard of Weights and Measures;

To provide for the Punishment of counterfeiting the Securities and current Coin of the United States;

To establish Post Offices and post Roads;

To promote the Progress of Science and useful Arts, by securing for limited Times to Authors and Inventors the exclusive Right to their respective Writings and Discoveries;

To constitute Tribunals inferior to the supreme Court;

To define and punish Piracies and Felonies committed on the high Seas, and Offences against the Law of Nations;

To declare War, grant Letters of Marque and Reprisal, and make Rules concerning Captures on Land and Water;

To raise and support Armies, but no Appropriation of Money to that Use shall be for a longer Term than two Years;

To provide and maintain a Navy;

To make Rules for the Government and Regulation of the land and naval Forces;

To provide for calling forth the Militia to execute the Laws of the Union, suppress Insurrections and repel Invasions;

To provide for organizing, arming, and disciplining, the Militia, and for governing such Part of them as may be employed in the Service of the United States, reserving to the States respectively, the Appointment of the Officers, and the Authority of training the Militia according to the discipline prescribed by Congress;

To exercise exclusive Legislation in all Cases whatsoever, over such District (not exceeding ten Miles square) as may, by Cession of particular States, and the Acceptance of Congress, become the Seat of the Government of the United States, and to exercise like Authority over all Places purchased by the Consent of the Legislature of the State in which the Same shall be, for the Erection of Forts, Magazines, Arsenals, dock-Yards, and other needful Buildings;—And

To make all Laws which shall be necessary and proper for carrying into Execution the foregoing Powers, and all other Powers vested by this Constitution in the Government of the United States, or in any Department or Officer thereof.

Section. 9.

The Migration or Importation of such Persons as any of the States now existing shall think proper to admit, shall not be prohibited by the Congress prior to the Year one thousand eight hundred and eight, but a Tax or duty may be imposed on such Importation, not exceeding ten dollars for each Person.

The Privilege of the Writ of Habeas Corpus shall not be suspended, unless when in Cases of Rebellion or Invasion the public Safety may require it.

No Bill of Attainder or ex post facto Law shall be passed.

No Capitation, or other direct, Tax shall be laid, unless in Proportion to the Census or enumeration herein before directed to be taken.

No Tax or Duty shall be laid on Articles exported from any State.

No Preference shall be given by any Regulation of Commerce or Revenue to the Ports of one State over those of another; nor shall

Vessels bound to, or from, one State, be obliged to enter, clear, or pay Duties in another.

No Money shall be drawn from the Treasury, but in Consequence of Appropriations made by Law; and a regular Statement and Account of the Receipts and Expenditures of all public Money shall be published from time to time.

No Title of Nobility shall be granted by the United States: And no Person holding any Office of Profit or Trust under them, shall, without the Consent of the Congress, accept of any present, Emolument, Office, or Title, of any kind whatever, from any King, Prince, or foreign State.

Section. 10.

No State shall enter into any Treaty, Alliance, or Confederation; grant Letters of Marque and Reprisal; coin Money; emit Bills of Credit; make any Thing but gold and silver Coin a Tender in Payment of Debts; pass any Bill of Attainder, ex post facto Law, or Law impairing the Obligation of Contracts, or grant any Title of Nobility.

No State shall, without the Consent of the Congress, lay any Imposts or Duties on Imports or Exports, except what may be absolutely necessary for executing it's inspection Laws: and the net Produce of all Duties and Imposts, laid by any State on Imports or Exports, shall be for the Use of the Treasury of the United States; and all such Laws shall be subject to the Revision and Controul of the Congress.

No State shall, without the Consent of Congress, lay any Duty of Tonnage, keep Troops, or Ships of War in time of Peace, enter into any Agreement or Compact with another State, or with a foreign Power, or engage in War, unless actually invaded, or in such imminent Danger as will not admit of delay.

Article. II.

Section. 1.

The executive Power shall be vested in a President of the United States of America. He shall hold his Office during the Term of four Years, and, together with the Vice President, chosen for the same Term, be elected, as follows:

Each State shall appoint, in such Manner as the Legislature thereof may direct, a Number of Electors, equal to the whole Number of Senators and Representatives to which the State may be entitled in the Congress: but no Senator or Representative, or Person holding an Office of Trust or Profit under the United States, shall be appointed an Elector.

The Electors shall meet in their respective States, and vote by Ballot for two Persons, of whom one at least shall not be an Inhabitant of the same State with themselves. And they shall make a List of all the Persons voted for, and of the Number of Votes for each; which List they shall sign and certify, and transmit sealed to the Seat of the Government of the United States, directed to the President of the Senate. The President of the Senate shall, in the Presence of the Senate and House of Representatives, open all the Certificates, and the Votes shall then be counted. The Person having the greatest Number of Votes shall be the President, if such Number be a Majority of the whole Number of Electors appointed; and if there be more than one who have such Majority, and have an equal Number of Votes, then the House of Representatives shall immediately chuse by Ballot one of them for President; and if no Person have a Majority, then from the five highest on the List the said House shall in like Manner chuse the President. But in chusing the President, the Votes shall be taken by States, the Representation from each State having one Vote; A quorum for this purpose shall consist of a Member or Members from two thirds of the States, and a Majority of all the States shall be necessary to a Choice. In every Case, after the Choice of the President, the Person having the greatest Number of Votes of the Electors shall be the Vice President. But if there should remain two or more who have equal Votes, the Senate shall chuse from them by Ballot the Vice President.

The Congress may determine the Time of chusing the Electors, and the Day on which they shall give their Votes; which Day shall be the same throughout the United States.

No Person except a natural born Citizen, or a Citizen of the United States, at the time of the Adoption of this Constitution, shall be eligible to the Office of President; neither shall any Person be eligible to that Office who shall not have attained to the Age of thirty five Years, and been fourteen Years a Resident within the United States.

In Case of the Removal of the President from Office, or of his Death, Resignation, or Inability to discharge the Powers and Duties of the said Office, the Same shall devolve on the Vice President, and the Congress may by Law provide for the Case of Removal, Death, Resignation or Inability, both of the President and Vice President, declaring what Officer shall then act as President, and such Officer shall act accordingly, until the Disability be removed, or a President shall be elected.

The President shall, at stated Times, receive for his Services, a Compensation, which shall neither be increased nor diminished during the Period for which he shall have been elected, and he shall not receive within that Period any other Emolument from the United States, or any of them.

Before he enter on the Execution of his Office, he shall take the following Oath or Affirmation:—"I do solemnly swear (or affirm) that I will faithfully execute the Office of President of the United States, and will to the best of my Ability, preserve, protect and defend the Constitution of the United States."

Section. 2.

The President shall be Commander in Chief of the Army and Navy of the United States, and of the Militia of the several States, when called into the actual Service of the United States; he may require the Opinion, in writing, of the principal Officer in each of the executive Departments, upon any Subject relating to the Duties of their respective Offices, and he shall have Power to grant Reprieves and Pardons for Offences against the United States, except in Cases of Impeachment.

He shall have Power, by and with the Advice and Consent of the Senate, to make Treaties, provided two thirds of the Senators present concur; and he shall nominate, and by and with the Advice and Consent of the Senate, shall appoint Ambassadors, other public Ministers and Consuls, Judges of the supreme Court, and all other Officers of the United States, whose Appointments are not herein otherwise provided for, and which shall be established by Law: but the Congress may by Law vest the Appointment of such inferior Officers, as they think proper, in the President alone, in the Courts of Law, or in the Heads of Departments.

The President shall have Power to fill up all Vacancies that may happen during the Recess of the Senate, by granting Commissions which shall expire at the End of their next Session.

Section. 3.

He shall from time to time give to the Congress Information of the State of the Union, and recommend to their Consideration such Measures as he shall judge necessary and expedient; he may, on extraordinary Occasions, convene both Houses, or either of them, and in Case of Disagreement between them, with Respect to the Time of Adjournment, he may adjourn them to such Time as he shall think proper; he shall receive Ambassadors and other public Ministers; he shall take Care that the Laws be faithfully executed, and shall Commission all the Officers of the United States.

Section. 4.

The President, Vice President and all civil Officers of the United States, shall be removed from Office on Impeachment for, and Conviction of, Treason, Bribery, or other high Crimes and Misdemeanors.

Article III.

Section. 1.

The judicial Power of the United States shall be vested in one supreme Court, and in such inferior Courts as the Congress may from time to time ordain and establish. The Judges, both of the supreme and inferior Courts, shall hold their Offices during good

Behaviour, and shall, at stated Times, receive for their Services a Compensation, which shall not be diminished during their Continuance in Office.

Section. 2.

The judicial Power shall extend to all Cases, in Law and Equity, arising under this Constitution, the Laws of the United States, and Treaties made, or which shall be made, under their Authority;—to all Cases affecting Ambassadors, other public Ministers and Consuls;—to all Cases of admiralty and maritime Jurisdiction;—to Controversies to which the United States shall be a Party;—to Controversies between two or more States;—between a State and Citizens of another State;—between Citizens of different States;—between Citizens of the same State claiming Lands under Grants of different States, and between a State, or the Citizens thereof, and foreign States, Citizens or Subjects.

In all Cases affecting Ambassadors, other public Ministers and Consuls, and those in which a State shall be Party, the supreme Court shall have original Jurisdiction. In all the other Cases before mentioned, the supreme Court shall have appellate Jurisdiction, both as to Law and Fact, with such Exceptions, and under such Regulations as the Congress shall make.

The Trial of all Crimes, except in Cases of Impeachment, shall be by Jury; and such Trial shall be held in the State where the said Crimes shall have been committed; but when not committed within any State, the Trial shall be at such Place or Places as the Congress may by Law have directed.

Section. 3.

Treason against the United States, shall consist only in levying War against them, or in adhering to their Enemies, giving them Aid and Comfort. No Person shall be convicted of Treason unless on the Testimony of two Witnesses to the same overt Act, or on Confession in open Court.

The Congress shall have Power to declare the Punishment of Treason, but no Attainder of Treason shall work Corruption of Blood, or Forfeiture except during the Life of the Person attainted.

Article. IV.

Section. 1.

Full Faith and Credit shall be given in each State to the public Acts, Records, and judicial Proceedings of every other State. And the Congress may by general Laws prescribe the Manner in which such Acts, Records and Proceedings shall be proved, and the Effect thereof.

Section. 2.

The Citizens of each State shall be entitled to all Privileges and Immunities of Citizens in the several States.

A Person charged in any State with Treason, Felony, or other Crime, who shall flee from Justice, and be found in another State, shall on Demand of the executive Authority of the State from which he fled, be delivered up, to be removed to the State having Jurisdiction of the Crime.

No Person held to Service or Labour in one State, under the Laws thereof, escaping into another, shall, in Consequence of any Law or

Regulation therein, be discharged from such Service or Labour, but shall be delivered up on Claim of the Party to whom such Service or Labour may be due.

Section. 3.

New States may be admitted by the Congress into this Union; but no new State shall be formed or erected within the Jurisdiction of any other State; nor any State be formed by the Junction of two or more States, or Parts of States, without the Consent of the Legislatures of the States concerned as well as of the Congress.

The Congress shall have Power to dispose of and make all needful Rules and Regulations respecting the Territory or other Property belonging to the United States; and nothing in this Constitution shall be so construed as to Prejudice any Claims of the United States, or of any particular State.

Section. 4.

The United States shall guarantee to every State in this Union a Republican Form of Government, and shall protect each of them against Invasion; and on Application of the Legislature, or of the Executive (when the Legislature cannot be convened), against domestic Violence.

Article. V.

The Congress, whenever two thirds of both Houses shall deem it necessary, shall propose Amendments to this Constitution, or, on the Application of the Legislatures of two thirds of the several States, shall call a Convention for proposing Amendments, which, in either Case, shall be valid to all Intents and Purposes, as Part of this Constitution, when ratified by the Legislatures of three fourths of the several States, or by Conventions in three fourths thereof, as the one or the other Mode of Ratification may be proposed by the Congress; Provided that no Amendment which may be made prior to the Year One thousand eight hundred and eight shall in any Manner affect the first and fourth Clauses in the Ninth Section of the first Article; and that no State, without its Consent, shall be deprived of its equal Suffrage in the Senate.

Article. VI.

All Debts contracted and Engagements entered into, before the Adoption of this Constitution, shall be as valid against the United States under this Constitution, as under the Confederation.

This Constitution, and the Laws of the United States which shall be made in Pursuance thereof; and all Treaties made, or which shall be made, under the Authority of the United States, shall be the supreme Law of the Land; and the Judges in every State shall be bound thereby, any Thing in the Constitution or Laws of any State to the Contrary notwithstanding.

The Senators and Representatives before mentioned, and the Members of the several State Legislatures, and all executive and judicial Officers, both of the United States and of the several States, shall be bound by Oath or Affirmation, to support this Constitution; but no religious Test shall ever be required as a Qualification to any Office or public Trust under the United States.

Article. VII.

The Ratification of the Conventions of nine States, shall be sufficient for the Establishment of this Constitution between the States so ratifying the Same.

The Word, "the," being interlined between the seventh and eighth Lines of the first Page, the Word "Thirty" being partly written on an Erazure in the fifteenth Line of the first Page, The Words "is tried" being interlined between the thirty second and thirty third Lines of the first Page and the Word "the" being interlined between the forty third and forty fourth Lines of the second Page.

Attest William Jackson Secretary

Done in Convention by the Unanimous Consent of the States present the Seventeenth Day of September in the Year of our Lord one thousand seven hundred and Eighty seven and of the Independence of the United States of America the Twelfth In witness whereof We have hereunto subscribed our Names,

G°. Washington
Presidt and deputy from Virginia

Delaware
Geo: Read
Gunning Bedford jun
John Dickinson
Richard Bassett
Jaco: Broom

Maryland
James McHenry
Dan of St Thos. Jenifer
Danl. Carroll

Virginia
John Blair
James Madison Jr.

North Carolina
Wm. Blount
Richd. Dobbs Spaight
Hu Williamson

South Carolina
J. Rutledge
Charles Cotesworth Pinckney
Charles Pinckney
Pierce Butler

Georgia
William Few
Abr Baldwin

New Hampshire
John Langdon
Nicholas Gilman

Massachusetts
Nathaniel Gorham
Rufus King

Connecticut
Wm. Saml. Johnson
Roger Sherman

New York
Alexander Hamilton

New Jersey
Wil: Livingston
David Brearley
Wm. Paterson
Jona: Dayton

Pennsylvania
B Franklin
Thomas Mifflin
Robt. Morris
Geo. Clymer
Thos. FitzSimons
Jared Ingersoll
James Wilson
Gouv Morris

THE BILL OF RIGHTS

The Preamble to The Bill of Rights

Congress of the United States

begun and held at the City of New-York, on

Wednesday the fourth of March, one thousand seven hundred and eighty nine.

THE Conventions of a number of the States, having at the time of their adopting the Constitution, expressed a desire, in order to prevent misconstruction or abuse of its powers, that further declaratory and restrictive clauses should be added: And as extending the ground of public confidence in the Government, will best ensure the beneficent ends of its institution.

RESOLVED by the Senate and House of Representatives of the United States of America, in Congress assembled, two thirds of both Houses concurring, that the following Articles be proposed to the Legislatures of the several States, as amendments to the Constitution of the United States, all, or any of which Articles, when ratified by three fourths of the said Legislatures, to be valid to all intents and purposes, as part of the said Constitution; viz.

ARTICLES in addition to, and Amendment of the Constitution of the United States of America, proposed by Congress, and ratified by the Legislatures of the several States, pursuant to the fifth Article of the original Constitution.

Amendment I

Congress shall make no law respecting an establishment of religion, or prohibiting the free exercise thereof; or abridging the freedom of speech, or of the press; or the right of the people peaceably to assemble, and to petition the Government for a redress of grievances.

Amendment II

A well regulated Militia, being necessary to the security of a free State, the right of the people to keep and bear Arms, shall not be infringed.

Amendment III

No Soldier shall, in time of peace be quartered in any house, without the consent of the Owner, nor in time of war, but in a manner to be prescribed by law.

Amendment IV

The right of the people to be secure in their persons, houses, papers, and effects, against unreasonable searches and seizures, shall not be violated, and no Warrants shall issue, but upon probable cause, supported by Oath or affirmation, and particularly describing the place to be searched, and the persons or things to be seized.

Amendment V

No person shall be held to answer for a capital, or otherwise infamous crime, unless on a presentment or indictment of a Grand Jury, except in cases arising in the land or naval forces, or in the Militia, when in actual service in time of War or public danger; nor shall any person be subject for the same offence to be twice put in jeopardy of life or limb; nor shall be compelled in any criminal case to be a witness against himself, nor be deprived of life, liberty, or property, without due process of law; nor shall private property be taken for public use, without just compensation.

Amendment VI

In all criminal prosecutions, the accused shall enjoy the right to a speedy and public trial, by an impartial jury of the State and district wherein the crime shall have been committed, which district shall have been previously ascertained by law, and to be informed of the nature and cause of the accusation; to be confronted with the witnesses against him; to have compulsory process for obtaining witnesses in his favor, and to have the Assistance of Counsel for his defence.

Amendment VII

In Suits at common law, where the value in controversy shall exceed twenty dollars, the right of trial by jury shall be preserved, and no fact tried by a jury, shall be otherwise re-examined in any Court of the United States, than according to the rules of the common law.

Amendment VIII

Excessive bail shall not be required, nor excessive fines imposed, nor cruel and unusual punishments inflicted.

Amendment IX

The enumeration in the Constitution, of certain rights, shall not be construed to deny or disparage others retained by the people.

Amendment X

The powers not delegated to the United States by the Constitution, nor prohibited by it to the States, are reserved to the States respectively, or to the people.

Revolutionary War Timeline

1760 - George III becomes King of England.

1763 - The French and Indian War ends.

1764 - Parliament passes the Sugar Act (or the American Revenue Act).

1765 - Parliament passes the Stamp Act.

1766 - The Stamp Act is repealed.

1767 - The Townshend Duties are enacted; they are repealed in 1770.

1770 - The Boston Massacre takes place.

1773 - The Tea Act is passed

December 16, 1773 - The Boston Tea Party takes place

1774 - Parliament closes the port of Boston to all trade. The Coercive Acts are passed, intended to restrict Massachusetts government.

1774 - The First Continental Congress meets to protest the Coercive Acts.

1774 - The colonists organize a military force and begin to accumulate and store arms at Concord. Massachusetts Governor Thomas Gage sends British troops to destroy the arms.

April 18, 1775 - Paul Revere and others ride to Lexington and Concord to warn of the British invasion.

April 19, 1775 - The battles of Lexington and Concord take place; the American Revolutionary War begins

May 1775 - The Second Continental Congress meets, and declares war on Britain.

January 1776 - Thomas Paine's *Common Sense* is published, rallying colonists to the cause of independence.

July 4, 1776 - The Declaration of Independence is ratified by the Continental Congress.

August 1776 - The Continental Army loses the battle at Long Island, New York.

December 25, 1776 - Washington leads his troops by boat across the Delaware River to capture the Hessian army at Trenton, New Jersey.

September 1777 - British forces defeat Washington at Brandywine and take Philadelphia; the Continental Congress flees.

October 1777 - American forces defeat Burgoyne and the British at Saratoga, a major military victory.

Winter 1777-78 - The Continental Army endures the harsh winter at Valley Forge.

February 1778 - France agrees to an alliance with the United States, sending money, troops, and ships to the U.S.

1780 - The war moves to the South, with victories for Nathanael Greene in South Carolina.

1781 - American and French forces converge on Yorktown, Virginia, surrounding Cornwallis. He surrenders. The war is over.

1783 - The Treaty of Paris is signed, officially ending the war and granting the U.S. new territories to the west as far as the Mississippi River.

1787 - The Constitutional Convention writes and passes a national constitution.

1788 - The Constitution is ratified by the states.

1791 - The Bill of Rights officially become the first ten amendments to the Constitution.

Subject Index

This index contains the names and key words relating to entries in this volume. It also includes significant historical events covered in the text. Bold-faced type indicates the main entry on an individual (i.e., Adams, Samuel, **153-161**), or group (i.e., Quakers, **49-60**).

JEROME LIBRARY
CURRICULUM RESOURCE CENTER
BOWLING GREEN STATE UNIVERSITY
BOWLING GREEN, OHIO 43403

DATE DUE

OhioLINK
MAY 2 8 REC'D
OhioLINK
APR 1 4 2011
OhioLINK
FEB 1 7 2012
ILL 102490796
TN 215322
5/7/13
APR 1 8 2013
NOV 2 6 2013
FEB 1 6 2017

GAYLORD PRINTED IN U.S.A.

JUV 973.2 C7191

Colonial America and the Revolutionary War